CW01467129

COMPENSATION AND BENEFIT DESIGN

COMPENSATION AND BENEFIT DESIGN

Applying Finance and Accounting Principles to Global Human Resource Management Systems

BASHKER D. BISWAS

Vice President, Publisher: Tim Moore
Associate Publisher and Director of Marketing: Amy Neidlinger
Executive Editor: Jeanne Glasser
Editorial Assistant: Pamela Boland
Operations Specialist: Jodi Kemper
Marketing Manager: Megan Graue
Cover Designer: Chuti Prasertsith
Managing Editor: Kristy Hart
Project Editor: Elaine Wiley
Copy Editor: Keith Cline
Proofreader: Leslie Joseph
Senior Indexer: Cheryl Lenser
Compositor: Nonie Ratcliff
Manufacturing Buyer: Dan Uhrig

© 2013 by Bashker D. Biswas
Publishing as Pearson Education, Inc.

Pearson offers excellent discounts on this book when ordered in quantity for bulk purchases or special sales. For more information, please contact U.S. Corporate and Government Sales, 1-800-382-3419, corpsales@pearsontechgroup.com. For sales outside the U.S., please contact International Sales at international@pearsoned. com.

Company and product names mentioned herein are the trademarks or registered trademarks of their respective owners.

All rights reserved. No part of this book may be reproduced, in any form or by any means, without permission in writing from the publisher.

Printed in the United States of America

First Printing December 2012

ISBN-10: 0-13-438589-6
I SBN-13: 978-0-13-438589-1

Pearson Education LTD.
Pearson Education Australia PTY, Limited.
Pearson Education Singapore, Pte. Ltd.
Pearson Education Asia, Ltd.
Pearson Education Canada, Ltd.
Pearson Educación de Mexico, S.A. de C.V.
Pearson Education—Japan
Pearson Education Malaysia, Pte. Ltd.

Library of Congress Cataloging-in-Publication Data is on file.

This product is printed digitally on demand. This book is the paperback version of an original hardcover book.

Dedicated to the memory of my parents and my son.
And to a prosperous future for my granddaughter, Mayah.

Contents

Foreword

Bashker Biswas and I have known one another for over 40 years. We first met when he joined the corporate compensation and benefits practice at Control Data Corporation as a new college hire. Several years later we met again at Skopos Corporation, where he led the compensation practice for this computer-based human resources application start-up. About five years ago, he joined me at Zain as the director of the Corporate Total Rewards function. Zain is a multinational corporation based in the Middle East. In between, Biswas worked at Coopers & Lybrand and PricewaterhouseCoopers as a Director and a Senior Consultant in compensation and benefits design. He also managed to sandwich a parallel career as a college-level professor at various universities in the greater San Francisco Bay area since 1984.

Over these years, I have witnessed first hand Biswas' vast knowledge and repertoire of compensation and benefit design skills, at the national and international level. It is, therefore, a great honor for me to contribute this foreword and to share with the reader my own insights and appreciation for Biswas' contributions to the advancement of the practice of compensation and benefits design.

For most firms, people costs are the lion share of both direct and indirect expenses. Managing it requires sound accounting, financial management, and good business judgment. Biswas makes an excellent case for extending the HR skill set to include accounting, finance, and business management. I support the extension of the HR professional role from a technician's point of view to a business professional. As in most fields, there is art and science involved in HR. It has been said that within the classical HR functions, employee relations has the most art and the least science while compensation and benefits has more science than art. The book does a great job of capturing the science of compensation and benefit design.

Traditional human resources management has taught us that sound compensation and benefit programs ought to meet three important tests: (1) is it competitive? (2) is it fair?, and (3) is it consistent? Biswas has extended these tests by two additional measures: (1)

is it based on sound accounting and financial management principles? and (2) does it advance the firm's competitive advantage by making the programs commensurate with an organization's financial objectives? These latter measures make the book seminal and a must-read by students of the HR professional.

While traditional human resources management emphasized the importance of evaluating compensation and benefit programs based on their ability to attract, motivate, and retain superior human talent, the contemporary view expressed by Biswas is that they also need to be supported by sound accounting, financial, and business practice. In the past 25 years, it has become fashionable for HR professionals to describe their role as *business partners*. In my view, HR professionals can rightfully claim that title only when bestowed on them by their host organization. Senior management will recognize HR professionals as *partners* only when they demonstrate a working knowledge of the organization's financial and business imperatives and demonstrate the ability to link HR programs to the accounting, financial, and business results of the firm. Until then, the term, to many, has little or no value.

As competition worldwide continues to grow, finding, honing, and retaining a competitive advantage is becoming more and more elusive. Experience teaches us that HR has a great opportunity to contribute to this endeavor. How? If your firm has a more cost-effective compensation and benefits program, by definition, it has an economic advantage over less cost-effective firms. If your firm has a compensation program better tailored to advance the firm's objectives, again by definition, it has an operational advantage over firms that are unable to focus people's efforts. If your firm is more able to link rewards with both individual and organizational financial performance, by definition, it has an employee relations advantage over firms that are unable to pay for performance.

It is fashionable to hire compensation consultants from well known consulting firms to come in and do the compensation and benefit design work. My experience has taught me that what you will get, at best, is a good boiler-plate solution, and at worst, a flavor of the year, gimmicky proposal. External consultants, for all their technical knowledge, do not have an intimate knowledge of your firm, its aspirations, foibles, and driving force. They also often provide solutions that are difficult to implement or expensive to maintain, making the need for their service a never-ending dependency. Thus it becomes imperative for HR professionals to develop their finance and accounting skills. This book will help with that effort.

Finally, Biswas' book reinforces the importance of custom design. Every firm is unique! There are no two firms alike. Designing one size-fits-all compensation and benefit programs to match current fads or what is in vogue is foolhardy. His repertoire of design options is intended to promote the notion of linking compensation and benefit programs to the unique needs of the organization, from the accounting and financial perspectives. Biswas' work links design options with a number of critical legal requirements.

Tony Tasca, Ph.D.
Retired HR Executive & International Consultant
Palo Alto, California
December 2012

Acknowledgments

This book would not have been possible without the efforts of my colleagues at DeVry University–Keller School of Management, Sacramento Campus, where I currently teach as a visiting professor. A special thanks goes to Oscar Gutierrez, national dean, College of Business and Management, for introducing this publishing opportunity to the faculty. To Dr. Jose Michel goes much appreciation for facilitating the project. And to Mary Cole MS, MAFM, Professor and Business Manager, for so willingly approving the student support for the project and for facilitating my ongoing teaching career. Also, I want to thank my many students who have helped me in various ways, throughout the years, to improve the clarity of my thinking.

A special word of appreciation goes to Dr. Anythony Tasca for writing the foreword to the book. I have known Tony for 42 years. He knows the art and the science of Human Capital Management, having served as a Chief Human Resource Officer of a very large company, and also having been a distinguished Human Capital Effectiveness Management Consultant to many companies over a period of 38 years.

This project greatly benefited from the efforts of Nusrat Tinni, one of my hardworking graduate accounting students at Keller School of Management, who carried the burden of transcribing the manuscript. Occasionally, I received some research assistance from another brilliant student, Madison Voss. I also want to acknowledge the work of Sharon Evers, who provided additional valuable transcription support.

My appreciation goes to Jeanne Glasser Levine, executive editor at FT Press, for so ably guiding this project to completion. Here also, I wish to acknowledge the assistance I received from Project Editor Elaine Wiley and Copy Editor Keith Cline. They both were calm, collected, and competent. They are true human resource assets to their organization.

I want to especially thank and acknowledge Thomas Hestwood, my friend and colleague of many years. Our joint research and publishing efforts have found expression in two of the chapters in this book. Tom was a strong professional partner early in my career. Our connections have remained steadfast over the many years. I owe a deep gratitude to Tom for agreeing so readily to the use of two of our joint publications in this book.

Finally, and as always, I acknowledge the efforts of my wife of more than 40 years, Usha, who has steadfastly provided support for this project and for many others. On this project, her assistance was invaluable both with the administrative tasks and in the editing of the manuscript.

Bashker Biswas, Ph.D.
Lincoln, California
August 2012

About the Author

Bashker "Bob" Biswas, Ph.D., is the Principal of the Biswas Group Inc., a Global Management Consultancy. Dr. Biswas concurrently holds the position of Visiting Professor at Keller School of Management at DeVry University in Sacramento, California.

Dr. Biswas has over 40 years experience in Total Rewards Management; Finance; Accounting; Executive Compensation; Base, Incentive, Sales and Equity Compensation; Human Resource Strategy; Human Resource Information Systems; International Human Resources; and International Compensation.

The companies he has worked for are Control Data, Bechtel, Memorex, Maxtor, Hitachi Data Systems and BioGenex, and Zain. Dr. Biswas has held positions at the Director level and above since 1982. At Maxtor and BioGenex he was a Vice President. While at Memorex and Zain, he worked out of London and the Middle East/Africa respectively. He has traveled to over 30 countries on various compensation and benefits related projects.

During his tenure in the Middle East, Dr. Biswas conducted Total Rewards and Global Human Resource Management Seminars throughout the Middle East and Africa. He was a leading instructor in the Zain Human Resource Management Academy.

In addition, he has held consulting positions at Skopos Corporation, a venture investment backed HRIS start-up cofounded by Dr. Biswas in 1983, at Coopers & Lybrand, and at PricewaterhouseCoopers. At Coopers & Lybrand, he was a Director of Human Resource Consulting in the San Francisco office and National High-tech Leader for Human Resource Consulting. Dr. Biswas was also responsible for the firm's National Software Industry Compensation Survey. In total he has provided Compensation Consulting to over 40 companies.

Dr. Biswas has taught at various universities as an adjunct faculty member since 1984. He has authored and coauthored articles in Human Resource Management. Dr. Biswas also has presented at WorldatWork's National Conference and briefly taught in their Certification Program.

Dr. Biswas holds a B.A., M.B.A., and Ph.D., and a post-graduate diploma in Industrial Relations.

He has been a member of WorldatWork (American Compensation Association) since 1972.

Preface

Accounting is the language of business. *Human resource* (HR) management deals with the major asset of a business: the employee. Therefore, when dealing with employee issues, shouldn't HR professionals use the language of business? Shouldn't a connection exist between these important dimensions? Yet, as often noted by various people, HR management and accounting (finance also) come from different planets. This disconnect was discussed in an article published in the WorldatWork journal[1] a few years ago, "Finance Is from Mars, Human Resources Is from Venus," by Wade Lindenberger, CPA, and Kayoko Lindenberger, CBP, Employee Benefits Training and Solutions. But both of these planets are from the same solar system, and commonsense logic suggests that both should be connected by the same force field.[2]

So, why are they not connected? What are the main disconnects? What are the reasons for this disconnect? Why does the chasm exist? Why the gaps? What can be done to strengthen the links? What are the knowledge and skill gaps? What specific knowledge areas need to be addressed?

This book seeks to answer these questions, discussing in detail the specific connection points between accounting and finance and HR management.

Throughout this book, accounting and finance are combined into one discipline, although they are not necessarily the same. Simply stated, accounting people are record keepers, and finance people are the analyzers. However, both group's core foundations are the numbers of the organization. Both groups have to be proficient in the language of business: accounting. Accountants keep the records of the numbers and are responsible for reporting those numbers using

---

[1] WorldatWork is a premier association, globally, for compensation and benefits professionals.

[2] Lindenberger, W., and K. Lindenberger, "Finance Is from Mars, Human Resources Is from Venus," *Workspan, The Magazine of WorldatWork,* January 2009, pp. 41–44.

the guidelines and rules laid out for them by the rule-setting bodies (GAAP, IFRS, SEC, AICPA,[3] and others). Finance people are analyzers and interpreters of the record. Therefore, a case can clearly be made that accountants and finance people are from the same planet, whereas HR professionals are from a different planet. The goal in this book is to bring these two force fields closer together by imparting to the HR community the finance and accounting skills needed (in a comprehensive manner) to talk the language of business. But why are these groups so far apart? After all, HR professionals also have to talk the language of business if they want to make strategic business decisions.

HR management as a function started off in the enlightened period of management, when employee productivity enhanced through improvement in morale, motivation, and commitment. During this period, work behavior started to be considered an important element in overall organizational success. The origins were in Western Electric via the Hawthorne studies. For the first time, studies showed that management had to pay attention to the welfare of employees if they were to achieve organizational success. From those early days, management got a new focus: employee relations. Management hired people to help them with employee welfare. These early employee welfare professionals were usually called employee relation specialists. *Specialist* here was a stretch. These early staffers were mostly administrators helping managers with the tasks associated with employee welfare. But, then workers started seeing that they could raise their bargaining power with their employers if they joined forces to form unions. Managers started seeing that they needed staffers to help them handle union-related issues, and thus came the advent of labor relation specialists.

Along with the growth in labor relation professionals, organizations during this period saw the growth of personnel administrators. Managers hired personnel administrators to assist them with employee management responsibilities. And so grew the functional

[3] GAAP (Generally Accepted Accounting Principles), IFRS (International Financial Reporting Standards), SEC (Securities and Exchange Commission), AICPA (American Institute of Certified Public Accountants).

specialties of personnel management: recruitment, wage and salary administration, policies and procedures, training and labor relations.

After Douglas McGregor's bestselling book *The Human Side of the Enterprise* started gaining traction, the personnel department was renamed to HR management. The idea was to bring in more consideration to the *human* side of an organization. Therefore, managers hired and sought the guidance of "people specialists": the HR professional.

HR people would be "people persons" (touch-feely or soft-skill experts). They would be guardians of the people side of the business. They would be advocates to management for the employee's view of things and simultaneously represent to employees the management view of things. But the HR functions would continue to be responsible for helping managers with the day-to-day employee management issues, such as recruiting, compensation, benefits, training, development, and employee relations.

The skills and knowledge HR professionals needed to have to do their jobs effectively remained uncertain, and still does. Senior managers decided that HR professionals mainly needed people skills or soft skills. However, what were really the required core competencies vital for the HR professional? The answer was not clear and remains unclear still today.

During the past 20 years, attempts have been made to define HR core competencies. David Ulrich's landmark book is a case in point, *Human Resource Champions.*[4] Over the past 50 years, whether you are an internal HR staff member or an outside HR consultant or even an HR professor, it can safely be said that there still remains uncertainty as to what knowledge, skill, and core competencies are needed for the HR professional. Also, we remain unsure as to whether HR management is indeed even a profession.

Let's look at what the criteria are for a particular occupation to be regarded as a profession. For a class of activities to be considered a

[4] Ulrich, D. *Human Resource Champions: The Next Agenda for Adding Value and Delivering Results*, Harvard Business School Press, 1997.

profession, the class jointly should have the following characteristics, among others:

- The public must recognize the occupation as a profession.
- There needs to be a central regulatory body.
- There needs to be a code of conduct.
- There has to be a careful management of knowledge.
- The activities the profession engages in should satisfy an essential societal need.
- There must be an official recognition of professional status by the government.
- There needs to be standards of competence.

From further analysis, consider these two intriguing characteristics:[5]

- "A profession is based on one or more undergirding disciplines from which it builds its own applied knowledge and skills."
- "Preparation for and induction into the profession are provided through a protracted academic program, usually in a professional school on a college or university campus." This should be accentuated with rigorous testing and examination. Based on these criteria, many organizational activities certainly cannot be considered a profession.

Over time, things have changed. Indeed, the times are still changing. Now organizations all over the world are in a period of turmoil. Some call it *creative destruction*. Pressures have increased to create efficiencies, to reduce expenses, to manage costs, to stay focused on business strategies, to improve financial performance. This is the era of the "lean mean fighting machine." Intense global competition, scarcity of resources, dried-up funding sources—all represent real organizational success impediments. In most organizations, labor costs are typically the largest cost component.

---

[5] Adapted from a post written by R.J. Kizik, found at www.adprima.com/profession.htm.

Over the past few decades, there has been a great deal of talk about the fact that HR professionals need to become a strategic business partner. But this has not become reality. More so than ever, it is now imperative that HR professionals understand and participate directly in the strategic initiatives of their organizations. HR has to move from a counseling role to a more primary role. Now financial realities exert relentless pressures. Customers are more demanding, and there is incessant pressure to reduce costs. Cost-effectiveness, conserving resources, and regulatory pressures have great impact on business operations. Turnover of critical talent remains a major concern. Globalization requires human resources to think and act globally. Now more so than ever, overhead departments are being asked to justify monies being spent for those departments. These departments are being asked to justify their value add. Foremost under this scrutiny is the HR function. The perception is that in the HR department a bunch of people sit around and do things that the senior management cannot clearly understand; that is, the "line of sight" is unclear between expenses made for this department and their staffs and the organization's overall financial success. Senior managers are asking tough questions: Why are we doing this and that in the HR department? Can we outsource these activities and save money? Why do we need to staff this department with so many people? Are the large salaries being paid to these HR folks really worth it? Are they doing us any good? Can we do without them? Many business leaders wonder whether they even need HR departments. And so, HR departments are being asked to justify their activities using the language of business: accounting and finance. An interesting article appeared on this subject in the *Fast Company* magazine in August 2005 titled, "Why We Hate HR." This article looks critically at the role of HR departments[6] and stirred up a lot discussion and debate when it came out.

Here is the dilemma: HR professionals realize that their survival depends on "coming to the table" (that is, being business savvy). It also means directly tying in HR activities with business strategies in the long term. At the same time, it also means tying these activities and their associated expenditures with the short-term bottom line.

---

[6] "Why We Hate HR," by *Fast Company* staff, August 1, 2005.

The dilemma occurs when we realize the current HR professional has come to this line of work from a whole host of different backgrounds. There are no common threads of knowledge, know-how, and skills in the current repertoire of the HR professional. This is not true with the accounting or finance professional. To work in their fields, accounting and finance professionals must have professional qualifications (CPA/CMA, BA/MA in accounting, MBA in finance, and so on). If they do not possess these qualifications they would have to secure professional credentials from a recognized credentialing body. This focused qualification credentialing does not exist in a comprehensive manner for the HR professional.

The various professional HR associations have started credentialing efforts, but these efforts remain voluntary. The WorldatWork organization has successful credentialing programs for the compensation and benefits professional (for example, *Certified Compensation Professional* [CCP] and *Certified Benefits Professional* [CBP]). In addition, there are no specific college degree requirements for working in the HR department. People working in HR departments have college degrees starting from theater arts to advanced graduate degrees in electrical engineering. Also, many successful HR folks have no college degrees whatsoever.

The orientations of the HR departments vary from organization to organization. No common threads can be discerned. As evidence of this, consider the mind-numbing plethora of terms and expressions that HR departments use: *talent management, succession planning, organizational development, performance management, rewards management, work-life balance, total rewards, onboarding, downsizing, delayering, resizing, competency framework, internal consulting, assessment centers,* and what not. No wonder HR consulting remains a growth industry. This is not true in accounting and finance departments. Every accounting department has to keep the books, develop and report financial information via standard financial statements, and follow the standards developed by standard setting bodies (such as the Federal Accounting Standards Board and the Securities and Exchange Commission in the USA). Every finance department has to analyze financial conditions using these standard rules and standards.

So, here we are: The HR professional is being required to talk the language of business, but the HR professional does not necessarily know the language of accounting and finance. Many organizations have efforts underway to develop the accounting and finance skills of HR professionals. In a January 2009 article in the *Workspan* magazine of the WorldatWork,[7] authors Wade Lindenberger, CPA, and Kayoko Lindenberger, CBP, talk about American Express Company's mandatory effort through a training program to develop the "financial acumen of our HR professionals."

But we think this knowledge gap is huge. WorldatWork in its credentialing education courses does have a course titled "Accounting and Finance for the Human Resource Professional." But this general course covers subjects in a broad manner without going into the specifics and details of the connections between HR management topics and accounting and finance. This book is designed to fill this gap.

The HR department has many functions, including recruitment, compensation and benefits, and training. Among them, compensation and benefits is the most technical, requiring hard skills. This is because this function involves dealing with numbers. The activities involved in compensation and benefits are therefore the most affected by accounting and finance implications.

Also compensation and benefit expenses are often the largest individual line item expense in any organizational setting.[8] Relevant data shows that total compensation expenses in organizations fall within 20% to 60% of gross revenue. In the service sector, this percentage is in the 50% to 60% range. If one considers salaries as a percentage of operating expense, the range can be from 15% to 50%. Data from the Bureau of Labor Statistics in 2008 suggests that in the healthcare industry the salaries to operating expenses ratio was as high as 52%. In for-profit service organizations, the ratio was 50%. In durable goods manufacturing, construction/mining, and oil/gas, the ratio was 22%. And in the retail sector, the salaries to operating expenses ratio was as low as 18%.

---

[7] Lindenberger, W., and K. Lindenberger, "Finance Is from Mars, Human Resources Is from Venus," *Workspan: The Magazine of WorldatWork,* January 2009, pp. 41-44.

[8] In fact, in the national economy, wages represent nearly three quarters of total costs.

Compensation and benefits is the largest expense item for any organization. Therefore, there is a need to clearly understand and articulate the links between compensation and benefits and accounting (finance). It also suggests a need for a closer alignment of accounting (finance) with the activities of compensation and benefits.

Note, as well, that many financial problems can be explained by compensation systems or by the specifics of the tax code. When one cannot explain a firm's behavior with economic logic, the real answer may often lie in compensation systems. We will explore these connections in more detail throughout the book.

This book's main objective is to fully examine the connection between compensation and benefits and accounting (finance). This book explores various aspects of accounting and finance as they relate to compensation and benefit analysis.

HR-related accounting and finance implications are usually captured in accounting and finance texts in an unconnected manner. In contrast, this book brings into focus in one single publication all of these compensation and benefit and accounting (finance) topics, discussing the major compensation and benefit subfunctions one by one. Within each subtopic, you learn the relevant accounting and finance implications.

Throughout this book, the compensation and benefit topics that have major accounting (finance) implications are discussed. Each chapter deals with a specific compensation and benefit topic, with no particular connective flow between the chapters. A lot of topics covered came from the author's college lectures teaching accounting and finance and from compensation and benefit courses.

In recent years, there has been a transformation from independent applications of various compensation and benefits elements. Now organizations focus on the total compensation system to manage total compensation costs and to educate employees on the true costs of their total compensation package. A new term has been used recently: *total rewards.* Total rewards nomenclature is just a different way of referring to total compensation. Keeping this total compensation focus in mind, this book covers the major elements and program costs wherever necessary.

Before going into the detailed analytical connections between compensation and benefits and accounting (finance), it is important to understand the basics. So, defining terminology is an important first step. The basic framework for the connection that currently exists between the functions also needs to be understood. The first chapter lays the foundation before detailed analytical connections are explored.

When talking about compensation and benefits, you must consider that a total compensation program consists of various elements. Normally, a total compensation structure includes the following elements:

- Base
- Cash incentives or bonuses
- Equity compensation
- Cash-based long-term incentives
- Executive compensation
- Sales compensation
- Expatriate compensation
- Risk benefits
- Retirement benefits
- Perquisites
- Other Benefits

This book analyzes the accounting and finance implications for most of the elements of a total compensation structure. Note here that some of the compensation and benefit topics are more influenced by accounting and finance know-how than others. So, in this book, the topics that have more of an accounting and finance angle are covered in more detail. A good example of this is employee share plans and pension accounting; these topics are covered in longer chapters.

Part I of this book discusses terms and key concepts to lay a conceptual framework for the book.

- Chapter 1, "Introduction: Setting the Stage, covers the foundations of the total compensation system. Terms are defined, concepts are explained, and connections to finance and accounting are established.

- Chapter 2, "Business, Financial, and Human Resource Planning," presents the connection between business/financial planning and compensation and benefit planning. Assuming that compensation and benefit expenses are indeed the highest expense category of any organization, Chapter 2 emphasizes the importance and explains the connections between the two critical planning processes.

- Chapter 3, "Projecting Compensation Costs," introduces a financial projection model for forecasting fixed compensation costs. Again, the fixed element or the base salary of the compensation package can be the highest cost element in any organization. So, this discussion recognizes its importance by explaining a detailed cost forecasting model and process.

- Chapter 4, "Incentive Compensation," deals with one of the most important elements of the total compensation package: incentive compensation. In an era of limited resources and cost reduction, incentive compensation has become important. A concept called *pay at risk* is being discussed a lot. This concept suggests reducing the fixed or base component of the pay package below the market average and then increasing the incentive component. The goal being the total cash compensation (base plus incentive) will be targeted much above the average in the market. If the financial goals of the company are met or exceeded, the employee's total compensation will be above the market averages. The financial and accounting dimensions of incentive compensation are explained. Some financially rigorous metrics to be used as the triggering mechanisms for incentive and compensation programs are introduced. These concepts are economic value added, free cash flow, and residual income.

- Chapter 5, "Share-Based Compensation Plans," discusses all the accounting and finance issues for share-based compensation plans. This area of a total compensation system has many finance and accounting implications, and therefore the discussions in this chapter are quite extensive.

- Chapter 6, "International and Expatriate Compensation," covers all the finance and accounting dimensions of international compensation programs. This chapter focuses especially on expatriate compensation, which has many finance and accounting nuances.

- Chapter 7, "Sales Compensation Accounting," provides a detailed analysis of the various accounting and finance issues that impact the effective development, design, and administration of sales compensation programs. Sales commission plan administration accounting is covered. This chapter briefly looks at the software packages available for administering sales commission plans.

- Chapter 8, "Employee Benefit Accounting," discusses the accounting and finance issues impacting employee benefit programs. The accounting standards framework for employee benefit plan accounting is also discussed.[9]

- Chapter 9, "Healthcare Benefits Cost Management," covers employee healthcare benefits and costing. Because healthcare benefits cost is the compensation cost component with the highest inflation, this whole chapter is devoted to employee healthcare benefit cost containment. This topic is a hot-button issue in many contemporary debates and discussions.

- Chapter 10, "The Accounting and Financing of Retirement Plans," covers retirement program financing and accounting in its entirety and discusses defined contribution and benefit plans in detail. This is another area of a total compensation system dominated by accounting and finance implications, so we devote a great deal of attention to thoroughly discussing all of these implications. After studying this chapter, you can appreciate all the finance and accounting nuances of defined benefit retirement programs

---

[9] Financial reporting standards under U.S. *Generally Accepted Accounting Principles* (GAPP) and the *International Financial Accounting Standards* (IFRS) are covered.

Part II of the book looks at various nontraditional concepts with regard to finance and accounting implications for global HR management. Key here are discussions about changing the accounting and finance paradigm and considering HR investments, a financial asset, that can be capitalized (rather than completely expensed as a period expense[10]).

Recently, *human capital* has been a widely discussed concept. Such an expression implies that the human assets of a company are capital assets, assets that generate value to an organization for a longer time period than just a single year. However, current accounting practice expenses these investments in the period in which they occur. Researchers have suggested that this is a flawed assumption. HR expenditures, they say, are investments, just like other intangible assets, whose value is derived over a period of time. The basis of this argument lies as the foundation of the concepts covered in Part II:

- Chapter 11, "Human Resource Analytics," discusses the concept of HR measurements or HR effectiveness measures. In keeping with senior management's demands to justify the business value, the use of appropriate effectiveness measures becomes very important. This chapter examines the various appropriate HR effectiveness measures.

- Chapter 12, "Human Resource Accounting," covers the paradigm-shifting concept of HR accounting. Although this concept has been around for a while, the accounting profession has not yet endorsed it. Nevertheless, this chapter analyzes HR accounting methodologies and discusses their pros and cons.

Accounting standards are referred to quite often in this book. Currently in the United States, the governing standards are referred to as the *Generally Accepted Accounting Principles* (GAAP).[11] In the global environment, the governing standard is the *International Accounting Financial Standards* (IFRS). The movement to converge

---

[10] Human asset contribution to organizational value generation increases over time.

[11] These standards are developed and promulgated in the United States by the *Financial Accounting Standards Board* (FASB).

these standards into one is well on its way. With the advent of the global economy and preponderance of multinationals, the accounting profession realizes that it does not make sense to operate within a dual standard framework: U.S. GAAP + IFRS. Therefore, an effort is ongoing to converge the standards. A roadmap has been laid, and a transition plan has been implemented. Therefore, both these standards are discussed, when relevant, throughout this book.

Although this book is U.S. centric, it also has wide coverage of accounting and finance issues with implications for global HR management.

Finally, note that the tax accounting implications for global HR systems are discussed wherever appropriate in each chapter. If you want to learn more about relevant tax issues, refer to legal and tax publications.

Part I

We start this part of the book with some foundational concepts. First, we cover the basics within the total compensation structure. Second, we discuss the concept of planning and the need to connect total compensation planning with the strategic and operational planning of the organization. Third, we discuss base compensation cost forecasting, and we cover forecasting other total cost elements in specific chapters.

Part I of the book deals with topics that cover the entire total compensation structure. These include base, incentive, sales, international, and equity (share-based) compensation. We also cover topics within the total compensation structure that are commonly known as employee benefits, concentrating mainly on health and retirement plans.

Our focus is to cover the finance and accounting principles within each compensation element. The discussion for each topic stays within the framework of accounting principles and standards as established by the Generally Accepted Accounting Principles (GAAP) and International Accounting Financial Standards (IFRS).

We do not discuss the normal concepts and techniques of designing or developing the elements of the total compensation structure. The normal concepts and techniques are built around the following principles: internal and external equity, motivation theories, ability to pay, and competitive practices. This discussion is left up to other texts. The sole purpose of Part I of this book is to highlight and then discuss in detail the accounting and finance principles that are integral to all the elements of the total compensation structure.

1

Introduction: Setting the Stage

Aims and objectives of this chapter
- Set the stage for the discussions in this book
- Discuss the concept of costs versus expenses
- Explain the concepts of OPEX and CAPEX
- Examine various compensation and benefit elements
- Discuss in detail the concept of base salary
- Discuss the treatment of compensation and benefit elements within current accounting systems and structures
- Discuss the current accounting for human resource cost outlays
- Explain the current payroll accounting process for hourly and salaried employees

This introductory chapter examines how finance and accounting principles apply to compensation and benefit program design. The discussion analyzes the current connections and proposes various connection enhancements. In this chapter, you also learn the terms commonly used with regard to compensation and benefits. The chapter also proposes modifications to the accounting process to accommodate a revised classification of compensation and benefit cost outlays and transactions. Thus, the chapter lays the foundation for the finance and accounting analysis of compensation and benefit transactions.

The words *cost* and *expense* are often used interchangeably. Are *human resource* (HR) outlays costs or expenses? What is the difference? Where in the accounting structure and system can one find HR expenditures? Are the current classifications within the accounting framework appropriate? What changes can one anticipate in the current expense/cost classification resulting from the changes in how work is currently done and how it will be done in the future? These and other questions need to be answered before discussing the various specific techniques and analytical mechanisms within the finance and accounting structure that affects HR mandgement (and specifically compensation and benefits).

In this chapter, after answering some critical questions posed here, the basic flow of compensation and benefits outlays,[1] as defined by HR departments, is traced through the accounting framework and structure.

The Cost Versus Expense Conundrum

The words *cost* and *expense* are used interchangeably in accounting. But a cost incurred can be an asset or expense depending on the timing of accounting transactions and the concept of periodicity.

Especially in transactions like the acquisition of a physical asset, the cost classification can become an important decision. When a physical asset is acquired, many costs might be involved (for example, purchase price, freight costs, and installation costs). So, the accountant has to decide which cost to include as an asset and which costs to expense immediately. Those costs that are expensed immediately can be called revenue expenditures. And costs that are not expensed immediately but are included in asset accounts are referred to as capital expenditures. Some firms call these expenses *operating expenses* (OPEX) and *capital expenses* (CAPEX). You'll read more about these classifications later in this chapter.

An expense is, in actuality, a cost used up while producing the sales revenue for the business. In other words, expenses are those monetary outlays that flow through to the income statement. In contrast, costs that have not been used up remain a cost and are reported on the balance sheet as an asset. Expenses are those costs that are necessary to make sales within a specific period. A company can incur a

---

[1] This discussion uses the word *outlay* for HR monetary outflows because, as covered here, some questions exist as to the proper classification of these outflows within prevailing accounting definitions of the terms *cost* and *expense*.

cost and spend cash to pay rent in advance for a six-month period, for example. On the day this transaction is made, however, a debit entry is made to an asset account called Prepaid Rent. Only after a month is over and the premises have been occupied for that month does an expense transaction occur, and for that month only; five months of the cost incurred for prepaying the rent stays on the balance sheet as an asset.

Let's take another example. Suppose a restaurant is gearing up for a Christmas banquet for a big corporate event. The owners go out and buy nonperishable restaurant supplies such as napkins and so forth. The cost of this cash purchase is $5000. Now let's suppose they use up 30% of these supplies for this big corporate banquet. In this case, $1500 is classified as an expense for that period (the month and year when financial statements are prepared) and the remaining $3500 will still be a cost but will be reported on the balance sheet as Restaurant Supplies (an asset). In this case, this cost—an outlay of cash—is both an asset and an expense.

Now, suppose that a business buys a piece of land to build a factory. The cost of that land never becomes an expense. That cost continues to be classified as an asset (because land is never depreciated).

If a hospital buys an MRI machine, any cash or credit purchase is first carried as an asset on the balance sheet. Then, after that, a periodic depreciation expense is recognized in the income statement. So, here again, the entire cost of that MRI machine is not an expense at the time of purchase. Instead, the expense is spread over the useful life of the MRI machine. As a matter of fact, the historical cost of acquiring the MRI machine is always shown on the balance sheet. Depreciation taken each period is recorded as a period expense and also recorded as a contra-asset in an account called accumulated depreciation.

Now consider manufacturing businesses: Cost outlays within a given period for direct materials, direct labor, and manufacturing overhead directly used in making products that were sold within that specific time period are considered expenses for that period and are termed *cost of goods sold*. Cost of goods sold flows into the income statement and is matched with revenue earned during that period. But direct materials, manufacturing overhead (which includes indirect labor), and direct labor remaining in finished goods or in work in process are considered assets. Therefore, here again, not all costs are expenses. Some are assets (balance sheet), others are expenses (income statement). So, in current accounting practice, some employee monetary outlays are assets, some are expenses.

Furthermore, other transactions in a manufacturing company are considered selling, general, and administrative expenses for a specific period. Compensation outlays for the truck driver who delivers materials to the factory are considered expenses for a period. In contrast, electricity used in the factory might be either an asset or an expense depending on whether manufacturing overhead, including factory electricity, is assigned to products as cost of goods or as work in process inventory or finished goods inventory. But all electricity used in the administrative offices is considered an expense for a particular period.

Adding to the confusion, let's consider monetary outlays for research scientists. Suppose that a firm buys a laboratory machine for a research lab. The cost of this machine might be $20,000, with an additional $5,000 expense for installing the machine. As of the date the firm acquires this machine, the accounting system increases an asset account by debiting that account with the total purchase cost of the machine plus all costs necessary to make the machine ready to use. And then the accountant periodically records a debit entry to a depreciation expense account spread over the useful life of the machine, using an acceptable depreciation schedule. This expense is then reported in the income statement, matching it against the current period revenue.

If the same firm were to hire a research scientist during the same period, however, the costs that the firm incurred to hire that scientist—recruitment advertising, search fees (which can be quite large), interviewing costs, and other hiring costs—will all be currently expensed and reported in the income statement. This can lead to a distortion in income measurement because the research scientist's service will extend over more than one year. But currently, the accounting rules require that all the HR cost outlays be expensed during the current period.

Compensation-related outlays for these scientists are all considered expenses for the current period. In accounting systems, though, the cost outlays for physical products (the machines the scientists use) are considered assets and are expensed only over a period of time (their useful life).

The issue of reporting intangibles also needs to be discussed in connection with the recording of HR outlays. Under current accounting standards, intellectual property that an employee brings and utilizes within the employment setting is not considered a recognizable asset. The current accounting system records as assets only certain other intangibles such as copyrights, patents, and trademarks. The irony is that the intangibles are the outputs of the employees with specifically valuable intellectual property.

In many cases, a big difference can exist in book value versus market value of the assets. For example, in a recent year Google had stockholder equity of $22.7 billion, whereas its market value during the same period as determined by multiplying Google's market price of its shares by the number of outstanding shares was about $179 billion. Such a wide difference undermines financial reporting. It can be assumed that most of this big difference results from nonrecognized intangibles. And one of the biggest intangibles is the value of Google's human assets. Part II of this book discusses this concept in greater detail.

So, one can safely say that confusion abounds within current accounting standards frameworks as to how and where HR monetary outlays are classified in accounting systems.

CAPEX Versus OPEX

The expressions *capital expenses* and *operating expenses* are often used in accounting and finance. Cost or expenditure outlays can either be capitalized (spread out over a period of time) or taken into a specific time period's profit/loss—in other words, in the time period they were incurred (revenue and expense recognition). This is the difference between *capital expenditures* (CAPEX) and *operating expenditures* (OPEX).

With reference to these classifications, employee-related expenditures are classified differently by different groups. The HR-related cost or expenditures can be classified either as CAPEX or OPEX.

CAPEX remain capitalized (a balance sheet classification) until these transactions become expenses for a specific time period. HR accounting proponents suggest that for effective management reporting it might be better to aggregate these accounting entries into one account. If done, it gives business decision makers a more complete picture when making strategic and operational decisions affecting employees.

The Current HR Cost-Classification Structure

Let's now examine the fundamental elements covered in this book. First, it is important that you understand the terminology commonly used in compensation and benefit analysis. After reviewing this terminology, the discussion turns to these terms within the context of the current accounting framework.[2]

Compensation and Benefit Elements

The most commonly used terminology related to compensation and benefits within the organizations are as follows:

- **Base salary:** Base or basic or fixed pay describes the "fixed" part of pay. This pay element is mainly paid to employees to come to work (to attract employees). It is also paid to employees to do the assigned work by applying the required skills, knowledge, and abilities using normal effort and demonstrating necessary work behaviors. Basic pay is usually the largest component of the total pay package. In other words, basic pay is the amount of nonincentive wages or salaries paid over a period of time for work performed. It may include additional payments that are not directly related to the work effort.

  Compensation professionals use the following methods to determine base pay levels:

[2] When the term *accounting framework* is used, it means here the accounting structures and framework as established under *Generally Accepted Accounting Principles* (GAAP) and the *International Financial Accounting Standards* (IFAS).

- Job-based pay
- Skill- or competency-based pay
- Market-based pay
- A combination of these three

Compensation books adequately explain these methodologies.[3] The professional organization WorldatWork[4] conducts seminars and develops various publications explaining these methodologies. Some compensation specialists have tried to define precisely the distinctions between the terms *base pay* and *basic pay*.

Chuck Czismar, in a blog post[5] from January 6, 2010, attempts to create a distinction between the terms *base pay* and *basic pay*. He says that base pay refers only to "non-incentive wages and salary paid out over a twelve month period for work performed." He goes on to define basic pay as "the amount of non-incentive wages or salary paid out over a twelve month period for work performed, but including additional payments not directly related to work effort." He seems to be referring to additional variable pay allowances and to 13th and 14th month payments, prevalent in various countries.

The term *fixed* is used to distinguish this pay component from others that are of a variable nature, such as bonuses, incentives, and various contingent payments.

Base compensation has other flows (or changes), as well. Here is a list of the cost flows (changes) that affect the base pay in total:

- Part-time status to full-time status
- Full- time status to part-time status
- Change of status to nonpaid leave
- A temporary allowance (on and off)

---

[3] Milkovich, G.T., and Newman, J. *Compensation,* 2008, McGraw-Hill, Irwin, New York.

[4] WorldatWork is the largest professional association of compensation and benefit practitioners in the world.

[5] www.internationalhrforum.com/2010/01/06/base-salary-not-so-basic/.

- A temporary adder (on and off)
- Exempt employee to nonexempt and vice versa in the United States
- Promotion increase
- Annual performance increment or merit increase
- Salary reductions
- Overtime payments
- Workers' compensation (on and off)
- Salary differentials (on and off)
- General increases
- Step increases
- Cost-of-living adjustments

All these variables affect the total base pay expenses and therefore the total costs for employees in an organization. To understand the real impact of employee-related expenditures, there is a need to record and analyze all these expense triggers. Also to forecast or budget these expenditures, all these inflows and outflows need to be documented, tracked, and analyzed. But the current accounting systems do not identify these flows separately in any detail. The payroll systems aggregate these pay transactions into a composite gross rate. To the accounting structure, it is not important to keep track of the various employee flows (although some of these flows could be tracked separately by payroll systems but not by accounting systems).[6] If the salary is stated in monthly terms, these individual expense transactions are tracked in the aggregate monthly stated salary.

- **Incentive compensation:** Incentives or bonuses payments are paid to an employee for achieving time-bound goals and objectives. Terms such as *incentive targets, objectives (bonus objectives), measurements*, and *ratings* are all contextual terms used in most organizations. Incentive compensation refers to

---

[6] The HR inflows and outflows referred to here are important to track for HR management but not for finance and accounting. An intermediate step is therefore needed to track costs of the inflows and outflows for the use of HR professionals.

contingent payments paid to employees only when certain predetermined financial or individual objectives are met.

- **Allowances:** Allowances are usually temporary adders to the basic pay. Housing allowance, transportation allowance, and education allowance are common. Allowances are widely used in various countries. Allowances are paid for special situations or conditions.

- **Pay adders:** Adders to base pay are common in the United States. Overtime pay, callback pay, on-call pay are examples of pay elements and are provided for work that is done beyond normal working hours. These adders are governed by wage and hour laws in most countries.

- **Risk benefits:** Risk benefits are payments made for medical, disability, and life (actually death) situations. The benefits in this category are provided to employees in lieu of direct cash payments to mitigate the various life risks for employees and their families.

- **Retirement benefits:** Retirement benefits are common compensation elements that organizations provide to assist employees with their post-employment lives. Retirement benefits can take the form of defined benefit or defined contribution plans.

- **Equity compensation:** Employee equity programs in the past had been mostly provided to senior executives to motivate them to increase shareholder value. This component of pay has seen sweeping accounting changes over the past ten years or so. There has been a growth of many different structures for these plans; nonqualified stock options, incentive stock options, restricted stock options, stock appreciation rights are a few. Accounting, tax, and legal implications are integral to the design, development, and administration of these programs. More recently, issues surrounding executive compensation excesses, earnings management, insider trading, ownership culture, stock option pricing and expensing, dilution effects, and overhang have all clouded this pay element with a lot of debate and discussion.

- **Perquisites:** Perquisites are elements of compensation that are normally paid to senior executives. The practice is widespread around the world. Most common are first-class travel, executive jets, country club memberships, executive physicals, and financial planning. Perquisites can be direct cash payments or are compensation payments in the form of expense reimbursements for approved executive benefits.

- **Expatriate compensation:** Expatriate compensation is made to employees who are sent by companies to live and work abroad. Within this overall category, there can be many subcategories of payments. Among them are cost-differential payments, housing differential payments, education allowance, tax protection or tax equalization payments, moving expense allowances and foreign-service premiums, and hardship and special area allowances. An expatriate assignment occurs when an employee is transferred to a foreign jurisdiction (different from the headquarters country or the employee's country of permanent domicile).

The appendix at the end of this chapter describes all the terms and words used in the field of total compensation. This will set the stage for a comprehensive analysis of the finance and accounting implications involved in compensation and benefit plan design.

The Current Accounting for Compensation and Benefit Cost Elements

Now that you know the commonly used terms in compensation and benefits, let's explore how these compensation and benefits cost elements are reflected in accounting systems.

If an employee's job entails directly producing a product (as part of a manufacturing operation), accounting systems classify that employee as direct labor. Another common identifier for this grouping is touch labor. *Touch labor* refers to those people required to touch the product during the manufacturing process. Those employees who are involved in the manufacturing process but are involved in a supporting activity (such as the manufacturing manager or the janitor who cleans the factory floor) are included in manufacturing overhead. A commonly used term for this category is *indirect labor*.

In cost accounting, manufacturing overhead is absorbed into unit product costs through various mechanisms, such as job order costing and process costing. All the specific compensation elements are lumped together by the accounting process into two accounts, normally called direct labor or indirect labor. Both of these account categories become a part of the cost of goods sold cost.

For manufacturing companies, the gross profit is calculated by subtracting cost of goods sold from the revenue. In accounting, therefore, the employees directly involved in making a product contribute toward the achievement of the gross profit of an organization. And in manufacturing, companies' monetary outlays for those employees not involved in making the product are considered period expenses. Normally these expenses are part of the selling, general, and administrative expense account. The selling, general, and administrative expense and other indirect expenses are deducted from gross profit to derive the net income or loss.

Cost of goods sold in the service industry refers to the cost of the employees or machines directly involved in providing the service. Other items like electricity to run the machines and those employees who are not directly connected to providing the service are usually included as part of selling, general, and administrative expenses. This is an overhead or indirect expense. And as stated before, these expenses are deducted after the gross profit is calculated, to arrive at the net profit or income.

Let's look at an example for a construction company. In a construction company, the compensation paid to workers directly involved in construction activities is a part of cost of goods sold, whereas employees who support them (estimators, clerks, material handlers) are included in the selling, general, and administrative expenses.

Note that the actual practice of classifying employee expenses either in cost of goods sold or in overhead expenses can vary from company to company.

In a merchandising business, there are no raw materials, work in process, or finished goods accounts. There is only a merchandise inventory account. All purchases of goods bought for resale become a part of the merchandise inventory account. Only when a specific item sells is the acquisition cost of that item then transferred from the merchandise inventory account to the cost of goods sold account. It is then subtracted from sales revenue to derive gross income or profit. In merchandising businesses, all employee expenses are classified into general expenses, which appear on the income statement after the calculation of gross profit or income.

In financial reporting, some employee costs are included in the asset section of the balance sheet. In addition, employee-related monetary transactions are often included in the balance sheet in a liability account called salary or wages payable. This suggests that some earned wages have not been paid to employees.

A case can be made that most HR cost outlays can be classified as assets. This argument might have some merit if you consider that the compensation paid to software engineers, scientists, electronic engineers, and development engineers is a CAPEX. A case can be made that these types of employees are indeed the true assets of a company, especially in high-technology and biotechnology firms. They have rare skills, and losing one of these critical skills might result in a decrease in the value of a business. But current accounting thinking does not concur with this line of thought. Current accounting standards state that expenditures should be included in financial statements only if they are clearly measurable in monetary terms and there is reliability and relevance. The accounting profession asserts that there are problems in determining relevant and reliable values for human assets. Accountants believe that human capital measurements are not up to par on reliability and accuracy. If accurate measurements are found, perhaps human capital values can be included in financial statements. But most likely, they would appear as footnote disclosures.

The point to note here is that the HR and payroll systems are identifying employee expense outlays differently from accounting systems. Accounting systems do not capture the true cost flows for the HR financial outlays.

Exhibit 1-1 summarizes all the compensation and benefit cost flows. In one place, it shows the accounting flows of all total compensation elements and also indicates the accounting classification most likely used to record these transactions.

Exhibit 1-1 A Summary of the Flows

HR Classification	Accounting Classifications
Base pay	Direct labor, indirect labor, selling, general and administrative expenses
	---
	Could be an income statement expense
	Could be an asset on balance sheet
Benefits	Direct labor, indirect labor, selling, general and administrative expenses
	---
	Could be an income statement expense
	Could be an asset on balance sheet
Incentives	Direct labor, indirect labor, selling, general and administrative expenses
	---
	Could be an income statement expense
	Could be an asset on balance sheet
Allowances	Direct labor, indirect labor, selling, general and administrative expenses
	---
	Could be an income statement expense
	Could be an asset on balance sheet
Adders to base	Direct labor, indirect labor, selling, general and administrative expenses
	---
	Could be an income statement expense
	Could be an asset on the balance sheet
Retirement Benefits	
Define benefits	Pension expense on income statement
	Net pension liability or asset on balance sheet
Define contribution	Pension expense
Stock related	Stock option expense
Perquisites	Expense: selling, general, and administrative expense
Expatriate compensation	Selling, general, and administrative expense

The Accounting of HR Cost Outlays – How Payroll Systems Work

Now that you understand cost and expense classifications in general and the HR designations of employee cost outlays, this section covers how accounting systems currently report employee cost transactions in the accounting cycle.[7]

Payroll departments are responsible for making payments to employees. But not all employee payments are transmitted from the payroll department. Some payments are made as expense reimbursements.

Exhibit 1-2 shows the payment transactions normally disbursed from payroll departments.

Exhibit 1-2 Payment Transactions Made from Payroll Departments

Employee Payment Category	Accounting Disbursement Point
Base pay	Payroll
Overtime	Payroll
Pay adders	Payroll
Incentives and bonuses	Payroll
Allowances (including international allowances)	Payroll
Sales commissions	Payroll[*1]
Stock program transactions	Stock administration
Perquisites	Payroll or accounts payable
Risk benefit outlays	Accounts payable and TPAs[*2]
Workers' compensation disbursements	Accounts payable and TPAs
Retirement program disbursements, plan contribution	Account payable, TPAs for 401(k)

*1 All payroll disbursements are those that involve tax-related deductions and involve accounting transactions.

*2 Third-party administrator

[7]   By accounting cycle it is meant: source documents are classified into the appropriate account from the charter of accounts; then entries are journalized; then entries are posted to the ledger; then the trial balance is developed; then period end adjustments are recorded; then the post-adjustments trial balance is developed; then the financial statements are created; then closing entries are entered; and then finally post-closing trail balance is developed.

Exhibit 1-3 indicates in summary form how a typical payroll process works, which we explain in more detail.

Exhibit 1-3 Payment Transactions Made from Payroll Departments

The Typical Payroll Process Involves
Calculating gross earnings
Calculating employee withholding taxes
Preparing paychecks
Preparing the payroll register
Updating employee payroll registers
Preparing governmental filings
Journalizing into the general ledger payroll, payroll taxes
Posting these transactions to the general ledger
Preparing payroll reports

In addition, payroll systems track payment transactions differently depending on how pay is recorded in HR processes and systems. Employee designations commonly use designations such as salaried, monthly, weekly, or hourly. It should be noted that these are payroll-related computational designations rather than what is conventionally thought–an employee ranking or status designation. If an employee is designated as an hourly employee, the computations in the payroll system might be as in the following example.

Suppose that John Peters is one of six hourly (non-exempt) employees who work for Bagan, Inc. Bagan has a biweekly payroll process. Let's also say that the biweekly period starts on March 16 and ends on March 30. The first week of this period started on March 16 and ended March 23. And during this period, John worked for 46 hours. Federal law in the United States stipulates that any nonexempt employee who works for more than 40 hours a week needs to be compensated at a time-and-a-half rate for those extra hours.[8] In this

---

[8] Note that in the USA, there are many differences between federal wage and hour laws and state wage and hour laws.

case, 6 hours are over the 40-hour limit. Suppose John's hourly rate is $25.20. In that case, his weekly gross pay is calculated in this manner:

40 hours @ $25.20 = $1,008.00

6 hours @ $25.20 × 1.5 or $37.80 = $226.80

Total gross earnings for the week = $1,234.80

In the United States, tax is withheld from the gross wage income (which for John Smith is calculated based on his documented deductions on his W-4 form and withholding tax publication–Circular E, provided by the Internal Revenue Service). After that, state income tax withholding is also deducted from gross pay. In addition, the payroll department must withhold Social Security taxes or FICA (*Federal Insurance Contribution Act*). This tax is actually two taxes. One tax is called the *Old-Age, Survivors, and Disability Insurance* (OASDI), and the other is known as Medicare (hospital insurance). The rates for OASDI and Medicare are, respectively, for 2012, 6.2%[9] and 1.45% of gross wages. In addition to these deductions, other deductions will be needed, such as the employee portion of an employee health insurance program (if there are any for the organization).

To further illustrate the gross earnings to net earnings calculation, now let's assume that for the second week, the March 26 to March 30 pay period, John worked 40 hours.

So, here is the gross to net calculation:

Week 1 gross (which includes 6 hours of overtime pay)	1,234.80
Week 2 gross (40 hours × $25.20)	1,008.00
Total gross for the pay period	2,242.80
Deductions:	
Federal income tax (assumed numbers in this example)	215.74

---

[9] There is currently a "tax holiday" in place that relieves employees of this deduction.

Note

The federal withholding tax is derived after the employee completes and submits Form W-4, Employee's Withholding Allowance Certificate. This amount is based on marital status and the total number of dependant allowances claimed on the certificate. The amount of tax withheld is provided in the wage bracket table, published by the IRS in Circular E.

State income tax	179.43

Note

The state income tax withholding is calculated in a similar manner using allowances provided on the W-4 form and by using state publications published for the purpose of calculating withholding taxes.

OASDI tax (6.2% of gross pay)	139.05
Medicare tax (1.45% of gross pay)	32.52
Medical insurance copay (assumed number for this example)	54.00
Total deductions	620.74
Net pay	1,622.06

Other possible payroll deductions and adjustments include the following:

- City and county taxes, if any
- Before-tax employee contributions
- 401(k) employee contributions (disbursed to TPAs*)
- Health savings account (disbursed to TPAs*)
- Flexible spending accounts (disbursed to TPAs*)

Employer Payments

Also note the potential employer payments made on behalf of an employee:

- *Federal Unemployment Tax* (FUTA)
- *Statement Unemployment Tax* (SUTA)
- Employer-matching contributions for 401(k) plans
- Workers' compensation premiums
- Employer portion of Social Security taxes paid on behalf of an employee

Accounting Record Keeping

In the accounting process, employee payment transactions are journalized, posted to the ledger, and recorded in the financial statements in the manner shown in Exhibit 1-4.

Exhibit 1-4 Employee Payment Transactions

Account Title Affected	Category	Account	Financial Statement
Product or service expense	Expense	Debit	Income statement
Payroll tax expense	Expense	Debit	Income statement
Workers' compensation insurance expense	Expense	Debit	Income statement
FICA payable	Liability	Credit	Balance sheet
FICA Medicare payable	Liability	Credit	Balance sheet
FIT payable	Liability	Credit	Balance sheet
SIT payable	Liability	Credit	Balance sheet
FUTA payable	Liability	Credit	Balance sheet
SUTA payable	Liability	Credit	Balance sheet
Medical insurance payable	Liability	Credit	Balance sheet
Wages salaries payable	Liability	Credit	Balance sheet

This is not necessarily the case in manufacturing companies, where employee payments can be a part of work in process, finished goods, or cost of goods sold. Exhibit 1-5 gives a description of the accounting entries recorded for payroll transactions.

Exhibit 1-5 Accounting Entries for Payroll Transactions

Date	Cost of goods sold		xxxxx	
	General selling and admin expense		xxxxx	
		FIT payable		xxxxx
		SIT payable		xxxxx
		FICA OASDI payable		xxxxx
		FICA Medicare payable		xxxxx
		Medical insurance payable		xxxxx
		Wages and salaries payable		xxxxx
		To record payroll for a period		xxxxx
Date				
	Payroll tax expense		xxxxx	
		FICA OASDI payable		xxxxx
		FICA Medicare payable		xxxxx
		FUTA payable		xxxxx
		SUTA payable		xxxxx
		To record payroll tax expense for pay period, xx/xx/xxxx, and then when payment is made to employees		xxxxx
Date				
	Wages and salaries payable		xxxxx	
		Cash		xxxxx
		To record actual payment of current payment accruals		xxxxx

Note here that after these transactions are incurred they become payables and remain on the balance sheet until those outlays are paid out from cash. At that point, those transactions become income statement accounts.

Accounting for Payments Made to Salaried Employees

For employees who are classified as salaried, the payroll status is normally stated as a monthly wage. This is not a job-level designation. It indicates that in the payroll system these employees' compensation payments are recorded on a monthly basis. In the United States, salaried employees are usually exempt from the provisions of the Fair Labor Standards Act. In other words, they do not have to be paid overtime for any hours they work over 40 hours in a week.

Federal law in the United States that governs overtime earnings is called the Fair Labor Standards Act, which is part of the federal wage and hour legislation. All employers engaged in interstate commerce have to adhere to the Fair Labor Standards Act. There are also state wage and hours legislation with which employers must comply.[10]

The payroll system pays these employees their fixed monthly salary on each pay date. If the pay period is biweekly, these salaried employees are paid their monthly rate divided by two. The stated salary rate will be gross pay from which the employee's specific payroll deductions are subtracted. These deductions are similar to those used for hourly employees (as described earlier in this chapter).

Other Technical Payroll Accounting and HR Issues

First, there is the issue of thirteenth- and fourteenth-month payments made in many countries outside of the United States. Normally, in the United States, the workday is 8 hours in duration. In a 52-week year, that makes 2,080 work hours in a year:

8 hours a day × 5 days a week × 52 weeks in a year = 2,080 hours

In the United States, the number of hours employees can work is 2,080. But we know that most employees take at least two weeks of vacation during the year. Those two weeks are paid vacation days. Therefore, in the 52-week year, the employee does not necessarily work the entire 2,080 hours. If the employee takes a two-week

---

[10] FLSA states that any nonexempt (not exempt from the law) employee who works more than 8 hours in a day or 40 hours in a week has to be paid time and a half for those additional hours. In a state such as California, if the employee works more than 12 hours in a day or on the seventh consecutive day in a week, his or her pay must be double time for those hours.

vacation, he or she actually works 2,000 hours. But, employees are paid their annual stated salary. This is because a salaried employee's stated salary is an annual amount. It could also be stated on a monthly basis. In the latter case, you just have to multiply the monthly salary by 12 to get the annual stated salary. Therefore, in the United States, paid vacation is built in to the annual or monthly stated salary. Holiday pay is treated in the same manner.

In some countries, the monthly or annual salary covers only hours actually worked. The vacation is paid as an extra month: the 13th month. The 13th-month payment is identified differently in different countries. In some countries, it is a bonus granted to all employees. In other countries the Christmas bonus is a legal requirement. The additional-month payment adds to wage costs. In Greece, which is in economic chaos, the payment of the 13th month has become a political issue.

The main purpose of this chapter was to explain how the accounting process and the HR process classify compensation and benefit elements. As you learned, to accurately understand and record HR financial transactions, processes have to be developed to record these expenditures to better understand their impact on operational and strategic business decisions. For example, the critical strategic and operational decision about workforce reductions is often made based on accounting data, which is much narrower in scope than HR inflows and outflows classifications. If a more broadly scoped HR accounting data-gathering process were adopted, business decision makers might not be as willing to terminate the services of thousands of people so readily. As you know, workforce reduction results in devastating consequences for those employees who lose their jobs and for society as a whole.

Key Concepts in This Chapter

- Flow of compensation and benefits cost outlays
- Costs versus expenses
- CAPEX
- OPEX

- Compensation and benefits cost elements
- Understanding base pay
- Base pay outflows
- Current accounting for compensation and benefit cost elements
- Payroll accounting
- Record keeping of HR cost elements within the accounting cycle
- Technical issues with respect to compensation and benefit cost elements
- The definition of all compensation and benefit terms

Appendix: The Terms

This appendix describes compensation and benefit terms in more detail than described in the main body of this chapter:

- **Base, basic, fixed, "come to work" pay:** The "fixed" part of pay. This element is provided to employees to come to work and do the job by using the required skills, knowledge, abilities, and appropriate work behaviors. Usually, this component is based on market rates combined with some measure of the internal ranking for the job or position, normally through a job-evaluation system.

  Base pay can also be identified in many other ways:
  - **Wage:** A fixed regular payment typically paid on a daily or weekly basis by an employer to an employee classified as a manual or unskilled worker. In economics, wage is the part of total production that is the return to labor as earned income as compared to dividends received by owners. Some contend that wages are paid to daily workers who are not necessarily employees. The implication is that the word *wage* is used to define the money a worker receives in exchange for labor (that is, physical labor). There seems to be a connotation that wages are given in exchange for physical labor and not brain power (physical strength in contrast to intelligence).

- **Salary:** A fixed regular payment typically paid on a monthly or biweekly basis but often stated as an annual sum. This is payment made by an employer to an employee as opposed to a worker. In other words, it is a payment made to a professional or a white-collar worker. A salary is a form of periodic payment from an employer to an employee, as stated in a recruitment contract. The payment differs from wages. In wage payments, each job or hour is paid separately. The distinction between salary and wages flows from the fact that for salaried employment the effort and output of "office work" is hard to measure in hourly terms.

- **Compensation:** The money received by an employee from an employer as a salary or wage. Therefore, the word *compensation* is used as an encompassing word covering both wages and salaries. But the pure definition of this word is money awarded to a person to compensate that person for his or her time, effort, abilities, knowledge, experience, and skills provided to an employer. This is the basis for an exchange; employer pays compensation, the employee provides the employer various personal attributes. When the exchange is not fair from the point of view of either party, there is dissatisfaction. Effective compensation is based on various motivational theories. A discussion about the theories is beyond the scope of this book.

- **Pay:** Pay means the giving of money to someone that is due to him or her for work done. In other words, it explains the giving of a sum of money in exchange for work done. It also alludes to giving what is due or deserved. The notion of payment arose from the sense of pacifying a creditor. I want to pay him for his work (reward him, reimburse her, compensate him, give payment to him or her, or remunerate him or her).

In the current context, this concept needs some thought. It is not just wages or salaries that are being provided. Organizations are paying their human resources; they are rewarding, they are remunerating. The concept here is that the word *pay* should include both the perspectives of the giver and receiver of pay. This is a psychological transaction as much as it is an economic transaction. Both the supply (what the organization wants to provide) and the demand side (what the employee, who is the creditor being pacified) of the equation need to be considered to make the transaction fair to both parties.

All too often, organizations (both private and public) look at only the supply side and ignore the demand side (what the employee wants), and therefore pay remains one of the most emotionally disturbing work conditions.

- **Remuneration:** One will receive adequate remuneration for the work one has done (that is, a payment, pay, salary, wages; earnings, fees, reward, compensation, reimbursement; formal emoluments). So, this word is also an all-encompassing word.

- **Rewards:** A payment given in recognition of service, effort, or accomplishment. Today, the concepts behind the terminology listed here continue to evolve as part of a system of reward that employers offer to employees. Salary (also now known as fixed pay) is coming to be seen as part of a *total rewards* system, which includes variable pay (such as bonuses, incentive pay, and commissions), benefits and perquisites (or perks), and other schemes employers use to link reward to an employee's individual performance. Tying it into performance in a clear, understandable, and acceptable way remains a continuing challenge. Good in theory, but fraught with real-life issues.

- **Incentives or bonuses:** These payments are provided to employees for achieving time-bound goals and objectives. Words such as *incentive targets, objectives (bonus objectives), measurements,* and *ratings* are all contextual terms used in most organizations. In economics and sociology, an incentive is any factor (financial or nonfinancial) that enables or motivates a particular course of action. These payments or gifts are added to what is usual or expected. Incentives are often amounts of money added to wages on a seasonal basis, especially as a reward for good performance (for example, a Christmas bonus).

- **Allowances:** These items are not benefits but are additional cash payments for special circumstances. These types of allowances are widely used in various countries. They are sums of money paid regularly to a person, specifically to meet specified life needs or expenses. It is an amount of money that can be earned or received free of tax or tax neutralized; examples are housing, education, hardship, transportation, special area allowances, foreign service premiums, and tax protection or equalization payments.

- **Adders to base:** These payments are common in the United States. Overtime pay, callback pay, and on-call pay (also called *beeper pay*) are common elements provided for work that is done beyond normal work hours or under special circumstances. Overtime is provided for work done over standard legal working hours. Callback pay is special pay provided to technical workers who are called back to work after normal hours because they are needed to address a specific or an urgent situation. On-call pay is similarly an additional amount paid to employees who are required to be on-call by their employers to come into work when asked to do so. *Beeper pay* is provided to employees who have to keep electronic beepers on all the time so employers can access the workers on short notice.

- **Risk benefits:** Medical, disability, and life insurance. These benefits are provided to employees in lieu of cash to mitigate the various life risks faced by employees and their families. Employee benefits are regarded as nonwage compensation provided to employees in addition to their normal wages. Benefits can be regarded as transactions where the employee exchanges (cash) wages for some other form of economic benefit. This is generally referred to as a *salary-sacrifice* arrangement. In most countries, employee benefits are taxable at least to some degree. Some of these benefits are group insurance (health, dental, life, and so on), medical payment plans, disability income protection, daycare, tuition reimbursement, sick leave, vacation (paid and nonpaid), and Social Security. The purpose of the benefits is to increase the economic security of employees and protect them from unfavorable life situations.

- **Retirement plans:** Employers provide these benefits to assist employees with their post-employment lives. Usually there are two categories of retirement plans: the defined benefit plans and the defined contribution plans. Defined benefits plans are formula based, and defined contribution plans are contribution based. The contributions are made by participating employees. The fundamental objective of these plans is to provide an income-replacement payment. With this payment, participating employees should be able to replace a certain portion of their preretirement income during their retirement years.

- **Equity compensation:** This element in the past was mostly provided to senior executives to motivate them to increase shareholder value. But the equity compensation component of pay has seen many changes over the past ten years or so. There are many versions of these plans: nonqualified stock options, incentive stock options, restricted stock options, stock appreciation rights, among others. There are many accounting, tax, and legal implications to these plans. Some of the issues being discussed within this context are ownership culture, stock option pricing, dilution, and overhang. The equity compensation element has spawned specialists, legal experts, associations, and interest groups (each with their unique opinions and viewpoints). The important issues in equity compensation are (1) whether these programs have any value if distributed all across the whole employee population, even to the lowest employee levels, and (2) whether the organizations that distribute stock options widely to all levels of employees achieve an "ownership culture."

- **Perquisites:** Many companies provide executives a wide variety of perks. This practice is widespread around the world. The term *perks* is often used colloquially to refer to payments because of their discretionary nature. Often, perks are given to employees who are outstanding performers and those who have seniority. Common perks include company cars, hotel stays, free refreshments, leisure activities during work time (golf and so on), stationery, and lunch allowances.

2

Business, Financial, and Human Resource Planning[1]

Aims and objectives of this chapter

- Explain the connections between business planning, human resource planning, and compensation planning
- Develop the need for planning
- Examine the concept of strategic planning
- Explore the connections between strategic planning and operational planning
- Discuss the concept of HR planning
- Review an integrated HR planning process
- Discuss the concept of organizational planning and design
- Develop the connections between HR and compensation planning
- Explain the concept of talent management

This chapter deals with the strategic concept of planning. Effective compensation and benefits program design—from an accounting and finance point of view—requires a solid planning foundation.

Finance and accounting departments usually are the operational guardians of the organization-wide planning activities. Therefore,

---

[1] Adapted wholly or partly from a paper written by Biswas, B.D., and Hestwood, T., "Human Resource Planning and Compensation: A Developing Relationship." Conference presentation made at National Conference of the American Compensation Associates 1979.

before delving into the components of compensation and benefits program design (from an accounting and finance perspective), it is important to discuss the concept of planning and how it ties into *human resource* (HR) planning and then compensation and benefits planning.

Integrating HR, compensation, and benefits activities into strategic financial and operational plans is a key first step for the integration of the two disciplines (HR / compensation and benefits and finance / accounting). Therefore, this chapter explores these connections.

Business and financial planning, as well as HR and compensation planning, have not traditionally been thought of as codependent functions. This is reflected in how HR departments normally are organized. Even in organizations that usually have an HR planning function, it is normally teamed with organization planning and development function. This is because the organization planning and development is often commissioned to conduct organizational effectiveness studies. Compensation is a separate entity. In addition, experience suggests that even informal links between the two functions are few and far in between. Compensation specialists and financial or even HR planners rarely work together on projects and tasks.

However, both the planning and compensation functions can gain by being better aligned. This chapter looks at the reasons why planning is necessary. The focus then turns to a review of a standard structure for strategic business planning and the related strategic and operational financial planning. The discussion then suggests an HR planning model that flows from the inputs of the strategic and operational financial plans. This chapter also explores the specific benefits a total compensation system can derive from the planning efforts. The chapter ends with a look at how compensation can contribute to the overall planning effort.

The Overall Planning Framework

Exhibit 2-1 shows a flowchart of planning activities, and is a macro view of the planning process. This overall planning framework identifies the focus of this chapter.

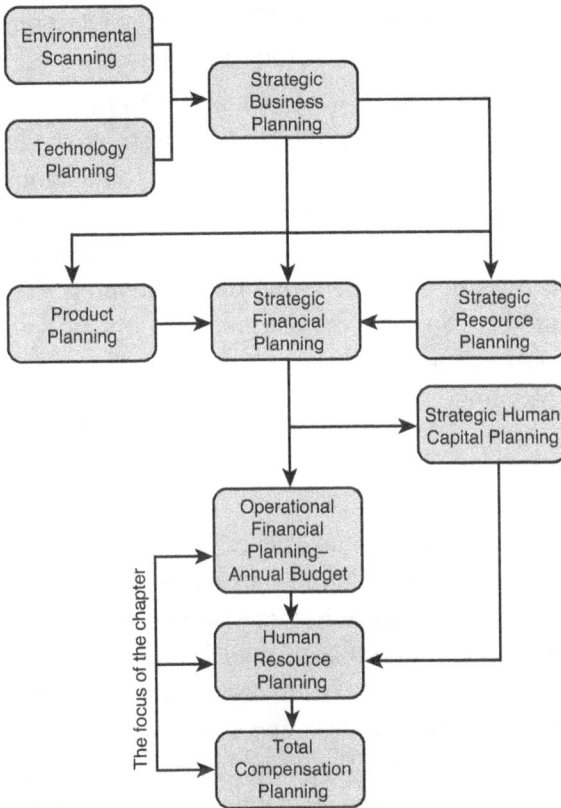

Exhibit 2-1 A Conceptual Framework for the Connections between Strategic Business and Financial Planning and HR and Total Compensation Planning

The Need for Planning

Organizations know that success requires planning with regard to both physical and financial resources. (In economics terms, these are the factors of production.) To state an obvious example, electric-generation companies must now plan more carefully than ever to ensure an adequate supply of coal at the right time and place. Electric generation plants require large quantities of coal to operate. It's not just shortages that promote planning, it's the complexity in the form of the global nature of business, of government regulations, of the exponential growth of technology, of human capital challenges, and all the other interests of various stakeholders. Managing the interconnectivity among these varying forces clearly requires planning.

Planning entails many dimensions, each connected to the other in an integrated approach to planning. Exhibit 2-1 suggests a form of this integrated approach. The exhibit suggests that clear connections do indeed exist between these planning processes. Strategic planning or longer-term planning is important, but this activity (at least an in-depth discussion about it) is beyond the scope of this chapter. The discussion here is limited to the connections between operational financial planning and HR planning and the subsequent connections to total compensation planning.

Strategic Planning

Let's briefly consider strategic planning here. Strategic planning refers to an organization's process of defining its strategy, or direction, and making decisions about allocating its resources to pursue that strategy. The strategic plan identifies and analyzes the current status, objectives, and strategies of an existing organization to determine the direction of the organization. It is necessary to understand the organization's current position and the possible avenues through which it can pursue alternative courses of action. An organization looks at strategy from a long-term perspective. Therefore, strategic planning is considered a process for determining where an organization is going over the next three to five years (long term).

When looking at the longer term, organizations examine existing or perceived *strengths, weaknesses, threats, and opportunities* (SWOT). Information about the future business and social environment the organization operates in is analyzed in connection with the marketing, production, and research capabilities, which then leads to strategy development covering the following issues:

- Vision
- Mission
- Values
- Strategies

- Goals
- Programs
- Objectives
- Resource allocation

Business plans are derived from strategic planning in terms of the products or services to be produced and the materials, people, and facilities necessary to produce them. All of this is converted to the language of business: finance and accounting.

An integral part of the strategic business planning process is the follow-on strategic financial plan, which codifies the strategic plan in monetary terms over the same long-term time horizon. The strategic financial plan then forms the basis for the short-term operational financial plan, often called the annual financial budget. Thus, strategic financial plans become the triggering point for the annual operational financial budget planning exercise. Operational financial planning is also often called profit planning. Exhibit 2-2 shows these connections in the planning process. It also illustrates how strategic financial planning flows through to the operating profit plans of an organization.

The annual financial budget or the profit plan is important for many reasons, including the following:

- It is a means of communication throughout the organization.
- The financial budgeting process facilitates management planning for resource usage.
- The financial budget is a mechanism that assists with the most efficient allocation of resources within an organization.
- It also assists in uncovering potential trouble areas, before they happen.
- The financial budget assists in coordinating the varied activities within an organization into an integrated focused effort that is in sync with the strategic business plans of the organization.
- The financial budget structure lends itself to the tasks of monitoring and controlling, which are necessary to ensure that progress is measured and all the required activities within an organization are on track.

Therefore, strategic and operational financial planning is certainly a key success factor for any organization. Within this context, the focus now turns to HR planning and the subsequent total compensation planning.

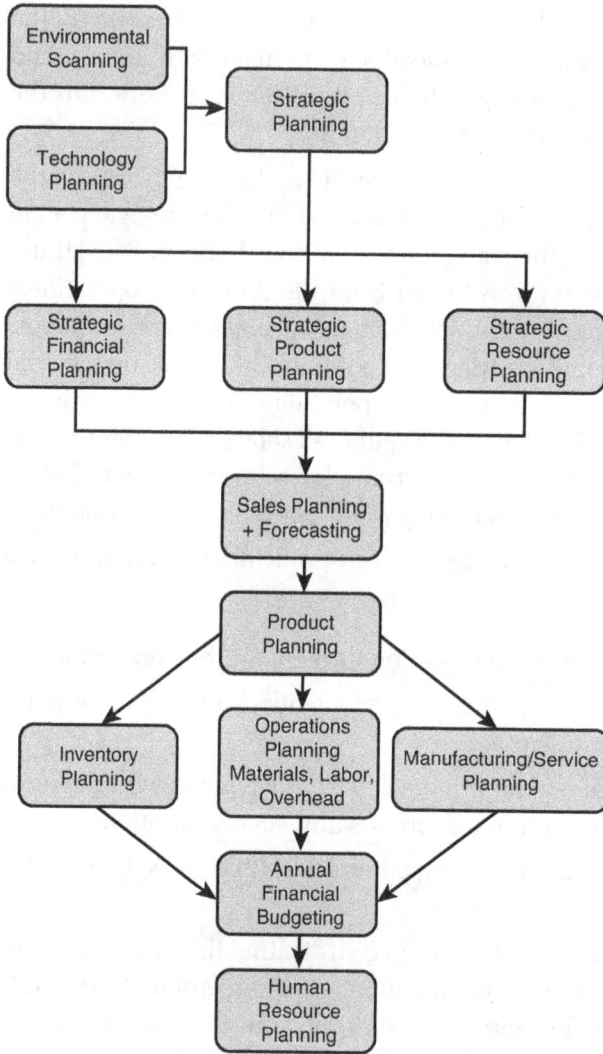

```
┌──────────────┐
│ Environmental│
│   Scanning   │
└──────────────┘──┐      ┌──────────────┐
                  ├─────▶│  Strategic   │
┌──────────────┐  │      │   Planning   │
│  Technology  │──┘      └──────────────┘
│   Planning   │
└──────────────┘
```

```
┌──────────────┐   ┌──────────────┐   ┌──────────────┐
│  Strategic   │   │  Strategic   │   │  Strategic   │
│  Financial   │   │   Product    │   │   Resource   │
│   Planning   │   │   Planning   │   │   Planning   │
└──────────────┘   └──────────────┘   └──────────────┘
```

```
┌──────────────┐
│Sales Planning│
│ + Forecasting│
└──────────────┘
```

```
┌──────────────┐
│   Product    │
│   Planning   │
└──────────────┘
```

```
┌──────────────┐   ┌──────────────┐   ┌──────────────────┐
│              │   │  Operations  │   │                  │
│  Inventory   │   │   Planning   │   │Manufacturing/    │
│   Planning   │   │Materials,Labor,│ │Service Planning  │
│              │   │   Overhead   │   │                  │
└──────────────┘   └──────────────┘   └──────────────────┘
```

```
┌──────────────┐
│    Annual    │
│  Financial   │
│  Budgeting   │
└──────────────┘
```

```
┌──────────────┐
│    Human     │
│   Resource   │
│   Planning   │
└──────────────┘
```

Exhibit 2-2 The Planning Connections

HR Planning

The HR function is on a continual talent hunt for the right human resources at the right times and the right places. This is similar to resource acquisition and consumption in other areas throughout the business world. All business functions, including the HR function, face supply issues and therefore must plan for such. This section covers a few of the reasons why such planning is vital.

First, organizations require a sufficient number and quality of the "right" talent (talent management) available to meet future organizational needs. With regard to this requirement, a number of factors make HR planning a necessity:

- **Technical obsolescence and associated technological innovations:** In many technical fields, a person's professional knowledge can become obsolete within five years. Firms that require the development of new or expanded technology must constantly retrain and reeducate their employee base. Of course, talent acquisition, training, and education take time. To have that time requires HR planning and a global view of the HR capital asset or resource.

- **Scarcity of the right type of talent:** In some occupations and areas, the unemployment rates for specifically skilled professionals is nearly zero. And this is in spite of the high overall current unemployment rates and the increasing numbers of structurally unemployed individuals. Managers and skilled professionals in such fields as specialized engineering programming, robotics, and biotechnology are still in short supply. Shortages in specific types of needed talent are going to continue for some time to come.

  Organizations confront some interesting attitudinal problems with an issue like this. Consider this analogy: Many motorists, as demonstrated by their driving patterns, still find it hard to believe that there is a diminishing supply of fossil fuel resources in the world. Similarly, many managers and HR professionals find it difficult to believe that there might be a shortage of the right talent to fill specific openings. If these shortages are real then organizations should be planning for the optimization of human capital resources.

- **Lack of an adequate level of geographic mobility:** Because of the employment needs of spouses and quality-of-life considerations, more people are unwilling to relocate. Because of this inability to motivate employees to relocate, the supply of qualified candidates may be inadequate to meet the needs of many organizations.

- **Transferability of skills:** As long as talent shortages remain and technological innovation continues, professionals in those fields will find it easier to transfer their skills and talents from company to company. Companies cannot count on people spending their whole careers in one organization.

Second, organizations must identify problems that are hindering the optimal use of human resources, leading to organizational ineffectiveness. To meet the needs of the future, employee and organizational effectiveness needs to be improved at every possible opportunity. The planning process provides an opportunity to identify shortages of skills, overstaffing or understaffing, and other human resource problems.

Third, HR planning integrates the goals and actions of the disparate HR functions and enables HR management to allocate resources to the functions capable of contributing most to the organization's needs. The activities of the separate functions (compensation, staffing, training, and so on) should be based on the objectives of the business. For example, recruiting may be rejecting applicants for technician jobs without knowing what training could be done in-house to make technical employees more effective and in tune with the current business needs. Compensation may be developing a system of flexible benefits, even though the real need is extra dollars of base pay to help get people in the door and to keep them there. Planning facilitates the use of a "systems approach" to HR management.

The last reason for HR planning is that it creates the ability to respond quickly to unexpected business and financial changes, such as mergers, acquisitions, financial consolidations, and product demand.

An Integrated HR Planning Process

Financial planning, HR planning, and compensation planning have a lot to gain by being more closely associated. Therefore, HR planning is the process by which an organization forecasts the future HR requirements of the organization and then develops and implements policies and programs to meet those requirements.

Now that we have established the need for HR planning, let's expand on the definition of the term and look at a model for the process.

HR planning is the process by which an organization forecasts the future HR requirements of an organization and develops and implements plans, policies, and programs to meet those requirements. This definition emphasizes the integration of HR plans with the development of the HR programs necessary to achieve those plans. The model of the planning process shown in Exhibit 2-3 illustrates this approach.

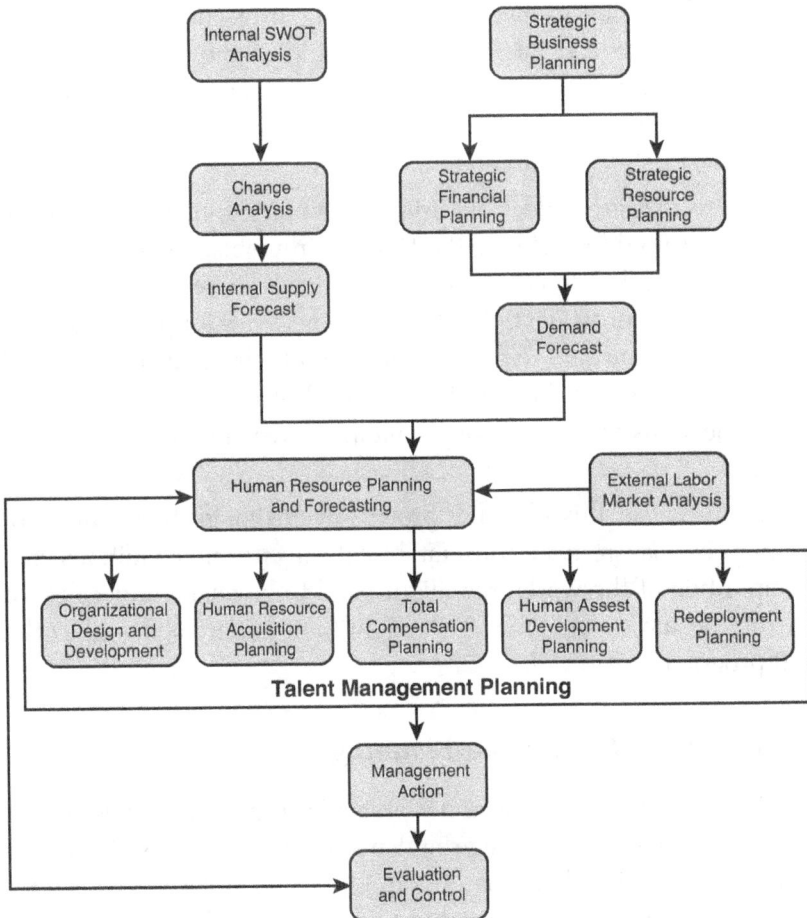

Exhibit 2-3 An Integrated Human Resource Planning Process

The model consists of four major components. The first component is the process of developing future HR requirements—the true planning part of the process. The second component is the establishment of HR policies and programs necessary to achieve those plans. We call this step talent management. The third component comprises the actions taken by HR professionals and managers to implement HR programs developed in the second component. The last component is the evaluation of the success or failure of the actions taken.

Demand Planning

HR plans are formed by comparing projections of expected demand for the HR talent (the right side of the model) and the potential supply of the talent (the left side of the model). Forecasts of demand are not going to proceed without an analysis of the capabilities of the existing workforce to meet them.

There is a great deal of variability among organizations in the procedures used for defining the HR requirements. Some companies have a team at headquarters that determines the needs by means of quantitative forecasting. Other organizations leave it up to division or department managers to forecast and plan their talent needs based on unit objectives and plans. The financial planning staff then totals the projections from these departments to develop an organization forecast.

Note that in this planning process even though the number of employees may remain constant based on current conditions, the composition of the workforce might need to be changed because of current business conditions. This might then require a change in the HR programs.

Organization Design and Planning

The next step in the planning process is organization design and planning. Organization design and planning is a process by which tasks are defined and grouped into positions and jobs and then integrated into an organization's structure (thus enabling the achievement of future business objectives). In other words, managers need to outline not only the number of employees they are going to require but also the required knowledge, skills, abilities, behavioral dimensions, experience levels, and competencies. Managers also need to develop the optimum organization structure based on guidelines provided about work levels and spans of control. Organization design and planning activities are becoming an integral part of the systematic talent management process. However, the trend has not been widely established, and many differences among organizations still exist as to what organization planning and development means and how it is implemented.

Also, the word *competency* has recently entered into the lexicon of HR management. In practice, though, there are multiple definitions and interpretations of this word. From among them all, the definition that makes the most sense states that competencies are the optimum set of knowledge, skills, abilities, and associated work behavior necessary to achieve the company's strategic and operational business objectives.

Organization design and planning is introduced into the HR planning process to deal with a common deficiency of many planning processes: the failure to define talent needs in terms specific enough for use by all the stakeholders: supervisors, managers, and the various HR functions. Talent forecasts are often stated only in quantitative terms. (For example, the marketing department will need 20 new people, and the accounting department will require 10 new people.) To ensure that a sufficient degree of detail is made available, managers must be asked to conduct organization design and planning exercises.

Forecasting Demand

Exhibit 2-4 presents a format for the development of a talent demand forecast—the next step in the planning process. This needs to be completed after the organization design and planning step. The exhibit presents future talent requirements, by department, for major job categories and job grade or salary levels. Special knowledge, skills, ability, experience, and competency requirements are noted in footnotes of the exhibit. An organization chart may be required as well. Large organizations may want geographic breakdowns or have other specific data-clustering requirements.

Exhibit 2-4 2013 Projected Additional Staff Requirements

Job Category Department	Executive Gr. 26+	Middle Management Gr 19–25	Management Gr 15–18	Supervisor Gr 11–14	Totals
Marketing					
Accounting					
Regional Sales Offices					
National Accounts					
Totals					

Supply Planning

Let's turn now to the supply side of the model. In this part of the model, we examine the quality and capabilities of the current talent pool. This is compared to the talent requirements needed over the forecast period. The comparative analysis will determine whether the workforce can meet the needs of the future.

We should not assume that the current talent pool is performing adequately or that it will meet future job requirements. One way to examine the quality and capabilities of the current talent pool is to conduct a talent review. The talent review is a systematic assessment of the qualifications and skills of individuals in the organization and the potential of those people to fill higher-level jobs. It involves questions such as these: Is the department meeting its goals and objectives? Are present incumbents performing adequately? If not, what actions can be taken? Are there enough resources in the current talent pool to fill key positions if current incumbents leave? Is our current talent pool being adequately trained to do their jobs in the future?

Often, information useful to compensation comes out of these discussions. Examples include information about perceived job-classification problems or the problems associated with high-potential employees, who are not being paid in line with market rates. Compensation specialists should become part of the team that conducts the talent review to ensure that issues affecting them are fully appreciated.

The next step on the supply side of the model is to determine the talent changes expected over the course of the planning cycle. In this part of the process, you always examine key segments of the talent pool. The analysis can be extended to the total talent pool if the future supply of workers is unstable. Forecasted changes include terminations, retirements, and layoffs. The data on these changes can be derived, especially in the case of terminations, from an extrapolation of historical trends in turnover grouped by termination reason. In the case of retirements, recent company experience can guide you. The talent changes should be projected by location, division, and job-family categories.

To integrate the potential internal supply information with the demand requirements, the information from each department or division is summarized on a table such as the one presented in Exhibit 2-5.

Exhibit 2-5 2013 HR Plan

	Current 12/31/12	Planned 12/31/13	Add/ Growth	Replace	Terms	Promotion
Marketing						
Accounting						
Sales						
Engineering						
Other selling, general, and administrative (SG&A)						
Management						
Executive						
Totals						

This exhibit shows data for each talent group, the current staff, the planned talent pool, additions to the pool, and the number of replacements that may have to be hired to reach a total year-end talent level. To provide a complete picture of the talent situation, each department or division can provide a narrative summary of the HR problems and challenges they anticipate confronting over the forecast period. They should explain how they plan to deal with the problems. By combining qualitative and quantitative information in this fashion, the organizational planning process can better meet the needs of all HR functions and, of course, those of the business as a whole.

External Labor Market

Organizations must also consider the projected availability of the right type of workers in the external labor market. The unemployment rate for different kinds of workers, labor force participation rates, and the external demand for similar skills and experiences can all have a major impact on an organization's HR plans. The external dimension will affect the organization's ability to attract new talent. The conditions in the external labor market affect an organization's turnover. The more opportunities there are in the external labor market, the higher the internal turnover. Therefore, organizations must keep track of the external market because it can affect the internal talent tool. This data is often available in local newspapers. For example, a manufacturer studied labor market conditions in a Southeast Asia location and found them ideal. There was a high rate of unemployment among skilled workers and a good labor pool to draw on. When the manufacturer opened a plant in that city, they found that other firms had also looked at the favorable conditions there and had decided to exploit the same location. The end result was that when all of these new businesses arrived, an acute labor shortage developed.

Planning information is gathered at different levels, in different degrees of detail, and over different time frames based on the type of organization. For example, in industries with relatively stable product markets, such as the airline industry, planning can be carried out on an overall company level without significant problems in the accuracy of the information. In more volatile industries and where the information needs to be specific, such as the technology sector, planning is more likely to be initiated at the division or department level. Divisional and departmental plans are rolled up to derive the company total.

Management Action/Evaluation and Control

Before we look at the relationship of planning to compensation, let's look at the two last segments of the model. Management action is the implementation by line managers of the programs developed by the HR department. The most sophisticated programs in the world will not be successful if improperly implemented and administered. The commitment of top management, the involvement of line managers in policy and program development, and the clear and careful communications are still the most important elements for the successful implementation and administration of programs.

The final step in the model is the evaluation of the contributions that each HR function makes to the achievement of the talent management goals of the business. Data needs to be collected on the actual achievement results compared to the objectives that were set in the planning process. This is where HR effectiveness measures come into play. Chapter 11, "Human Resource Analytics," discusses these measures in more detail. Procedures should be developed for taking corrective action for deviations from planned objectives.

The theory of constraints can be an effective method used during the evaluative phase. The theory of constraints calls for determining the weakest links and then focusing corrective attention on those areas.

HR Programs

The relationship between HR planning and the functional areas of human resources (compensation, benefits, recruiting, training, and employee services) can be clearly discerned. Recruiting uses the information to plan programs such as college recruiting, difficult recruiting efforts, and major recruiting campaigns such as those necessary to staff new programs, plants, or divisions. Training and development uses it to identify the kinds of talent that are being added to the organization and the training and developmental needs the talent pool is likely to require. The relationship between planning and compensation is less obvious and is the one examined in some detail in this chapter.

Compensation

To start our look at this relationship, let's identify the major compensation activities. We will then discuss those components that can derive benefits from HR planning. The compensation activities that have been identified are as follows:

- **Program development:** This is the design of salary ranges, salary-increase guidelines, incentive plans, and other techniques used by managers to determine individual employee salaries.
- **Program costing:** The next chapter covers this important component.
- **Job analysis and classification:** This is the process companies use to ensure internal equity or pay consistency within the organization.
- **Program administration:** These are the processes used by managers and HR departments to administer salary programs.
- **Executive compensation program development:** These are special compensation programs designed exclusively for the senior management in an organization.

Program Development

Compensation departments engage in some planning activities when developing salary programs. Typically, compensation planners collect data on the rate of inflation, changes in the cost-of-living indices (a measure that is used to gauge changes to the inflation rate is the change in the cost-of-living index), and union settlements. Compensation planners use such data to develop salary programs. However, most of the planning activities done currently are for the short term, normally a year. Short-term plans by their very nature are a response to immediate problems such as turnover, complaints about inflation (not in the USA now), or recruitment difficulties. One cannot ignore these immediate problems, but it is also important to analyze the longer-term implications of the actions taken.

An example of inadequate planning in program development is evident in the experience of a West Coast company. Although overall market average salaries for highly skilled engineering personnel in the labor market were increasing, the salaries of new college engineering graduates were not moving as fast as those in the general market because of the relatively high number of unemployed fresh college engineering graduates. Reacting to a short-term problem, the company decided, therefore, to move their range minimums less than the midpoints and maximums to control the cost of adjusting the salaries of employees low in the range. The company should have examined the future long-term trends in the external labor market by looking at long-term surveys of business activity. Had they done so, they would have found that the situation would reverse in the near future and that there would be a growing shortage of the specific types of engineers the company needed and that hiring salary rates would go up. Several months later, the failure to adequately adjust range minimums made it difficult to hire new college graduates in engineering. So, the company had to make reactionary mid-year salary-range adjustments. (Note this example is from a situation observed a few years ago.)

Information about the types and numbers of employees who will be added to the organization is also useful in developing increase guidelines and salary ranges for different job families. For example, suppose that your firm will increase its number of experienced engineers by 5% next year. The unemployment rate for those specific engineers is near zero, and turnover in your firm is significant. Even though your firm is already paying above market rates, you might have trouble finding and absorbing a large number of engineers without salary-compression problems.

Salary-compression problems occur when new employees come in at salary levels that put pressure on the salaries of existing employees. Under these circumstances, an organization will likely have to allocate more dollars to the engineering salary program than to the other programs by designing more liberal salary-increase guidelines and making bigger range adjustments for the engineering job family. If these additions are unknown (and therefore not being planned for), the organization might find it hard to attract the talent it needs without causing serious internal compensation problems.

The HR planning process can also provide information about jobs that are becoming more important or less important to the organization because of changes in the nature of the business. Compensation specialists can then be sure that important jobs are being included in benchmark job samples used to measure external competitiveness. For example, an international biotechnology company is planning to become more involved in development of genetic engineering solutions for medical technology. Because of the plan, genetic engineering specialists should be included in salary surveys and the resulting information considered in the design of the engineering salary program.

In a rapidly changing environment, organizations need to supplement normal sources of compensation information such as salary surveys and studies of expected salary changes in other organizations with information derived from the HR planning process. Exhibit 2-6 illustrates this concept. The most important information from the planning process is information about additions to staff, turnover statistics, and information about the future demand for talent from the external labor market.

Information for Salary Development

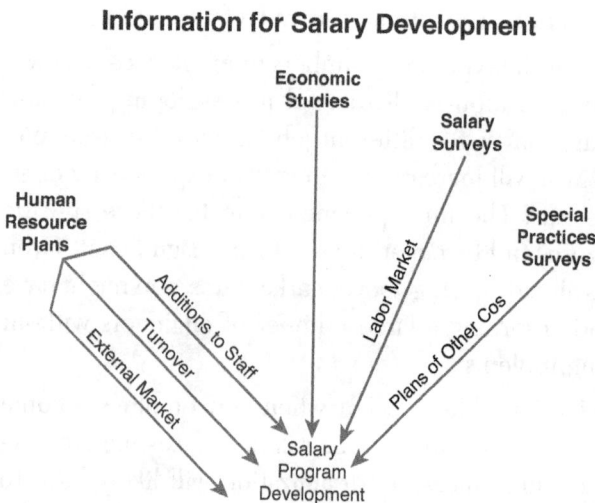

Exhibit 2-6 Information for Salary Development

Ideally, compensation specialists need to be able to simulate the future consequences of their pay programs. Exhibit 2-7 illustrates in simple terms this kind of analysis. If the average increase is 3% rather than 5%, the consequences in terms of cost and turnover should be projected. The impact of change in economic conditions might be examined in a similar way.

Exhibit 2-7 Consequences of Salary Increase Alternatives*

	8%	10%	12%	14%
Total cost				
Turnover				
Employee relations				
Productivity				
Compression problems				

* Numbers would be placed within each cell.

Job Analysis and Classification

Analyzing, describing, and evaluating jobs is probably the most time-consuming of all compensation activities. Moreover, it is often done under time constraints that make a thorough and well-prepared analysis difficult. Many times, however, the last-minute requests are not the result of last-minute decisions. They often were approved months ago; it's just that the manager has an immediate and pressing need to hire and promote someone. Therefore, they need the compensation department to classify the job immediately to determine the appropriate salary level.

How does one deal with such crises? First, compensation specialists need to be involved in the HR planning process through participation in organization planning and effectiveness studies and, more important, in organization design decisions. If compensation specialists have assisted managers in organization design decisions, they will be in a much better position to accurately and quickly describe, evaluate, and market-price the jobs. They will not have to go over the rationale behind the creation of each job, and they will understand reporting relationships, skill, knowledge, abilities, and competency requirements. Exhibit 2-8 shows the sequence by which jobs are developed and where further involvement by compensation specialists fits into the process.

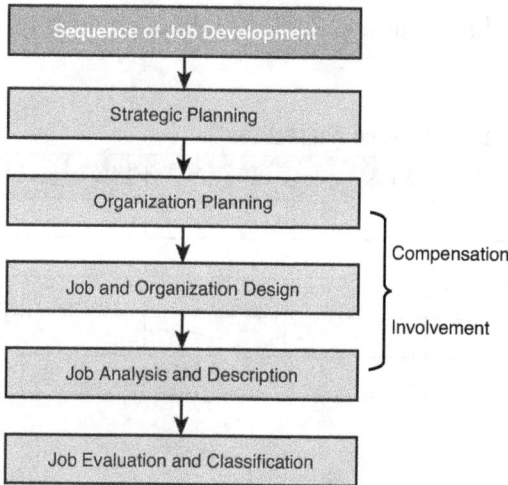

Exhibit 2-8 Sequence of Job Development

Organization Planning and Design

Organization planning is distinguished from job and organization design mainly by the detail of the analysis undertaken. Organization planning attempts to define job and organization needs for the future and, consequently, must be quite general in nature. Job and organization design, in contrast, deals with the here and now and requires decisions on specific work assignments and reporting relationships.

There is no right way to design an organization. The old organization norms, which suggested one supervisor for every seven subordinates (span of control) and clear distinctions between the responsibilities of line and staff, are no longer adhered to strictly. Although there is no one right way, there are ways of organizing that are more effective than others depending on the stability of the environment in which the organization functions, the type of technology, and the talent profile of the organization. For example, if a firm (or a division within a firm) uses a process production technology, has a stable product environment, and has relatively little need for high individual initiative and creativity, it should have a traditional, mechanistic type of organization. A flexible and more complex organization requires the reverse. These are extremes in a whole continuum of options, but they are the types of issues the organization has to address. Exhibit 2-9 illustrates these considerations. The compensation function may be the most logical area in which to facilitate organization design activities because it is the repository of information on jobs and job relationships.

By being involved in job and organization design activities and having a better connection to the planning process, compensation specialists can be more effective and responsive in carrying out job analysis and classification responsibilities. Job analysis and classification is often a necessary activity to establish appropriate salary levels within an organization.

Program Administration

Pay programs are required to motivate the organization's talent perform at superior levels, to attract and retain them, to be legally administered, and to be structured within the organization's ability to pay. There are various ways to measure the achievement of these goals, such as examining salary-related turnover, looking at the distribution of increases in relation to performance, and measuring direct compensation costs as a percentage of some indicator of organization success such as revenue or other key financial ratios (a subject to be discussed in Chapter 11). Although useful, where these measures fall short is that they do little to help proactively anticipate problems. Employees do not terminate the minute they perceive a problem. The talent leaves when they think there is no possibility for any corrective action for their concerns. When action is actually taken, it is often too late to modify a program or to address pay inequities with large salary adjustments.

The talent review portion of the HR planning process can also contribute information about attitudes toward program administration that will help compensation specialists anticipate problems. The talent review and assessment can generate a wealth of information.

However, for the review process to serve this purpose, it must be structured to elicit relevant information. Exhibit 2-9 outlines some of the issues related to compensation that you might address.

Exhibit 2-9 Compensation Issues to Be Examined in a Talent Review

- Competitiveness of salaries of key people
- Attitudes of key people toward the compensation program
- Administrative problems of the compensation program
- Ability and willingness to pay for performance
- Future compensation issues: compression, reclassification, and so on

Executive Compensation

Executive incentive plans should be tied to the planning activities of the business. As the needs of the business change, so also should the criteria for payments under the incentive plan. With regard to business plans, in one year the major concern may be market growth, in another year profit growth may be the primary focus, and in yet another year cost control may be the emphasis. Unfortunately, many executive incentive plans continue to pay out on the same financial results year after year, with *earnings before interest taxes depreciation and amortization* (EBITDA) being the most common measure of financial performance used in incentive plan design. The measures used are also those that are commonly used in financial analysis and are part of both internal and external financial reporting systems. The tendency is to apply measures that are conveniently available and conventionally used. Instead, the goals chosen for incentive rewards should emphasize the goals of the business as reflected in short- and long-range business plans, not just those traditionally used in financial analysis and reporting. By obtaining information from the planning process as described in this chapter and finding out what the organization's key success factors are from both the long-term and short-term perspective, organizations can develop executive incentive compensation triggering measures. Short-term, long-term, and value-enhancement measures should all be considered. Designing executive incentives only around short-term success measures can result in attempts to do earnings management under the accrual accounting structure. There needs to be more of an emphasis on long-term goals in executive incentive plans. Strategic measures that focus on sustained value creation should figure prominently in executive incentive compensation design. Chapter 4, "Incentive Compensation," explores the finance and accounting implications of incentive compensation program design.

What Can the Total Rewards Function Contribute to the Strategic and Operational Planning Efforts?

The total rewards function not only receives benefits from planning activities described in this chapter but also provides valuable inputs to the planning process.

It can provide information in the form of an accurate and comprehensive system of job descriptions, job levels, and classifications. Effective organization planning and design relies on the job-classification system because job classifications provide the framework that management uses to establish job relationships within their operations. The job-classification system also provides a foundation for career planning and internal promotional opportunities by establishing a sequence of jobs by which internal talent mobility is facilitated. In addition, the classification system serves as the basis for HR planning, both from a qualitative and quantitative point of view.

The compensation function is usually the custodian of the job-classification system. So, developing the most appropriate job-classification system, maintaining it, and communicating it effectively is a key way in which the compensation function can contribute to the organization-wide planning effort.

The second area by which the compensation function can help planning is in the design, development, and administration of an effective performance management process. The mechanism to make decisions on deviation from business plans on a qualitative (and sometimes quantitatively) basis is the performance management process. The compensation function is often the custodian of this critical activity. An effectively designed performance management process should be able to facilitate constructive dialogue between management and the employees they manage.

The third area of contribution to the planning process is salary costing and budgeting. Employee compensation cost outlays represent a significant resource-allocation item in the financial structure of most organizations. In some organizations, such as service organizations, employee-related expenditures are the highest allocation item. Therefore, the compensation function activities to accurately cost programs and forecast expenditures are an organization-wide strategic imperative. This becomes crucial when one considers that employee expenditures are considered to be fixed expenditures in most cases. So, the compensation function needs to develop and maintain effective mechanisms for monitoring compensation expenses not only against budgets but also against other key relevant financial indicators of organizational success. Compensation specialists should implement cost monitoring systems that can serve an important role in business planning efforts.

This chapter stressed the importance of planning as we explored the connections between strategic business planning and operational financial planning. The chapter also looked at the connections between operational financial planning and HR planning. We then reviewed a detailed model for HR planning. The chapter then took a closer look at the relationships between financial and HR operational planning and the compensation function, ending with an exploration of the contributions the total compensation function can make to add value to the corporate-wide planning effort. The chapter concluded by reviewing how the compensation function can contribute to the organization-wide planning effort by taking on the task of providing timely and accurate financial plans and forecasting on total compensation expenditures. The next chapter explores this last point in more detail.

Key Concepts in This Chapter

- Talent management
- Organization planning and design
- Human resource planning
- Compensation planning
- Operational planning

- Demand planning
- Supply planning
- Forecasting demand
- External labor market
- Job analysis and classification
- Program administration

Appendix

Exhibit 2-10 presents another strategic model for the HR planning process and the positioning of compensation and benefits planning within it.

Human Asset Life Cycle Model

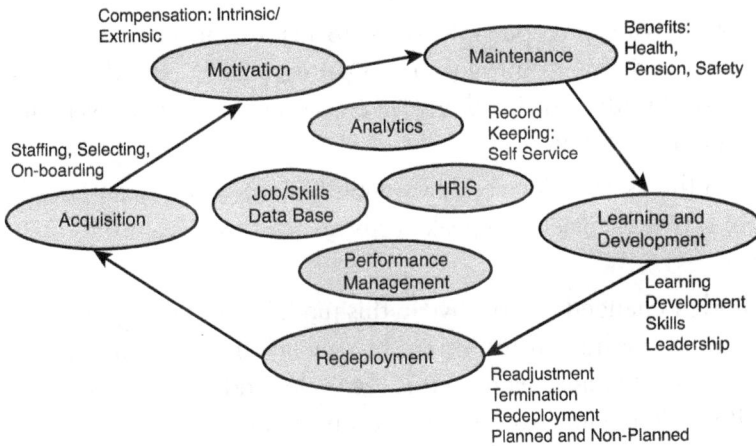

Exhibit 2-10 Human Asset Life Cycle

This model suggests that human capital investments can be considered capital expenditures and as such, an organizational asset. This is a recurring theme in this book.

If you then consider human resources as assets like all other assets, they also have life cycles. This model depicts a life cycle view of human resource assets.

Just like other assets, the human capital assets of an organization are acquired, motivated (specifically in the case of human resources), maintained, developed (for improved productivity) and redeployed to other effective uses when current effectiveness diminishes. The current functional activities have been mapped into the changed paradigm in the model.

Notice that when human resources are considered assets from an accounting and finance point of view, these critical assets then are viewed differently in the longer term, similar to product life cycles.

Here follows a brief description of the components of the model.

Acquisition efforts are not just recruiting efforts. When a human asset is acquired, the organization insures through proper planning that the human asset has a defined life cycle within the organization.

Then activities are put in place through on-boarding efforts to insure that the human asset is optimally motivated for peak performance through effective reward programs (both intrinsic and extrinsic).

Next activities are put into place to insure the human asset is adequately maintained through benefit programs to provide for the human asset's life risk incidence needs, such as illness, disability, safety, and retirement.

Then the asset is developed through lifelong learning and development activities to achieve peak performance throughout the asset's life cycle.

Another changed perspective in this model is the concept of summarily removing human resources (by way layoffs and terminations) for short-term financial gain. In this life cycle model (which takes the asset life cycle perspective), human resources are not easily disposed off, but are assigned to other appropriate best uses with adequate deployment efforts, which includes retraining and internal placement. This is similar to a hard asset retooling effort. Such a view of things, some postulate, will save organizations money over the long haul. Part II of this book revisits this point.

All of these life cycle phases of the human capital asset are supported in the HR department by certain core activities: an adequate job and skills database, a valid performance management system, an effective human resource information system, and a system of measurements with appropriate human resource analytics.

3

Projecting Base Compensation Costs

Aims and objectives of this chapter

- Explain the importance of projecting base salary costs
- Explain the connections of financial planning and budgeting to compensation planning
- Explain the various components of base compensation flows
- Explain the methods of improving the accuracy of base salary projections
- Demonstrate the formula for the various components of base compensation
- Explain the cash flow impact of base compensation increase programs
- Explain the concepts of payroll level rise and cost to payroll

Total compensation costs are often the highest direct and indirect expense in any organization. However, an analysis of the various elements of the total compensation is not always accomplished in whole or in part with analytical thoroughness. But because it can be the highest line item expense, understanding and projecting the true costs is of strategic and operational importance. This chapter presents a framework for analyzing each component of the total base compensation equation. It also provides analytical techniques to plan and forecast these expenses.[1] The chapter also covers base salary

---

[1] Adapted from an article written by Biswas, B.D., and Hestwood, T. in the *Compensation Review Journal* in 1979. Copyright currently held by Sage Publications. Author use accepted by Sage Publications.

projections. Other chapters, where appropriate, deal with projecting the other elements of the total compensation system.

You need to understand the various expense elements to accurately forecast compensation expenses. This understanding is important because these expenses are critical for long-term financial planning. Projecting these expenses is of strategic importance because accuracy here assists with the setting of the right "selling price" for a product or service, which then leads to determining the optimum financing and investing strategies. Furthermore, accuracy here leads to effective talent management strategies. Forecasting these expenses with accuracy also enables better annual financial budgeting and cash budgeting. The appendix, at the end of this chapter, provides a specific example of the direct relationship of salary planning to the determination of the annual cash requirements of a business.

Now, it is important to understand the connections between accurate compensation cost planning and financial planning. Exhibit 3-1 demonstrates these connections.

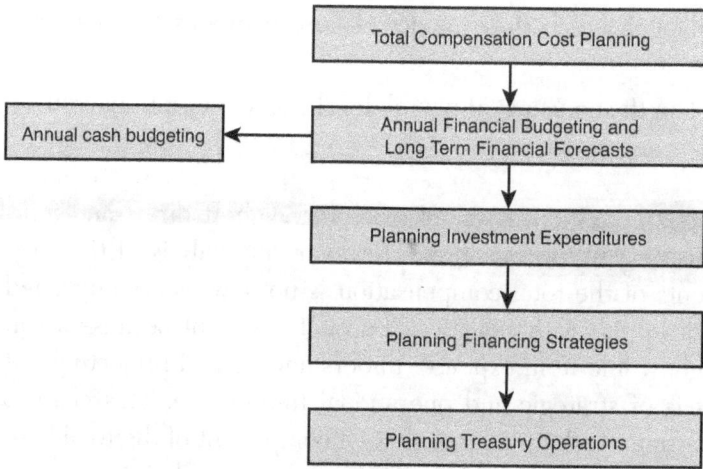

Exhibit 3-1 The Important Connection between Compensation Expense Planning and Financial Planning

Note here that if total compensation expenditures are indeed the most significant element of total expenditures, then being accurate with those projections will enhance the credibility and accuracy of the total financial planning system.

Before we start the planning exercise, it is again important to take a look at the various compensation and benefits cost elements. We do so in Exhibit 3-2.

Exhibit 3-2 Elements of the Total Compensation Framework (continuing the discussion from Chapter 1)

Major Category	Subelements
Base salary	The salary determined at the hiring point
	Annual increases—performance/merit, other types
	Performance/merit/other types
	Promotion increases
	Turnover effect
	Other charges, flows, and allowances
Benefits	Health programs
	Life insurance
	Disability insurance
	Retirement/Pension
	Expenses and investments
	Other benefit programs requiring monetary expenditures
Incentive compensation (cash incentive schemes)	Executive bonus
	Management bonus
	Other types of cash incentive programs
Expatriate compensation programs	Foreign service premiums
	Cost-differential allowances
	Hardship premiums
	Special area allowances
	Tax protection and equalization program

In the discussions about the projections of total compensation forecasting, expenditures normally paid via expense reimbursements or those directly paid by third-party administrators (TPAs) are excluded. These expenditures are as follows:

- Executive perquisites (the imputed value of which would be included as taxable income)
- Pension payments
- Medical insurance reimbursements
- Other insurance payments paid by TPAs and insurance companies
- Expatriate tax payments
- Company reimbursement to service providers on behalf of employees

The focus here is on all payments processed by the payroll department. Employee payments processed by payroll departments are subject to federal and state tax withholding requirements, whereas payments made by expense reimbursement are not subject to withholding taxes.

Base Salary Costs

An organization begins by comparing its salaries with those of its competitors. These competitors need to be both labor market competitors and product market competitors. From such an analysis, the organization makes a decision on the preferred market position. Having made the positioning decision, the organization must establish procedures for distributing increases among employees and then projecting those costs accurately. The specifics of the mechanics of the salary increase distribution will ultimately be a major determinant of the costs. The types of salary increases and the distribution methods, along with the net salary change flows (for example, new hires and terminations), help determine accurate program costs.

Organizations execute these actions in a variety of ways. One way to allocate increases is a salary or merit increase matrix. These are guidelines that assist in the determination of individual increases based on performance and the employee's salary range position. Using these guidelines, organizations forecast the cost of the salary increase program. Yet another method used to distribute increases to employees is based on performance ratings and resulting in a specific yearly average amount and also the time between increases. This average can vary for different groups of employees. The cost is calculated by multiplying the annual increase percentage by the base salary for each employee group at the beginning of the year.

Nevertheless, existing costing procedures are normally deficient in one or more of the following areas:

- They do not account for employee turnover.
- They ignore or inaccurately predict the net changes in employee population.
- They overlook deviations from approved practices.

Employee turnover can have a significant impact on anticipated salary expenditures because of the differences in the salaries of employees leaving and those employees joining the organization. Turnover lowers costs because employees who terminate usually are compensated at higher levels than those who replace them. In fact, because of turnover in some companies, salary programs add zero dollars to total payroll.

However, the impact of turnover is generally more involved than that, because there is rarely the simple replacement of one employee by another employee. Employees are not always directly replaced by other employees for the same job. There is a constant change in the mix of various kinds of employees and jobs. The effect of turnover can best be determined by an analysis of the relationship of new hire and terminee salaries.

The cost effects of population changes can prove particularly difficult to forecast because they often vary substantially from year to year depending on business, financial, and economic conditions. This information can be gathered from an organization-wide human resource (HR) planning and forecasting system (as discussed in Chapter 2, "Business, Financial, and Human Resource Planning"). But where forecasting data is not available, or where the forecasting process is not synchronized with compensation planning, the information must be derived from historical trend data for employee demographic changes.

Irrespective of the spending controls established, deviations from expected levels of spending often occur. It occurs quite often when managers are slow to adjust their spending to reflect the program changes and new programs. Some companies actually encourage deviations from policy in special employment cases. There is a belief that supervisors should not be subjected to strict spending controls. If measurable deviations occur consistently, provisions should be made for anticipating the cost impact by reviewing the historical relationships between authorized and actual merit increases.

Improving the Accuracy of Base Salary Expenditure Projections

The mathematical model described here captures the various elements of base or fixed compensation transitions and thereby suggests ways to improve the accuracy of base compensation forecasting. Exhibit 3-3 shows a suggested forecasting formula. It is assumed in the examples that follow that costs are to be projected for a 12-month period or an annual fiscal period.

$$\left(\frac{(BMP) \times AAI \times PR}{12} \pm PC\&T + PRO \times 78 = CTP \right)$$

Where: BMP = Beginning month payroll
AAI = Averaged annualized increase
PR = Participation rate
PC&T = Population change and turnover cost
PRO = Promotion cost
CTP = Cost to payroll

Exhibit 3-3 Payroll Forecasting Formula

Beginning month payroll (BMP) is the total base monthly payroll at the beginning of the program year. Most organizations have this information available in various HR and financial (payroll) electronic systems.

To demonstrate the forecasting methodology, let's consider an example. This example assumes that there are 100 employees with a payroll of $500,000 a month.

The average annualized increase (AAI) combines the effect on payroll of the expected average time interval between increases and the average amount of the increase during a given year or fiscal year. The annualized increase calculation determines the full-year impact of increases granted throughout the year. It also takes into account the higher base salary of employees who receive more than one increase within a year. This is because the interval between increases is less than 12 months for employees who receive more than one increase during a 12-month period. In the example, we assume that the expected average increase is 7%, with an interval between increases of 9 months. In most companies these increases would be based on performance (commonly termed merit increases). Exhibit 3-4 explains how the annualized increase is obtained.

$$\frac{\text{Average amount of increase} \times 12 \text{ months}}{\text{Average monthly interval between increases}} = \text{Average annualized increase}$$

$$\frac{.07 \times 12 = .093}{9}$$

A 7% increase granted with a nine month interval is annualized to 9.3%

Exhibit 3-4 Determining the Annualized Increased Component

When increases are granted at intervals that are not approved, the average will need to be adjusted. These deviations arise mainly in organizations that are decentralized with local autonomy. If there is historical evidence of a consistent deviation pattern in the increase interval, then an adjustment should be built into the calculations proactively.

In this case, the example assumes that an analysis of the data indicates a need for an adjustment in the expected interval between increases. You can obtain this information by analyzing the data on the historical relationship between the actual and approved interval between increases.

You might find, for example, that last year the actual average interval was 11.5 months but the approved interval was 12 months. This year, the approved program's average interval is 9 months. If the past relationship between the approved and actual interval is a valid guide for the future, you can set up a simple ratio equation and solve for the expected actual interval for the forecasting exercise.

Exhibit 3-5 presents this calculation. In the example, the expected interval is 8.63 months. This corrected interval can be inserted in place of 9 months in the annualizing formula to yield an AAI of 9.7% rather than 9.3%.

$$\frac{\text{Past year's approved interval}}{\text{Past year's actual interval}} = \frac{\text{Next year's approved interval}}{\text{Next year's actual interval}}$$

$$\frac{12}{11.5} = \frac{9}{x}$$

$$\frac{11.5 \times 9}{12} = 8.63 \text{ months}$$

Exhibit 3-5 Adjustment for Approved Versus Actual Interval

Participation rate (PR) is defined as the ratio of actual salary actions (increases) granted to employees compared to all employees eligible to receive increases. Participation is significant because if not all the possible salary increases are awarded, a smaller portion of base payroll than expected is actually increased. If this situation occurs, an adjustment must be made that reduces the projected expenditure. Unless an organization sets a specific participation rate objective, this information has to be obtained from a historical comparison of what actually occurred at year end to the number of possible actions for the year. Consequently, if it is anticipated that only 90% of the employees are going to receive a salary action, the annual merit increase cost must be multiplied by .90 to eliminate the 10% not participating.

After the participation rate is considered, the resulting cost is divided by 12 to obtain a monthly cost. So far in the example, the calculation would read as follows:

($500,000 × .097 × .90) ÷ 12 = $4,041.67 per month – Monthly payroll increase.

The effects of population change and turnover (PC&T) on salary expenses are considered together. In the example we are looking only at an increase in population. However, with minor changes, the procedure can be made to account for declines in population, as well. For this analysis, it is assumed that population change information is derived from historical trends maintained in the human resource information system. The effects of turnover on costs also would be obtained from historical data.

To determine the effects of population change and turnover require that an organization record monthly the salaries of new hires and terminees. Preferably, this data should be collected for at least five years. Exhibit 3-6 illustrates the type of information that should be collected each month.

Exhibit 3-6 Data for PC&T

	Month	Year	N	Monthly Base Payroll
New hires			6	$6,000.00
Terminations			4	4,500.00
			+2	$ +1,500.00
				Net monthly addition to payroll

To determine the average monthly additional cost to payroll, all monthly changes to payroll are averaged. Therefore, if the monthly net addition to payroll is $1,500, as shown in the calculation, that amount is added to the formula as the PC&T expense.

If population changes are not expected to follow historical patterns, there must be a way to separate turnover and growth. In the example shown in Exhibit 3-6, it is assumed that all new hires come in at the new-hire average salary of $1,000 per month and that there were two more new hires than terminees (these hires are presumed to be for positions that are newly created). Therefore, in this case, population growth accounts for a change in payroll of $2,000 ($1,000 × 2). But, turnover normally acts to reduce payroll. Because new-hire salaries are lower than those of terminees, there was a cost savings of $125 per replacement hire (average new hire cost of $1,000 versus average terminee cost of $1,125, a savings of $125 per replacement hire). This savings multiplied by the number of persons directly replaced (we assume four of the six new hires were replacing four who terminated) gives total monthly turnover savings of $500. Thus, the two growth hires were brought in at a cost of $2,000 ($1,000 × two brand new employees) and the four who were replaced came in at a lower salary ($1,000 per month), but they replaced four employees whose salaries averaged $1,125 per month, which gives a savings of $125 per replacement hire for a total of $500 for four employees. The $2,000 per month additional hire cost is reduced by $500 per month to result in a payroll increase of $1,500 per month.

Promotion (PRO) expenses are determined by examining historical data to find the number of employees getting a promotion each month and the average promotional increase. Exhibit 3-7 shows if 2.1% of the population is promoted each month and the average increase of those being promoted is 10%, the monthly promotional cost is $1,050.

Exhibit 3-7 Calculating Promotion Costs

BMP	×	Average proportion of employees promoted each month	×	Average promotional increase	=	Monthly promotional cost
$500,000	×	.021	×	.10	=	$1,050

The factor of 78 shown in the costing formula is used to convert the monthly expense to an annual expense; 78 is the total number of times the monthly expense has to be incurred if the expense is being determined for a year. For instance, the salary-increase dollars paid in January will be paid 12 times, the salary-increase dollars paid in February, 11 times, and so forth. This phenomenon is described in more detail in the appendix to this chapter.

The various components of the costing formula can now be shown together. If you insert the figures discussed previously into the formula shown in Exhibit 3-3, it reads as follows:

$$[(\$500,000 \times .097 \times .90) \div 12 + \$1,500 + \$1,050] \times 78 = \$482,625$$

Therefore, an additional $482,625.00 (CTP) will be spent on base salaries in the coming year. From an annual payroll of $6,000,000 at the start of the year, the expense rises to $6,482,625 at year end, an increase of 8.0% ($482,625 ÷ $6,000,000) on an annual basis and 14.85% ($6,188 × 12 ÷ $500,000) on a monthly basis. The $6,188 is calculated in this manner: $[(\$500,000 \times .097 \times .90) \div 12] + \$1,500 + \$1,050 = \$6,188$

Another example demonstrates the calculations discussed so far. The costing technique described to project compensation expenses was introduced in the 1970s when the Nixon wage-price controls were in effect. At that time, the concepts of level rise and cost to payroll were introduced. In this cost analysis, the emphasis is on looking at cost increases from both a monthly and annualized basis. The ending monthly figure (as defined by the payroll level rise) indicates the beginning of the next year run rate. The annualized cost increase (as defined by the cost to payroll) indicates the increased annual base compensation expenditures for the current year.

Let's first take a look at these concepts graphically and then discuss them more fully.

Assume that Paresh Enterprises, Inc. (PEI) has a monthly base payroll of $5,000,000 on 12/31/12. And let's assume that PEI has an anniversary salary-increase program; that is, employees are granted increases on the anniversary of the hire date. In addition, PEI plans a 5% of base average salary increase program for 2013. So, graphically the base compensation costs of PEI are as shown in Exhibit 3-8.

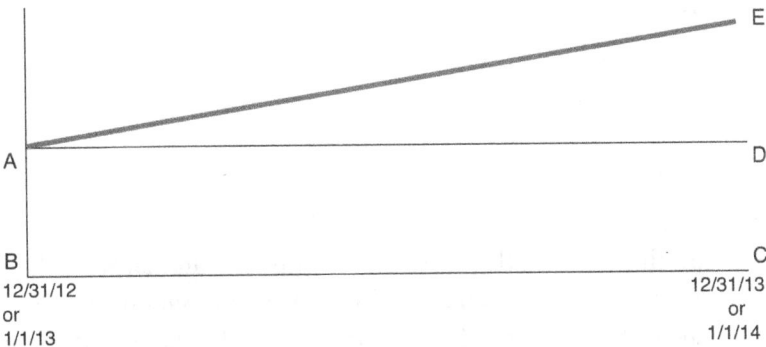

AB = Beginning monthly base payroll = $5 m
DE = Increase in monthly base payroll = $.250 m
ABCD = Annualized base payroll w/o salary increases = $60 m
CE = Ending monthly base payroll = $5.25 m
ADE = Annualized cost of base salary increase program = $1.625 m
ABCE = Annualized total base salary expense for 2012 = $61.625
And the calculations are:

AB   = $5m (given)
ABCD = $5m x 12 = $60m
DE   = $5m x .05 = $.250m
CE   = $5m + $.250m = $5.250m
ADE   = $.250m ÷ 12 x 78* = $1.625m

Exhibit 3-8 Base Compensation Costs for PEI

* Look for explanation of this factor in the appendix.

Here is the calculation in percentage terms:

$$\frac{\text{Ending monthly base payroll} - \text{Beginning Monthly Base Payroll}}{\text{Beginning Monthly Base Payroll}}$$

$$= \frac{\$5.250\text{ m} - \$5.0\text{m}}{5.0\text{ m}} = \frac{\$.250\text{m}}{\$5.0\text{m}}$$

$$= 5\% \text{ or } \frac{CE - AB}{AB} \quad \text{(in the graph)}$$

This figure is called level rise or the increase in the monthly base payroll level. This is a number that normally comes from an input provided to the compensation specialist by the budgeting people in the accounting department.

$$\frac{\text{Annualized Cost of Base Salary Increase Program}}{\text{Annualized Cost of Base Payroll w/o Base Salary Increase Program}}$$

$$= \frac{\$1.625\text{m}}{\$ 60\text{m}}$$

$$= 2.708\% \quad \text{(this percentage for an anniversary base salary increase will always be 54\% of the level rise)}$$

In the graph, $\dfrac{ADE}{ABCD}$

We call this statistic the cost to payroll of the annualized salary increase program. Such a technique for base compensation cost planning enhances the accuracy of the projections of the fixed costs to be incurred by an organization. Such costing accuracy facilitates accuracy cost estimations.

Organizations, both big and small, have to manage their operations by developing accurate financial budgets annually. A major expense that has to be planned by each manager is their employee expenses. And as you have seen, employee expenses can be the largest single line item expense for any organization. Note, as well, that base salary expenses form the major expense within the total compensation framework. Normally, the accounting and finance department provides to department managers budget guidelines for base salary increases that are not coordinated with the HR departments. There are many reasons for this lack of a connection. Common reasons include (1) the HR personnel's avoidance of anything to do with numbers and (2) the accounting department's reluctance to communicate with HR departments with respect to accounting and finance matters. However, one of the most important expense categories is people expenses, and therefore there needs to be accounting and finance cooperation on this activity. A financial planning model has been presented in this chapter, which, if put into practice, will greatly enhance fixed compensation estimation accuracy, understanding, and reporting.

Key Concepts in This Chapter

- Total compensation cost planning
- Payroll costing formula
- Average annualized increase
- Approved versus actual increase
- Participation rate
- Promotion costs
- Beginning monthly base payroll
- Payroll level rise
- Cost to payroll
- The 78 factor
- The cash flow impact
- Population change and turnover impact
- Ending monthly payroll

Appendix: Cash Flow Impact of Salary Increases

Companies usually distribute salary increases to employees on the annual service anniversary of the employee's hire date. The alternative is to distribute the annual salary increases on a specific date. The latter is called a focal increase. Note that there are significant cash flow issues with selecting the date on which increases are granted.

In a survey on compensation planning for 2008, Buck Consultants examined salary management practices among the 415 surveyed organizations (in particular, the timing of annual salary reviews). The Buck survey found that most organizations—over 80% (82.2%)—administer annual salary increases on a focal (or common) review date.[2] This means that in most organizations employees receive their annual salary increase on a common date, such as January 1, rather than on the annual anniversary of their hire date or when they were promoted into their current positions.

The Cash Flow Impact Analyzed

Suppose that a company has 12 employees and that they each earn $1,000 per month. Now suppose that one employee was hired each month of the year. In an anniversary salary increase program, each employee comes up for an increase at the beginning of each month, as illustrated in Exhibit 3-9.

Exhibit 3-9 Employee Salary Increase Dates

Employee 1	Increase date	-	1/1
Employee 2	Increase date	-	2/1
Employee 3	Increase date	-	3/1
Employee 4	Increase date	-	4/1
Employee 5	Increase date	-	5/1
Employee 6	Increase date	-	6/1
Employee 7	Increase date	-	7/1
Employee 8	Increase date	-	8/1
Employee 9	Increase date	-	9/1
Employee 10	Increase date	-	10/1
Employee 11	Increase date	-	11/1
Employee 12	Increase date	-	12/1

* This example is simplified to demonstrate the concepts.

[2] Koss, Sharon "Which is Best? Anniversary vs. Focal (Common Date)" Performance Reviews, SPHR, CCP (2009): www.kosshrexpert.com/Article-WhichisBest.pdf.

Now suppose that the annual increase for each employee is 10%. The true cash flow impact of this 10% increase program is demonstrated in Exhibit 3-10.

Exhibit 3-10 The Cash Flow Impact

Employee	Monthly Increase		Annual Cash Requirement	Cumulative Cash Requirement
1	$100	× 12	$1,200	$1,200
2	$100	× 11	$1,100	$2,300
3	$100	× 10	$1,000	$3,300
4	$100	× 9	$900	$4,200
5	$100	× 8	$800	$5,000
6	$100	× 7	$700	$5,700
7	$100	× 6	$600	$6,300
8	$100	× 5	$500	$6,800
9	$100	× 4	$400	$7,200
10	$100	× 3	$300	$7,500
11	$100	× 2	$200	$7,700
12	$100	× 1	$100	$7,800
Totals	**$1,200**	78[3]		**$7,800**

Therefore, an anniversary salary increase generates a cash flow requirement of $7,800 in this hypothetical example, whereas if all employees were granted their annual increases on January 1 the cash flow requirement would be $1,200 × 12 = $14,400. If all employees were granted increases on a focal date of July 1, the cash flow requirement would be $1,200 × 5 = $7,200. And if all employees were granted increases on September 1, the cash flow requirement would be $1,200 × 4 = $4,800.

Note that this is cash flow analysis and not accrued expense analysis. Also note that this type of accounting analysis conducted by a compensation department will add real value to the accounting department's efforts to do required cash budgeting and planning.

---

[3] Thus, the 78 used in Exhibit 3-3.

Cash management is a critical accounting activity that keeps many a chief financial officer under continuous stress and anxiety. The HR and compensation professionals will certainly "come to the table" when they support the business with this critical cash budgeting and planning activity. The activity becomes all the more important when one considers that in any organization of any size, the distribution of annual salary increases to employees can be one of the highest cash outflow activities.

4

Incentive Compensation

Aims and objectives of this chapter

- Explain the accounting issues involved in incentive compensation programs
- State the different types of cash incentive compensation plans currently in use
- Explore the prevalence of incentive compensation plans
- Discuss the various key incentive compensation metrics
- Explain the need to use sustaining financial value creation metrics
- Discuss the free cash flow measure as an incentive compensation metric
- Discuss the economic value added measure as an incentive compensation metric
- Discuss the residual income measure as an incentive compensation metric
- Discuss the use of a balance scorecard system as an incentive compensation triggering mechanism

An Introduction to Incentive Compensation Programs

One important element of the total compensation system is the short-term annual incentive compensation program. Most organizations have some form of this element of the total compensation

71

system. The structure of short-term incentives can take many forms. This chapter presents a detailed analysis of incentive compensation programs. The focus is on, as it is throughout this book, the accounting and finance implications of incentive compensation.

The chapter discusses the following:

- The accounting for annual incentive compensation plans
- Key incentive compensation program metrics
  - Free cash flow as an incentive plan metric
  - Economic value added as an incentive plan metric
  - Residual income as an incentive plan metric
- The balance scorecard and incentive compensation

Cash incentive plans are also called cash bonus plans. Cash incentive compensation can fall into the following categories:

- Annual plans covering all employees or a large percentage of employees of the company
- Long-term cash incentive plans that are provided mostly to senior executives
- Cash profit-sharing plans
- Incentive plans for specific employee groups (such as engineers, scientists, and other key employees)
- Annual bonus plans specially designed for senior executives
- Nonqualified deferred compensation plans tied into an annual incentive plan
- Other types of cash incentive/bonus plans
  - Sign-on bonus
  - Referral bonus
  - Spot bonus
  - Retention bonus

Note that these cash plans can be either annual plans, triggered by an annual metric, or they can cover multiyear periods if the plans are designed to be triggered by multiyear financial performance.

The prevalence of annual cash incentive plans clearly demonstrates that a majority of companies, both public and private, offer such plans to employees. A term *pay at risk* has been introduced to indicate that companies are increasingly asking employees to share in the risk/reward playing field of a business venture. Companies are now reducing or controlling the fixed component of pay (the base pay) and increasing the incentive component. The idea is that if a company achieves its financial goals the employees who made that happen should be rewarded accordingly. Such a motivational philosophy clearly applies to senior executives, but more and more companies are including all levels of employees within this conceptual structure. There is a great appeal for the pay-at-risk approach in an era of expense-reductions, financial control, and austerity. So, there is an increasing incidence of these plans. Note, as well, that by reducing or controlling the "fixed" component of pay and increasing the short-term component, companies can reduce fixed expenses. Compensation expenditures are contingent on increasing financial results.

In a paper written for the *Coastal Business Journal*, authors Mike Schraeder and J. Bret Becton provide an overview of recent trends in incentive pay programs. The paper suggests the following with regard to incentive compensation programs:

- Increased use of incentives for employee groups, teams, and project teams.
- More use of both qualitative and quantitative measures in incentive compensation programs.
- Increased use of incentive compensation programs in entrepreneurial firms.
- Increased use of incentive compensation programs in service industries has also been observed.[1]

The authors suggest that an incentive program plays an important role in motivating staff to achieve organizational goals.

The authors further suggest that the process used to develop the incentive program is often as important as the specific elements of

---

[1] Schraeder, M., and Becton J.B., "An Overview of Recent Trends on Incentive Pay Programs," *The Coastal Business Journal*, Vol. 2, No. 1, Fall 2003.

the program. This is in keeping with motivation theories that suggest employees consider the programs fair when they know how pay outcomes are determined. Employees perceive that the process used in determining amounts to be paid is more important than the amount of pay received. The more the employees participate in program development, the more they are satisfied with the entire incentive program. The process is as important as the outcome.

In addition, short-term incentive plans are becoming more and more important as an element of the total compensation structure. Short-term plans help strengthen the connection between the execution of a business strategy and payouts received from the plan. Incentive plans are also being customized to reinforce mission-critical functions. This means it becomes possible to align incentives with sales and functions that are critical to the successful execution of business strategies.

You can read an excellent analysis of the prevalence of short-term cash bonus plans in a report produced by the professional association WorldatWork. This report comprehensively analyzes the various types of bonus plans used to incent to achievement of various types of strategic and operational business objectives.[2] The report focuses on bonuses granted to generate specific types of employee behavior outcomes.

Accounting for Annual Cash Incentive Plans

The accounting for short-term incentive plans is fairly straightforward. All expenditures for these plans are expensed in the period in which they are incurred. This is in keeping with the *matching principle* of accounting. These expenses are regarded as period expenses and carried to the income statement in the year they are incurred. The same principle applies to cash wages. The logic for this holds that most annual incentive plans are built around performance triggers that cover the current accounting or fiscal year. Therefore, these

---

[2] "Bonus Programs and Practices," a research report by WorldatWork, April 2011, Scottsdale, AZ.

expenses should be "matched" against the revenues earned during the same period—the matching principle.

Usually, though, the annual payouts are made in the year following the year covered by the incentive plan. The payouts are normally made within the first three months of the upcoming year. The reason for this is that the accounting transactions for the completed year has to be closed, audited, and reported before incentive payouts can be finalized. For example, if the incentive plan measurement period is the calendar year 2013, the incentive payouts will be made in the first quarter of 2014. So, for 12/31/13 financial reporting, the expense for incentives will be recognized in 2013.

Another accounting issue dealing with incentive plans is the need to accrue these expenditures on a proactive basis. This means as the bonus is earned during the year the requisite amount needs to be accrued as a payable and also recorded as an expense. The key consideration here is the determination of when the participant earns the incentive out. Some plans have monthly, quarterly, or semi-annual measurement periods. If the formal plan document specifically stipulates the measurement period to be other than annual, the accounting system needs to accrue the liability and recognize an expense before publishing interim financial reports. Exhibit 4-1 shows this process in tabular form.

Exhibit 4-1 Incentive Plan Measurement and Accounting Period Recognition

Incentive Plan Measurement	Accounting Period Recognition
Monthly	Monthly
Quarterly	Quarterly
Yearly	Yearly

Estimated incentive payouts need to be accrued during the year the incentive is being earned. Suppose, for instance, that the current year is 2013. During the course of 2013, the accounting department needs to work with the *human resource* (HR) department and estimate incentive payouts per the plan provisions. This estimation needs to be based on the actual results to date of the financial and operational measures used in the incentive plans. These measures or objectives should be those that are stipulated in the plan. Based on these estimates, the journal entries listed in Exhibit 4-2 need to be made.

Exhibit 4-2 Journal Entries Illustrated

Incentive expense for department "a"	xxxxxx	
Accrued incentive liability		xxxxxx

The calculation and journal entry needs to be made whenever performance on the financial or the other operational incentive compensation metrics matches or exceeds the planned levels in the incentive plans, for all categories of employees.

When the incentives are actually paid out, the accrual accounts should be cleared out in the manner shown in Exhibit 4-3.

Exhibit 4-3 Journal Entry Illustrated

Accrued incentive liability	xxxxxx	
Federal Income Tax Payable		xxxxxx
Social Security Tax Payable		xxxxxx
Medicare Tax Payable		xxxxxx
Federal Unemployment Tax Payable		xxxxxx
State Tax Payable		xxxxxx
State Unemployment Tax Payable		xxxxxx
Cash		xxxxxx

Note that estimating incentives could be a subjective exercise. This is because estimates are made by making a guess about the financial and operational performance in the future months. This way, companies might wait for some months to pass in the year before any accruals of the incentives are recorded. This will allow for a better estimation of the eventual payouts.

Also, if the incentive plan has a provision for reduced payouts when targets are not achieved (usually up to a minimum threshold), the estimate of future payouts should account for this possible occurrence.

Nevertheless, at the end of the year, when the actual performance of the financial and operational measures that were used in the incentive plans are known, the incentive compensation accrual should be adjusted as final.

Another noteworthy accounting issue with respect to annual incentive compensation accounting is termed the *circular effective.* Accountants, when determining projected year-end net income (for interim reports), make an estimate of incentive compensation to be paid out. Based on the final results on the performance against plans for the incentive compensation performance metrics, however, the estimates made by the accountant for the annual incentive compensation to be paid might need to be revised at year end, thus affecting year-end net income. So, during-year incentive compensation estimates might be one of the causes of the deviation of year-end net income from the earlier-in-the-year projections. If the projected versus actual net income deviations are large enough, the accounting department might come under scrutiny for the inaccuracy in estimating incentive compensation payouts. These deviations are a further reason for the practice of earnings management.

Although the accounting treatment of these annual cash incentive plans is straightforward, accounting-related and finance-related issues need to be discussed, as we do throughout the remainder of this chapter.

Key Incentive Compensation Metrics

Although the development of key incentive compensation indicators is not a strictly accounting and finance issue, the selection and use of specific indicators does indirectly have finance and accounting implications. Key indicator or triggering metric determination is the most important design and implementation issue with respect to incentive plans.

Key indicators can be financial and nonfinancial, but financial indicators are usually given the highest weight in plan design. For executive incentive plans in public companies, the selection of these indicators requires board compensation committee and the entire board's approval.

The following financial metrics are commonly used in incentive plans:

- *Return on equity* (ROE)
- *Return on assets* (ROA)
- *Earnings per share* (EPS)
- *Net income* (NI)
- *Earnings before taxes* (EBT)
- *Earnings before interest and taxes* (EBIT)
- *Earnings before interest, taxes, depreciation, and amortization* (EBITDA)
- *Total shareholder return* (TSR)
- Gross sales
- Gross margin
- Expenses to budget
- Economic value added
- Intrinsic value (discounted free cash flow)

For private companies, the financial measure used might differ. An October 2007 research report by WorldatWork and Vivient Consulting[3] found the prevalence of financial metrics to be as shown in Exhibit 4-4.

Exhibit 4-4 Financial Metrics for Private Companies

Sales	49%*
Operating Income	44%
Net Income/EPS	34%
Economic profit	6%

*% of respondents

In another report from the premier compensation consulting firm Towers Watson, the incidence of financial metrics was reported.

---

[3] "Private Company Incentive Pay Practices," a research report by WorldatWork and Vivient Consulting, October 2007.

In this report, the change in the use of key metrics over a five-year period was demonstrated. Exhibit 4-5 shows the results of that report.

Exhibit 4-5 Prevalence of Financial Performance Measures[4]

	2010 Survey	2005 Survey
Sales/revenues	34%	31%
Earnings per share (EPS)	26%	29%
Cash flow	26%	19%
Operating income/operating profit	25%	28%
Earnings before interest and taxes (EBIT or EBITDA)	25%	19%
Net income/earnings/profit	24%	24%
Cost/expense control/reduction	17%	—
Return on investment/return on invested capital (ROI/ROIC)	8%	7%
Return on equity (ROE)	7%	9%
Operating measures (for example, operating margin)	7%	12%
Pretax income	5%	7%
Working capital	4%	—
Economic profit/economic value added (EP/EVA)	4%	3%
Gross margin	4%	—
Return on assets/return on net assets (ROA/RONA)	3%	4%
Total shareholder return	3%	—
Net operating profit after tax (NOPAT)	2%	

To more accurately assess an executive's performance, compensation plan designers should focus on organizational metrics that most closely resemble the company's operating fundamentals. Two such metrics are operating cash flow and EBITDA. Some incentive plan designers use these metrics to trigger incentive compensation plan payments because these metrics are also among the metrics used by business valuation specialists to value companies. Operating cash flow

---

[4] Data from Towers Watson; Executive Compensation Bulletin; Smith, Max, and Stradley, Ben; February 25, 2010; p. 4; reprinted with permission.

and EBITDA are regarded as better measures of the operating performance of a business.

Operating cash flow, rather than net income, can generally give plan designers a clearer picture of the company's sustainability. Moreover, operating cash flow takes into account a company's working capital (receivables, payables, and inventory) while eliminating noncash charges associated with depreciation. EBITDA is similar to operating cash flow; however, it does not take into account working capital or the firm's capital structure. In some cases, from an operational point of view the capital structure may be an important consideration, especially when companies are strategically attempting to deleverage. The control of excessive interest expense can also be a primary operational concern.

It can be safely concluded that financial metrics are generally used in defining the parameters for short-term incentive compensation or variable pay. They are also used for long-term incentives for companies in all stages of growth. Others are also currently advocating the need to include nonfinancial measures as incentive plan payment-triggering metrics.

Of all the financial metrics mentioned so far, two specific metrics, Economic Value Added (EVA) and Discounted Free Cash Flow, are effective measures for evaluating the performance of managers and other key employees vis-à-vis shareholder interests. These measures clearly emphasize sustaining value creation. However, these measures are not as widely used as financial metrics. Therefore, these measures need to be explored as valid incentive compensation metrics. So, the next sections discuss these two measures and comment on the validity of their use as incentive plan triggers.

These two metrics are effective as measures to assess long-term value creation for a business. So, using them to evaluate management and key employee performance (and therefore incentive compensation) is highly desirable. However, these metrics are seldom used. Instead, the use of short-term performance metrics is more common (for example, EBIT, NI, and EBIDTA). These measures currently being used are earnings-based measures. Arguably, managers and other key employees of corporations are hired to improve the sustainable value of a business and so they should be compensated on value creation and not just on short-term earnings measures. The true financial measure of sustaining value creation for a firm is the free cash flow generated. The sustaining value of this measure is the intrinsic value. Economic value added is also regarded as a valid value-creation measure. Incentive plans designed around these value measures can prove very effective for all concerned stakeholders.

Managers and shareholders alike need to know how alternative actions being contemplated are likely to affect stock prices. Intrinsic value as a measure clearly demonstrates the connections between managerial decisions and action and the firm's value. Therefore, using an intrinsic value measure to trigger managerial compensation makes a lot of sense.

The value measures also consider the cost of capital, as measured by the weighted average cost of capital. So, the cost of capital needs to be integrated into incentive plan design. Management will then be motivated to take all necessary actions to ensure that the company's return of invested capital exceeds the cost of that capital.

Let's now look at designing plans around these value measures.

Free Cash Flow as an Incentive Plan Metric

The value of a company is a function of the future cash flows it generates. Therefore, *free cash flow* (FCF) is an integral part of the analysis of the value enhancement for a firm. This is normally defined as after-tax operating profit minus the amount of new investment in working capital and fixed assets necessary for sustaining and maintaining the growth of the business. Managers make the business sustainable by increasing free cash flow. Therefore, an appropriate measure of managerial and key employee performance and thus incentive payouts is the increase in FCF from period to period and over the long run.

Calculating the FCF requires certain sequential calculations.[5]

---

[5] Ehrhardt, M.C., and Brigham, E.F., *Financial Management: Theory and Practice, 13e*, 2011, South-Western Language Learning, pp. 59–70.

First, the net operating profit has to be determined by multiplying EBIT by one minus the company's tax rate. Second, operating current liabilities should be subtracted from operating current assets, which will result in *net operating working capital* (NOWC). Third, the NOWC needs to be added to operating long-term assets to arrive at total net operating capital. Then, the year-to-year change in total net operating capital is calculated by subtracting this measure from one year to the next. This results in net investment in operating capital. Finally, the total net operating capital for the current year is subtracted from the NOPAT to derive FCF for the year. Sometimes, from operating cash flow (NOPAT + depreciation), the gross investment in operating capital (net investment in operating capital + depreciation and net investment) in working capital is subtracted to derive FCF.

To state the FCF measure in value-creation terms, we need to calculate the present value of the FCF over a fixed time period by applying a discounting factor using the *weighted average cost of capital* (WACC) for that company, as shown in Exhibit 4-6. The result of this formula is also referred to as the intrinsic value of a firm.

$$\text{Value of Firm} = \sum_{t=1}^{t=\infty} \frac{FCF_t}{(1+WACC)^t}$$

where,

FCF_t = the firm's free cash flow in year t

WACC = weighted average cost of capital

Exhibit 4-6 Intrinsic Value Calculation

The year-to-year change in this measure should be calculated and used in designing an incentive plan. Targets should be set for incentive payouts. Then, performance achieved against targets should establish the actual incentive payments.

Economic Value Added as an Incentive Plan Metric

Managers are the agents of the owners: the agency model. The owner's interest is to maximize the wealth that they have invested in the business. The board of directors, whom the owners elect to take care of their interests, hire professional managers to take care of the interests of all stakeholders.

The challenge for the board of directors is to align the managers' interests with those of the shareholders. Managers whose interests are not aligned with those of the shareholders will tend toward behavior that suits their interests, which might not necessarily be those of the shareholders. This is where the temptation to manage earnings arise. Management might channel investments that bring the most value to themselves personally through benefits such as perks and short-term profitability incentive payments. Management is tempted to do earnings management instead of making investments that create the most value for shareholders.

Therefore, it is in the interests of both the parties to align shareholder interests with those of managers. This can best be achieved by tying management compensation directly to a measure that indicates organizational value creation. EVA directly measures the value created by a company. It is a metric that considers both operating and capital costs.

EVA treats the opportunity cost of capital as a real cost that needs to be deducted from revenues to arrive at a more relevant "bottom line." A firm that is earning profits but is not covering its basic opportunity cost can use the capital in other areas. Therefore, many companies alter the management compensation paradigm and tie manager compensation to the EVA metric.

"Economic value added (EVA) is the spread between RoA and the cost of capital multiplied by the capital invested in the firm. It therefore measures the dollar value of the firm's return in excess of its opportunity cost."[6]

Clearly the EVA metric is an important measure to assess the maximization of shareholder wealth. Therefore, management (who are appointed nominees of the board of the directors and custodians of the interests of shareholders) should also be evaluated on their performance and rewarded based on EVA. In addition, EVA as a

---

[6] Bodie, Z., Kare, A., and Marcus, A., *Essentials of Investments, 8e*, 2010, McGraw Hill Irwin, New York, p. 452.

measure is not as global as the price of a stock. EVA measures can be developed for managers down the corporate ladder. EVA measures can be developed for a division, a business unit, a factory, or a store (for a retailer). Before we look at the connection of EVA to incentive plans, let's first review the calculations involved in developing the EVA measure.

The basic equation can be stated in various forms:

- EVA = Net income + Interest charges – Capital charge

  where

  Capital charge = (Notes payable + Current maturities of long-term debt + Long-term debt + Stockholders' equity) × Cost of capital[7]

  The cost of capital is the weighted average of the returns sought by stock investors and lenders.

- EVA can also be calculated by first calculating net operating profit after taxes, which is earnings before interest and taxes minus the effective tax rate. From this number, the total net operating capital multiplied by the weighted average cost of capital is subtracted to derive EVA.

- To derive economic value added or EVA, you can simply take the after-tax operating profit and remove a charge for the cost of the capital employed to deliver that profit. Specifically

  Net sales – Operating expenses = Operating profit (or EBIT)

  EBIT – Taxes = Net operating profit after tax (or NOPAT)

  NOPAT – Capital charge (Invested capital × WACC) = EVA

  Where the weighted average cost of capital is a firm's cost of capital for each category of capital proportionately weighted. All capital, common stock, preferred stock, bonds, and any other long-term debt are included in a WACC calculation.

---

[7] Harrison, Walter T., and Horngren, Charles T., *Financial Accounting, 7e,* 2008, Pearson Prentice-Hall, Upper Saddle River, NJ, p. 707.

After calculating the EVA for incentive compensation purposes, a formula needs to be set up to capture the year-to-year or interperiod change in the EVA measure. Such a model is described in "Using EVA to Align Management Incentives with Shareholders' Interests."[8] The author, Heather Balsley, identifies the following EVA-based incentive formula:

> Current year incentive = Target bonus + $y\%$ (Change in EVA less expected EVA improvement)

This is a unique incentive setup, in that the author is suggesting that the incentive participant should be paid his or her target incentive (a percentage of base salary) plus a percentage of the change in EVA that the participant helped generate, which is above the EVA improvement that was expected.

Setting up an incentive formula based on EVA improvement is quite appropriate. But another way to set up the scheme is as follows:

1. Set a numeric EVA improvement target at the start of the fiscal plan year. For a multiyear target, set up a cumulative interperiod EVA improvement target.

2. At year-end, calculate the plan to actual percentage. For a multiyear plan, calculate plan versus actual and do the calculations on the cumulative interperiod EVA improvement target.

3. If 100% of planned improvement is actually achieved, 100% of target bonus can be paid out. Then a sliding scale should be developed for the achieved versus the planned improvement percentage. There should be a minimum threshold and a maximum ceiling.

---

[8] Balsley, H., "Using EVA to Align Management Incentives with Shareholder Interests," December 2005, student paper, International Financial Management, Harvard Business School, pp. 1–2.

Exhibit 4-7 shows a payout matrix.

Exhibit 4-7 Payout Matrix

Percentage of Actual versus plan EVA improvement	Actual incentive Payout % Applied to target Incentive payout %
80%	80%
100%	100%
150%	150%

Fundamentally, EVA is a robust incentive compensation measure because it takes into account all the variables managers are responsible for: sales, operating expenses, and capital changes that offset the value added.

Residual Income as an Incentive Compensation Plan Metric

In both theory (the published literature) and actual current practice, *residual income* (RI) is sometimes used as an incentive compensation triggering metric. In general, RI is considered to be the net operating income that any economic unit earns above the minimum required return on the unit's operating assets. It is also defined as earnings before interest less a capital charge on total capital (debt and equity).[9]

Note that the residual income measure is similar in line with EVA and that some consider EVA an adoption of RI. Minor technical differences exist between EVA and RI. In the most practical sense, EVA is based on making some adjustments to the RI calculation. These are minor differences; for example, EVA could make an adjustment for research and development and treat R&D as an asset as opposed to the normal practice of expensing period R&D outlays. Ultimately, RI is basically the projected net operating income minus the dollar cost of capital. And, in essence, EVA projects what the company's NOPAT

---

[9] Commonly, RI is calculated by subtracting from net operating income average operating assets multiplied by the minimum required rate of return.

will be after subtracting the cost of capital. So, RI and EVA are fairly similar measures of business value creation.

In a research study conducted by James S. Wallace and published in the *Journal of Accounting and Economics*,[10] the author empirically established that RI is an effective incentive compensation metric. The study used data from 40 firms and analyzed the effectiveness of the decision making of managers who are under an RI incentive compensation system. The study considered (1) investing decisions (asset dispositions will increase and new investment will decrease), (2) financing decisions (share repurchases and dividend payouts will increase), and (3) operating decisions (total asset turnover will increase). The author concluded that those firms that used RI as an incentive compensation metric; "(i) increased their disposition of assets and decreased their new investment, (ii) increased their payouts to shareholders through share repurchases, and (iii) more intensively utilized their assets."[11]

The Balanced Scorecard and Incentive Compensation

Much has been written about the balanced scorecard form of evaluating corporate performance and tying the results to incentive compensation. This section reviews this concept.

A case can be made for tying incentive compensation, for all employees and (more important) executives, to balanced scorecard performance measures. However, all the evidence suggests that an organization should do this only after it has been using the balanced scorecard methodology for performance evaluation for some time. This period could be a year or more. The organization should feel confident that the balanced scorecard system is part of the corporate culture. And the organization as a whole should believe that the performance measures being used make sense. And, of course,

---

[10] Wallace, James S., "Adopting Residual Income-Based Compensation Plans: Do you get what you pay for?" Graduate School of Management, University of California, Irvine, October 1, 1996 pp. 275–300.

[11] Ibid pp. 275–300.

these measures should be clearly understood by all those whose performance is being evaluated using the balanced scorecard measures (because evidence suggests employees' often perceive that senior management might manipulate these measures). Furthermore, the data required to make the balanced scorecard methodology effective needs to be validated for relevancy of the performance measures and accuracy. In essence, compensation being a powerful psychological tool, an organization needs to be quite certain that it selects the right metrics for the balance score card and that the data being used to create a link is quite good.

As mentioned previously, many believe that a balanced scorecard methodology is an ideal tool for tying incentive compensation to organizational performance. This is because the balanced scorecard system facilitates clear communication of departmental, divisional, and corporate objectives and expectations, which flow directly from the organization-wide objectives and strategies. The balanced scorecard system's uniqueness lies in the fact that data from financial and nonfinancial drivers can be incorporated into the balanced scorecard system. So, the balanced scorecard superiority, it is believed, is the fact that *all* relevant organizational success measures (not just financial) can be used in an effort to improve overall performance, which ultimately will lead to improvement in financial performance.[12]

Before we look at a specific example of tying in incentive compensation to the balanced scorecard system, let's briefly analyze the balanced scorecard system itself.

A balanced scorecard system is an integrated set of performance standards that directly flow from the organization's overall strategy. In this system, the company translates overall organizational strategy in terms that can be understood by all levels of employees. In a balanced scorecard system, performance measures usually fall into four categories: financial, customer, processes, and learning and growth. Within each of these categories, the organization needs to define the strategic objectives, the metrics that will be used for performance evaluation,

---

[12] Atkinson, A.A., Kaplan, R.S., Matsumura, E.M., and Young, S.M; *Management Accounting: Information for Decision-Making and Strategy Execution, 6e,* 2012, Pearson, Upper Saddle River, NJ.

the targets for the chosen metrics, and both the strategic and operational actions required.

Fundamentally, the assumption is that financial measures are lagging measures. The leading measures are customer satisfaction and employee skills based on continual learning and growth. So, if an organization's employee base is skilled through learning and growth, they then will do what is necessary to satisfy customers. Satisfied customers will buy more from the organization, which will then lead to better financial performance (and hence the reason for the balanced scorecard). Internal processes are what the employees use to satisfy customers. The employees need to be trained to be skilled in the efficient use of internal processes. So, with continuous training, the employees will be motivated to improve the internal processes. Improved internal business processes used by trained and skilled employees is what increases customer satisfaction. The internal processes need to be improved before the final result is improved in financial performance. Continuous improvement is emphasized.

Financial measures are not sufficient in of themselves (but most incentive plans today are mainly centered on financial measures). They need to be integrated with nonfinancial measures in a well-integrated balanced scorecard system. Nonfinancial dimensions are often crucial to improving customer satisfaction. And improved customer satisfaction leads to improved financial performance.

Exhibit 4-8 lists performance metrics typically found in a balanced scorecard system.

Exhibit 4-8 Balance Scorecard Performance Metrics

Customer Satisfaction Measures
Customer satisfaction
Customer complaints
Returned products as a percentage of sales
Percentage of repeat customers from previous period
Internal Business Process Measures
Length of time taken to introduce new products
Time taken to answer customer calls (for example, answered within 30 seconds)
Response time for customer inquiries
Percent of on-time deliveries against all deliveries

Exhibit 4-8 Continued

Time to resolve customer raised problems, issues and complaints
Number of defect free units as a percent of all units
Delivery cycle times
Time to fill customer orders
Wait times for customer problem resolution
Throughput time
Manufacturing cycle efficiency
Percent of customer complaints settled the first time a contact is made
Employee Learning and Growth
Employee satisfaction measures
Voluntary employee turnover
Hours of training per employee
Suggestions per employee
Percentage of new hires based on employee referrals
Percentage of employees rating work environment as good to very good
Financial
Return on equity
Return on capital employed
Revenue growth
Discounted free cash flow generated

Companies should select performance measures carefully, selecting only those that fit the company's culture and unique characteristics. First and foremost, the measures selected should be clearly connected to the company's strategies and objectives. Second, the performance measures should be understandable to all constituents in a clear and concise manner. And finally, an organization should not use too many performance measures in its balanced scorecard.

From these, organization-wide measures, there should be a drill down of measures all the way to the individual level. This drill down exercise is not a trivial task. It will take concerted effort to develop connected balanced scorecard measures all the way down to the individual level. And it will take some time to develop this system for the entire organization and then follow up with a disciplined performance evaluation system built around the balanced scorecard measures. The system needs to be ingrained into the corporate culture, and that takes time. This is why before an organization uses balanced scorecard measures in incentive compensation plans it should first institutionalize the practice of using balance scorecard measures all the way from strategic objectives down to the individual level. And this balanced scorecard operating system should be in use for a while before tying the system to incentive compensation programs.

Each individual should have his or her own personal scorecard. These measures should be those that the individuals themselves can influence and affect. And the individual measures should be connected to the organization's overall scorecard. The individual needs to perceive as clearly as possible the "the line of sight." This means that the individual has to perceive that his or her individual efforts can indeed influence the results on the scorecard. They need to know that when their efforts produce positive results on the scorecard measures their individual performance evaluations will reflect such on the scorecard measures. In essence, they expect to receive positive recognition from their superiors for their efforts and actions.

If a balanced scorecard is constructed correctly, the performance measures should be linked on a cause and effect basis. For example, a high-end custom home builder might have a marketing strategy that involves enhancing the customer experience. The company believes that this will result in more sales. This high end custom home builder wants to offer more customized options to enhance the customer experience. In this case, the balanced scorecard process starts at the bottom. To execute the "more options" strategy, the internal processes involved in offering more options and in reducing the time to incorporate an option need to be improved. Along with improving the processes, employee skills in custom building need to be improved through additional training. So, when employee skill and competency enhancement has been addressed, the internal processes to build highly customized luxury homes and the time to build will also have been addressed. Then, customer satisfaction with custom building will improve. Customer satisfaction can be measured through customer satisfaction surveys. And now we can say that because of increasing customer satisfaction the number of expensive highly customized luxury homes sold will increase, and when the number of these custom homes sold increases, the financial numbers will show improvement. Such an integrated process is an example of how a balanced scorecard system works.

Balanced Scorecard and Compensation

As mentioned previously, before an organization considers using the balance scorecard measurement system as the incentive compensation triggering mechanism, the balanced scorecard system has to have been firmly in place as the performance management process for the organization for some time. The target-setting mechanism has to be firmly in place, as well. If these conditions have been met, the incentive compensation plan built around a balanced scorecard can be designed as follows:

- A target incentive compensation payout percentage must be established using salary surveys for each position in the organization. If it is too cumbersome to develop a target for every position, a target can be developed around job groupings, pay-grade levels, or salary bands.

- The target incentive percentage will be paid if the balanced scorecard measurement target is achieved.

- An incentive compensation payout range can be established (for example, 80% to 150%—80% being the minimum and 150% being the maximum payout levels). If the individual achieves a composite 80% of the balanced scorecard measures assigned, the individual receives 80% of the target incentive. And if he or she achieves 150% of the balanced scorecard measures, that individual receives 150% of the target incentive. Then, between 80% and 100% and between 100% and 150% proration can be done to derive the actual incentive payout. In other words, 80% is the minimum; no incentive will be paid out for performance below 80%. And 150% is the maximum; no incentive will be paid above 150% of the target incentive. The 150% is the ceiling. This ceiling is established to dissuade the establishment of easily accomplished performance measures.

Exhibit 4-9 shows the mechanics.

Exhibit 4-9 Mechanics of a Balanced Scorecard System

Performance measure 1	@ Achievement 100% = 20% of base compensation paid out as a bonus
	@ Achievement 80% = 16% of base compensation paid out as a bonus
	@ Achievement 150% = 30% of base compensation paid out as a bonus
	@ Below 80% achievement = No payout
	Above 150% achievement = the 30% maximum of base compensation paid out as a bonus
	An example: If achievement is 110%, payout will be 1.10 × 20% = 22% of base compensation.

When designing these plans, and in the light of financial reasonableness and adequacy, organizations sometimes establish an overall financial budget amount for the incentive program. If all individual payouts added exceed the budgeted amount, then even after the initial individual bonus tabulations have been made a downward recalibration calculation of the individual bonus amounts is made to keep the program within budget.

Note that, as mentioned earlier, tying the balanced scorecard to the organization's incentive compensation system is an involved and time-consuming process. To start this journey without the combined corporate will and without the wholehearted support of senior management risks failure.

The incentive compensation portion of the total compensation system is growing in significance. As economic uncertainties have plagued organizations over the past few years, many organizations have established incentive compensation programs. Incentive program payouts happen only when success targets are met. In a way, this puts employee pay at risk. Such a pay philosophy is finding acceptance because incentive compensation is directly connected to the organization's ability to pay. All employee groups, in both service and manufacturing organizations, are adopting these plans.

Incentive compensation is an important element of the total compensation structure. Therefore, it is important that incentive compensation is paid to managers in keeping with the interests of shareholders. Shareholders are keen on companies that increase their financial values period after period over a long term. Shrewd investors look for companies that have sustained value creation. Investors try to avoid companies that are fraught with volatility. Therefore, it is equally important to base executive and manager incentive compensation payouts on value-creation measures such as EVA, intrinsic value, RI. In addition, consideration needs to be given to a balanced scorecard system of organization performance evaluation. In summary, incentive compensation programs make a lot of sense from the finance and accounting point of view.

Key Concepts in This Chapter

- Economic value added
- Residual income
- Free cash flow
- Incentive compensation metrics
- Balanced scorecard and incentive compensation
- Prevalence of incentive compensation programs
- Financial measures used in incentive compensation
- Incentive compensation accounting
- Intrinsic value determination
- Balanced scorecard performance metrics
- Tying the performance measures to incentive compensation payouts
- Types of incentive plans
- Incentive plan circular effect
- Sustaining financial value metrics

5

Share-Based Compensation Plans

Aims and objectives of this chapter

- Explain all accounting and finance issues in share-based compensation
- Explain stock award plans
- Discuss the evolution of SFAS 123(R)
- Explain the accounting for restricted stock awards
- Discuss stock option expensing
- Discuss the debate on stock option expensing
- Explain the accounting for stock options
- Discuss stock plans with contingencies
- Explain tax implications of stock plans
- Discuss the APIC pool and deferred tax assets as they relate to stock option plans
- Explain the international tax implications of share-based employee compensation plans
- Discuss the differences between IFRS and GAAP in employee stock option accounting
- Discuss stock purchase plans
- Discuss stock appreciation rights
- Demonstrate the accounting for stock appreciation rights

A current common compensation practice is to include a share-based equity compensation plan as part of the total compensation package. The practice has been prevalent as part of an executive or senior management compensation programs, but now many companies around the world are including a share-based component in their total compensation package.

High-tech companies use these plans for all categories of employees. And if not for all employees, these companies use share-based plans to attract and retain key technical employees. Technical employees are the source of intellectual capital that high-tech companies need to succeed. Share-based plans are also almost always used to compensate outside board of directors.

Companies use share-based plans as a major component of the total compensation package because these plans motivate plan participants to act in the best interest of all shareholders.

The fact that the use of share-based plans is increasing is evidenced by the growth of professional organizations such as Global Equity Organization[1] and National Center for Employee Ownership.[2]

Share-based compensation plans have many dimensions covering eligibility, amounts of the grant, competitive practices, ownership culture, legal, tax, accounting, dilution (overhang), under-water options, and repricing of options. This chapter analyzes the accounting and finance issues that affect share-based compensation plans.

Share-based plans can consist of outright grants of shares, stock options, stock purchase plans, stock appreciation rights, or even cash payments tied to the market price of shares (phantom stock plans). Although the structure of these plans varies, the goal is the same: to compensate employees based on performance incentives. The accounting goals are also common across all plans: to establish a fair value of the compensation and to spread the calculated compensation value over the term of the receiving employee's service period.

Stock option expenses can be quite significant. After all, CEOs often hold stock options or stock grants with a value that is between 30 to 50 times their cash compensation. In addition, it has become common practice to distribute stock options and stock grants to a large percentage of the employee population, thus increasing stock option expenses.

[1]   www.globalequity.org.
[2]   www.nceo.org.

Stock Award Plans

Ever since the *Federal Accounting Standards Board* (FASB) issued its FAS 123 regulation, which now requires expensing of stock plans, companies have been adopting stock award plans. Award plans are grants of shares of stock subject to certain conditions. The conditions are normally called restrictions, and that is why these award programs are called restricted stock awards.

The restrictions are usually tied to continued employment for some pre-determined period. An employment restriction may state that if the employee terminates voluntarily or is terminated by the firm before the predetermined period ends, the shares awarded can be forfeited. The employee cannot sell the shares during the restriction period. The restrictions are designed to motivate the employee to stay with the company for a certain period of time or even motivate the employee to achieve certain preset performance goals.

On the grant date, the shares are transferred to employees subject to an agreement that the employee cannot sell, transfer, or pledge the shares until vesting occurs, which means until the employee earns these shares by way of removing the restrictions imposed. The shares can be forfeited if the restrictions are not satisfied. The company might retain the physical possession of the shares during the restriction period. The employee can be given all the rights of a shareholder subject to the restrictions and forfeiture requirements.

Advantages of restricted stock plans include the following:

- Restricted stock does not become worthless. No matter what happens to the market price of the underlining shares, the restricted stock retains some value.

- With restricted stock, dilution of current shareholder, interests is less of an issue as compared to stock options. In restricted stock plans, the number of shares granted is not as large as that granted in stock option plans. The reason for the lower number is that at the end of the vesting period the shares granted will have some value whereas under stock option plans the shares awarded might not have any value. In other words, the stock option values might be "under water" if the market price of a stock goes below the exercise price.

- Restricted stock plans align employee incentives better with the company's objectives. Often, the holder of restricted stock is also a shareholder, resulting in a better alignment with the long-term objectives of the company.

The compensation expense amount connected with a restricted stock is the market price of regular stock being traded on the date the restricted stock was granted. This amount is accrued as a compensation expense over the service period for which participants receive the shares, usually from the time the restricted stock is granted until the time the restrictions lapse or the restrictions are lifted. Once the restrictions are lifted, paid-in capital in restricted stock is replaced by common stock and paid-in capital in excess of par. The compensation expense is calculated on the date the grant is made, and the valued is based on the market price of the stock on that date. Market-price changes that happen after the grant date do not affect the restricted stock valuation.

For restricted stock plans, most companies base vesting on continued employment for a period of three to five years. Some companies might base vesting on some performance criteria, such as revenue, net income, or operating cash flows. Or the criteria can be a combination of various financial metrics. If the stock is a dividend-yielding stock, the participant collects the dividends, but those dividends can be forfeited if the participant terminates employment before the stipulated vesting date.[3]

Accounting for Restricted Stock Awards

Let's assume that on January 1, 2013, Zentec Corporation granted a restricted stock award of 80,000 shares with a term of four years, expiring on December 31, 2016, to four of its executives at 20,000 shares each. Shares have a current market price of $20 per share. The service period is four years. Vesting for the four executives occurs if they stay with the company for the entire four-year term. The par value of the shares granted is $5 per share for the restricted stock grant.

---

[3] Kiesco, D.E., Weygandt, J.J., Warfield, T.D., *Intermediate Accounting, 13e.*, Wiley, 2010.

Zentec makes the journal entry shown in Exhibit 5-1 on the date of the grant.

Exhibit 5-1 Journal Entry 1

Deferred compensation or unearned compensation (80,000 shares at $20)	1,600,000	
Common stock (80,000 at $5)		400,000
Paid-in Capital—excess of par		1,200,000

The credit entry of common stock and paid-in capital in excess of par indicates that stock has been issued. The debit entry of unearned compensation or deferred compensation is entered as a contra-equity account in the equity section of the balance sheet. This amount indicates that the company will recognize a compensation expense for each of the four years. Unearned compensation is a cost of service that has not been performed as yet. Therefore, it is not an asset.

At the end of each year 2013, 2014, 2015, 2016 (on December 31 of each year), Zentec will enter a compensation expense for that year. For example, for 2013 the entry is as shown in Exhibit 5-2.

Exhibit 5-2 Journal Entry 2

Compensation expense	400,000	
Deferred compensation		400,000

Note: $100,000 for each executive; $400,000 for 4 executives

If any of the four executives leave before the four-year period ends, he or she will forfeit rights to the shares and Zentec will reverse the accounting entries already recorded. For example, suppose that one executive leaves on April 3, 2015. No expense has been recognized for 2015 as yet. The reversing entry is as shown in Exhibit 5-3.

Exhibit 5-3 Journal Entry 2

Common stock (20,000 × $5)	100,000	
Paid-in capital in excess of par [($20 – $5) × 20,000]	300,000	
Compensation expense		200,000
Deferred compensation		200,000

Note: $400,000 applies to one executive for the entire grant

Zentec reverses the compensation expense of $200,000 recorded through 2013. Also, it debits common stock and paid-in capital in excess of par, in recognition of the forfeiture. Zentec also credits unearned compensation for the next 2 years, because of the termination of the one executive.

In the restricted stock plan, vesting did not occur at all for the executives so nothing was earned out. Therefore, reversal entries need to be made. One executive left before the continued employment requirement was met. Therefore, that executive's stock grant was forfeited.

Restricted stock plans have many advantages, not the least of which is the relative simplicity of the accounting just demonstrated. So because of the accounting, simplicity, and lower-per-unit grants, restricted stock has fast become a very attractive equity compensation element.

Stock Option Plans

In stock award programs, grants of stock are made, whereas in stock option programs, an option to purchase a stock is granted to participating employees. Over the past 40 years, stock option programs have become an integral part of the total compensation package for senior managers, executives, and key employees.[4] Although used first in the United States, companies across the globe stock now use option plans.

The accounting objective for stock option plans is to recognize an expense for these plans over the employment period of the employee who was awarded options under a stock option plan.

Options have been a controversial feature of the total compensation strategy. This is because stock options have made many CEOs exceptionally wealthy. Stock options have been legendary in the high-technology industry. There have also been various cases of malpractice

---

[4] A survey published in AICPA's Accounting Trends and Techniques, 2007, reported that of 600 companies, 590 companies stated that they had stock option plans.

with option-price backdating and grant amounts that defied logic. These factors have led to a great deal of scrutiny from various governmental agencies and resulted in these plans being immersed in tax and legal issues. (Note that this chapter focuses solely on the accounting issues related to stock option plans.)

Fundamentally, stock options give employees the option to purchase stock at (1) a specified exercise price (normally the market price on the date of the grant), (2) a predetermined period of time for vesting the option granted and for exercising the option, and (3) with a specified time for the contract period (option term).

The Stock Option Expensing Debate

The debate has been about what monetary value should be assigned to these options for expensing purposes. So, the controversy has been around how to measure the value of these options. Note that this form of compensation is noncash compensation.

In the past, options were valued (and not reported on the income statement, but rather were explained in footnotes to the financial statements) at their intrinsic value. That means, let's say, an option was granted at an exercise price of $10, but the market price on the date of the grant was $15. So, the option had an intrinsic value of $5. But, usually, options were granted at an exercise price that was the same as the market price on the date of the grant. Therefore, the option actually had a zero intrinsic value and as such there was no expense to be recognized. Before the stock option expensing regulation (FAS 123(R)) was promulgated, zero intrinsic valuation was assumed for expensing purposes even though the real value of these options could have been in the millions of dollars. This led a lot of people to start questioning the logic of recognizing zero expense when stock options were an integral part of an executives' compensation and indeed had value. In the absence of expense recognition, executives were raking in large sums of money when they exercised and sold their options. Although there is no cash impact for the company when it comes to the valuation of stock option plans, there is an implied expense involved. Because of the noncash nature of this implied expense, stock option expensing has been a matter of much debate.

Prior to 1993, stock options were being valued under the intrinsic value method under APB opinion 25. The FASB had been wavering all over on what standards for option expensing would be appropriate (the "right" way to determine the fair value of stock options). In 1993, the FASB issued a standard that would have required a fair value measurement process, but these standards were met with a lot of criticism from the public. FASB then agreed under pressure to encourage rather than require the use of fair value valuation.

Public pressure encouraged FASB to consider fair value valuation methods in the first place. The *Securities and Exchange Commission* (SEC) and the U.S. Congress urged the FASB to consider issuing standards that would use a fair value valuation method. These bodies became concerned at the lack of clear accounting for these high-payout compensation arrangements. In 1992, a bill was introduced in Congress that sought to require companies to report a compensation expense for stock options based on the fair value of the stock options. Responding to the public outcry, the FASB issued the new 1993 Exposure Draft. But because there were huge counterarguments put forth by the parties who did not want any expensing of options, the two schools of thought clearly diverged, leaving FASB with an unenviable dilemma. Supporters of the FASB Exposure Draft held to their views that these programs do have a value that needs to be recognized as a compensation expense. Supporters for fair value expensing came mostly from the academic community. The faction opposing expensing included executives (mainly from the high-tech industry), auditors, and members of Congress and of the SEC. Congress and the SEC were, in the beginning, in support of the Exposure Draft but changed their minds with the political winds and in the end opposed it.

After 2002 came a period of voluntary expensing. Many companies, on their own initiative, started using the fair value valuation methodology in their accounting for these stock options. However, public pressure continued against the excesses of executive compensation. A renewed interest surfaced for fair value expensing versus intrinsic value expensing.

The ongoing pressure on FASB to use fair value measurements grew again. Warren Buffet issued statements in favor of fair value expensing. More and more companies started using fair value expensing. (Note that the International Accounting Standards Board used fair value expensing.) However, vigorous opposition continued from the high-tech industry. High-tech companies were really concerned about the sudden erosion of their profitability position if fair value expensing were to be implemented. The inevitable happened when the FASB issued FAS 123 (finally revised in 2004). FAS 123 requires fair value valuation and associated expensing and completely does away with the intrinsic value methodology.

Note here that the valuation of stock options has nothing to do with cash flows. The only issue is expense recognition.

Finally, with the issuance of fair value expensing standards there has been a decrease in the incidence of stock option plans (because they were indeed expensive when fair value measurements were applied and these expenses are used to offset revenue).

In many cases, stock option plans have been replaced by restricted stock plans and cash-based plans.

Stock Option Expensing

Now we will analyze how stock options are expensed and accounted for based on the FAS 123 standard.

The accounting for stock options is similar to that of restricted stock. Compensation is measured at fair value and then expensed over the employment period of the employee. But the valuation of stock options requires the use of a mathematical equation.[5] This mathematical equation takes into consideration the following:

- The exercise price of the option. The exercise price is the price at which the employee can buy the option shares from the employer. Normally, the exercise price is the market price on the date the grant is made.

---

[5] The mathematical equation can take two forms: the Black-Scholes model and a Lattice model.

- Expected term of the option-exercise period.
- Current market price of the stock.
- Expected dividends.
- Expected risk-free rate of return during the term of the option.
- Expected volatility of the stock.

The mathematical model normally used for the determination of the fair value for stock options is the Black-Scholes option-pricing model. (Note that an alternative model—a lattice model, which is based on the on a binomial probability distribution—can also be used).

SFAS 123(R) called for the use of equations that would allow flexibility in modeling the ways in which employees might exercise options and also the employee-termination trends after the options vest.[6] Option pricing theory is often discussed in most accounting texts. This chapter's appendix provides you the theoretical framework.

Compensation expense calculated using the option pricing equation is expensed over the duration of employment for the employee. Also, employees receiving options are not allowed to exercise their options before the expiry of specific periods of time. These time periods are called exercise periods. And even after the expiration of the exercise time period the options can still be exercised before the expiration of the contract period. Compensation expense is spread out over a vesting period—the time period over which the options are earned out. So, from the date on which the options were granted until the first date on which the plan allows an employee to earn the option is called the vesting period. Exhibit 5-4 further explains these time periods.

---

[6] "Share-Based Payment," Statement of Financial Accounting Standards No. 123 (revised 2004), (Norwalk, CT: FASB 2004), par. A27–A29.

Exhibit 5-4 Stock Option Grant Timeline°

Five-year option

Three-year vesting

Ten-year contract term

1/3rd of grant 1st vesting date	2/3rd of grant 2nd vesting date	3/3rd of grant 3rd vesting date			
↓	↓	↓	↓	↓	(can continue exercising unexercised option]

Grant date	t_1	t_2	t_3	t_4	t_5	t_{10}
	Exercise date 1/5 of option grant	Exercise date 2/5 of option grant	Exercise date 3/5 of option grant	Exercise date 4/5 of option grant	Exercise date 5/5 of option grant	

° Note that in this example we have purposely separated vesting and exercising sequence. In reality, these two sequences would in most cases be the same.

This timeline example is for an option granted as a five-year grant. One-fifth of the number of options granted would be eligible for exercise on the annual anniversary date of the grant. Other plan provisions would indicate that if the employee did not exercise the options granted by the end of the fifth year, the employee would get another five more years to exercise, because these options, according to the plan, have a ten-year contractual duration. At the end of ten years, the option expires and the shares are forfeited.

You need to understand the following key terms related to the accounting of stock options and FAS 123(R):

- **Grant date:** The date from which the employee starts benefiting from or being adversely affected by changes in the price of the stock.

- **Measurement date:** The date at which the fair value determination is made. If it is an equity award, the measurement date is equal to the grant date. If it is a contingent award, like a restricted stock award, the measurement date is equal to the settlement date.

- **Service inception date:** The date on which the service period begins.
- **Tranche:** The lowest common denominator of an award. Tranches separate a grant into the components in which shares or units are actually earned.

In addition, there are two basic ways by which expense amortization occurs when it comes to stock options:

- **Graded amortization:** The grants are broken down into tranches such that a single tranche is viewed as an independent grant. Expenses within the tranche are straight-lined.
- **Straight-line:** Expenses are evenly distributed across a grant based on the total vesting period and total number of shares expected to vest.

The Accounting for Stock Options

To demonstrate the process for accounting for stock options, we look at two case examples. First, we continue with the Zentec Corporation example for all Zentec's executives. The second example introduces a different company: UMB Corporation. This case demonstrates expensing for an option where the exercise price differs from the market price on the date of the account.

Example 1

On January 1, 2013, Zentec Corporation granted options to their executives totaling 1,000,000 of the company's $5 par value shares with a four-year vesting and exercise period. The first vesting date is January 1, 2014. The exercise price is the market price on the date of the grant, which in the continuing example is $20. The fair value of the option was calculated to be $25 (using a mathematical model).

Journal entries were as follows:

January 1, 2013   no entry

Total compensation expense:

$25 estimated fair value per option as estimated using the Black-Scholes model × 1,000,000 options granted = $25,000,000 total compensation. This is a four-year grant, so expense per year is $25,000,000 / 4 = $6,250,000 per year recorded on December 31, 2013, 2014, 2015, and 2016.

In each year, the expense that will flow to the income statement is:

Compensation expense	6,250,000
Paid-in capital stock	6,250,000

The next few paragraphs cover situations that affect the accounting for stock options and therefore the compensation expense.

Forfeitures

Options are quite often forfeited before they vest. This is because of employee terminations and other reasons resulting in contract term violations. The fair value estimate needs to be adjusted for these incidents. If a forfeiture rate of 2% is expected because of historical trends, $25,000,000 would be adjusted to 98% or $24,500,000. The annual compensation would now change from $6,250,000 to $6,125,000. This forfeiture adjustment to the fair value-based compensation expense must be made on the original date of the calculation. If the forfeiture estimate needs to be changed during the four-year option term of the option, adjustments need to be made at that later date.

In the original example, on January 1, 2015, the forfeiture rate estimate, based on new evidence, is changed to 95% from 98%, and then the compensation expense for the four-year period needs to be $23,750,000 (or $5,937,500 per year). For 2013 and 2014, however, the compensation expense has been booked at $6,125,000 (or $12,250,000 for two years). However, it should have been booked at $5,937,500 per year and for two years $11,875,000. So, now only an additional $11,500,000 needs to be booked for the two remaining years, or $5,750,000 per year.

Calculation:

> Booked for the first two years = 12,750,000
>
> The four-year amount needs to be adjusted to = 23,750,000

So, for the next two years, the amount that needs to be booked = $23,750,000 − $12,750,000 = $11,500,000 (or $5,750,000 for each of the next two years). Of course, if estimates are changed mid-year, to be technically correct the proration of expenses should be done by the number of months in the year that the change affects.

Options Exercised

Let's assume that three quarters of these options (750,000 options) that were granted in the example were exercised by 2017 when the stock price reached $100 a share. (Wouldn't the employees love this scenario?) But the market price given here is not relevant when it comes to the stock option valuation. Fluctuations in the market price of the stock do not affect stock option valuations.

Exhibit 5-5 shows the required journal entries.

Exhibit 5-5 Journal Entry 3

Cash ($750,000 ×$20 exercise price)	15,000,000	
Cash = 750,000 shares, 3/4 of 1,000,000 × $20 per share exercise price or 750,000 × $20 = $15,000,000		
Paid-in capital – Stock Options	18,750,000	
Paid-in capital – Stock options –		
3/4th of $25,000,000 ($25 fair value × 1,000,000 Shares) = $18,750,000		
Common Stock at par (750,000 × $5 par value)		3,750,000
Common Stock = 750,000 at $5 per share par value = $3,750,000		
Paid-in capital in excess of par		30,000,000
(plugged-in number)		
Paid-in capital in excess of par = 15,000,000 + 18,750,000 =		
$33,750,000 − $3,750,000 = $30,000,000. We plug in this number.		

Options Expire

Sometimes employees let the options expire without exercising them. In this example, if we assume that one quarter of the options that remained were allowed to expire, the required journal entries would be as shown here.

Paid-in capital – Stock options	6, 250,000	
Paid-in capital – Options expired		6,250,000

In this example, we have ignored the forfeitures.

Example 2

To further demonstrate the accounting entries, here is another example. To reinforce the accounting aspects of stock option expensing, we again look at the accounting entries needed for the two most common occurrences after grant: option exercise and option expiration.

The top ten managers of UMB Corporation were granted 20,000 stock options each of the company's $5 par value common stock by the board of directors. The board granted these options effective January 1, 2013. These are options that vest over a five-year period, and the contractual term of the plan is seven years. So, the managers have seven years to exercise these options. The stipulated option exercise price is $30 per share, and the current market price for the shares is $40 per share. Therefore, these options are being granted at a discount from the market price (*discounted stock options*).

These options as of the date of the grant are in the money. In other words, the options have value on the grant date. These options cannot be distributed under a qualified *incentive stock option plan* (ISO), which has tax advantages compared to standard nonqualified stock option grants. As of January 1, 2013, they are in the money, but upon vesting they might not be in the money. It depends on the market price on the vesting dates. Also, whether the executive holds on to the stock or sells them will dictate the value that the executive will derive.

In this example, let's also assume that the option-pricing model (Black-Scholes) UMB Corporation utilizes values these options at a fair value of $35 per share, or a total compensation expense of $7,000,000 (10 managers ×20,000 shares each ×$35 a share) or $1,400,000 per year ($7,000,000 ÷ Five-year vesting period). Note that the market price of the shares on the date of grant does not affect option expensing.

At the date of the grant, January 1, 2013, no accounting entries are made. We assume also that the service period for these managers is the same as the five-year vesting period.

Entries on December 31, 2013:

Compensation expense	1,400,000	
Paid-in capital – Stock options ($7,000,000/5)		1,400,000

UMB Corporation is allocating these expenses evenly over the five years. So at the end of each year (2013 [shown above], 2014, 2014, 2016, 2017), $1,400,000 compensation expense will be recorded. After five years, $7,000,000 will have been expensed.

Options Exercised

If on July 1, 2018, UMB Corporation's managers exercise 100,000 shares of the 200,000 (10 managers × 20,000 shares each) granted (50% of the options; five and a half years after the grant date), the journal entries would be as follows:

July 1, 2018

Cash (100,000 ×$30 a share exercise price)	3,000,000	
Paid-in capital – Stock options (50% ×$7,000,000)	3,500,000	
Common stock (100,000 ×$5 a share)		500,000
Paid-in capital in excess of par		6,000,000

Options Expire

If UMB Corporation's managers do not exercise the remaining 50% of the original 200,000 shares granted and the seven-year contract term expires, the accounting entries are as follows:

January 1, 2019
Paid-in capital – Stock options	3,500,000	
Paid-in capital – Expired stock options		3,500,000

Note that forfeiture rules should be applied if necessary, as demonstrated in Example 1. Forfeiture rules are applied if there were service requirements that were not fulfilled by the executive or a performance targets were not achieved.

Stock Plan with Contingencies

Some stock plans have a contingency based on a performance condition or a market condition. These conditions need to be satisfied per the plan provisions before a participating employee can benefit from the stock awarded. These conditions or contingencies can be a stipulated performance measure on any financial metric, such as, target revenue, earnings per share, sales growth, net income, operating cash, and so on. Or a condition can be established based on stock performance. The stipulation could be set indicating that the stock option or award will not be earned by the participant unless the growth in the company's market stock price exceeds a hurdle based on a stock market index. (For example, the company's stock price has to exceed the growth in the Dow Jones Industrial Index by over 25%.)

There are two triggers for expensing of options or awards for the company when there are contingencies set: the probability of removing the condition or the contingency, and whether the condition or contingency was indeed removed.

The compensation expense estimates take into consideration the likelihood of forfeiture, in case the contingencies and conditions are not met, and also the likelihood of exceeding the performance targets.

Let's assume in the Zentec Corporation example that a performance target was established by stating the stock options or awards will be earned only if revenues grow above a 25% year-to-year growth rate. If it is determined probable that the 25% revenue growth target will be achieved, compensation expense recognition will occur, and it will be the same as in the previous example (1,000,000 shares × the fair value estimate of $25 per share, resulting in a compensation expense of $25,000,000 over the four-year term). If after two years it is determined that that 25% revenue target will not be achieved, the compensation expense estimate must be changed to zero. An accounting reversal needs to be made. The $12,500,000 amount already expensed will have to be reversed.

If the probability at the beginning of the option award four-year term is that the performance target is not going to be met, no expense needs to be recognized at the beginning of the term. Suppose, however, that in two years the probability is changed and it is determined that the performance target will be met. In that case, at that time compensation expense recognition needs to occur. However, we now know that the compensation expense estimate for the four-year period needed to be $25,000,000. So, at the end of the second year, the journal entries need to be as shown here:

For 2012 and 2013		
Compensation expense ($25,000,000 × .5)	12,500,000	
Paid-in capital – Stock options		12,500,000
For 2014 and 2015 each year		
Compensation expense	6,250,000	
Paid-in capital – Stock options		6,250,000

Tax Implications of Stock Plans

In the United States, the tax implications of stock option expensing are governed by two regulations: FAS 123(R) and SFAS 109. These are the accounting standards dealing with treatment of stock compensation for the purposes of calculating tax expense or the income tax provision.

For tax purposes, plans can qualify as an *incentive stock option* (ISO), under the tax code, or the plan could be designated as a nonqualified plan. Qualified plans are called incentive stock options, and nonqualified plans are designated as nonqualified stock option plans.

For a stock option plan to be designated as a qualified plan under the tax code, the exercise price of the option needs to be the same as the market price on the date of the grant. For such plans, no taxes need to be paid until the shares are sold, and the company granting those options does not get a tax deduction for those expenses.

For nonqualified stock option plans, taxes need to be paid at the time of exercise. At the same time, the company gets a tax deduction. The deduction is calculated based on the difference between the exercise price and the market price on the date of exercise. This creates a temporary difference between accounting income and taxable income. For accounting income, the expense is deducted in the current period, but the tax deduction is taken when the options are exercised. This creates a *deferred tax asset* (DTA). A DTA is an expectation that at a later date a tax deduction can be taken for the share-based award that was granted. The DTA is therefore an estimated tax benefit. This applies to stock option grants and also grants under restricted stock awards. For incentive stock option grants and a 423 Plan (a stock purchase plan), there is no "temporary difference" recognized, and no DTA needs to be recorded.

Before we analyze the tax issues in detail using our continuing example of Zentec Corporation, let's look at a simpler example that should explain the concepts being discussed. A nonqualified stock option grant of 1,000 shares is made at a fair value of $10 per share. The corporate tax rate is 40%, which results in a DTA of $4,000. Both the compensation expense ($10,000) and the DTA ($4,000) are recognized over the service period. This effectively reduces the cost of the option granted to $6,000.

Another important point to note here is that under FAS 123(R) there is a concept called the *additional paid-in capital pool* (the APIC pool). This account differs from the generic APIC account that is used for other specific purposes. Under FAS 123(R), when a tax deduction exceeds the compensation expense, the excess increases a temporary APIC pool. And, when the tax deduction is less than the compensation expense, the existing APIC pool is used to offset the difference. If the amount needed exceeds the remaining APIC pool, it becomes an additional tax expense.

Now let's look at the tax effects from our continuing Zentec Corporation example.

Assuming a 30% income tax rate, the following journal entries need to be made:

For the Zentec Corporation example for 2013, 2014, 2015, 2016 – calculation for each year:

Compensation expense	6,250,000	
Paid-in capital – Stock options		6,250,000
Deferred tax asset (30% of $6,250,000)	1,875,000	
Income tax expense		1,875,000

After tax impact on earnings 6,250,000 – 1,875,000 = 4,375,000 for each year.

Assume for the Zentec Corporation example that three quarters of the options granted (1,000,000 × .75 = 750,000) at the beginning of 2013 were exercised on December 31, 2018. Assume also that the market price of the stock is $50 a share on December 31, 2018. Note the exercise price for the Zentec Corporation example is $20 a share. In this case, the tax benefit will exceed the DTA.

Income tax payable	6,750,000	
[($50 – $20) × 750,000 × .30]		
Deferred tax asset (4 years × $1,875,000 × .75)		5,625,000
Paid-in capital – Tax effect of stock options[7]		1,125,000

Note that this was a four-year grant.

[7]   SFAS 109 (par. 36 c).

Now assume that the market price of the stock is $25 a share on December 31, 2019. Note the exercise price for the Zentec Corporation example is $20 a share. In this case, the tax benefit will be less than the DTA.

Income tax payable [($25 – 20) × 750,000 × 30%]	1,125,000	
Income tax expense or paid-in capital – Tax effect of stock options	4,500,000	
DTA (Four years × 1,875,000 × .75)		5,625,000

If the actual tax benefit is greater than the estimated tax benefit, this leads to an *excess*. More benefit comes to the company and this amount is posted to APIC.

If the actual tax benefit is less than the estimated tax benefit, a *shortfall* occurs, which provides fewer benefits to the company than originally projected. So, the company must either increase tax expense (income statement) or decrease APIC (balance sheet) to account for the shortfall. Most companies will want to decrease APIC. However, the company is permitted to decrease the APIC pool only to the extent that it exists. This creates a possible tax expense, which creates an offset against the existing APIC pool.

Here are two further examples that illustrate the concepts being discussed:

Example 1: Estimated DTA is greater than the actual tax benefit

NQ granted for 5,000 shares, price = $5

SFAS(R) expense = $4 per share × 5,000 shares = $20,000

DTA = 40% × $20,000 = $8,000

Shares exercised when market value = $10

Tax deduction = 5,000 shares × $5 gain per share = $25,000

Actual tax benefit = $25,000 × 40% = $10,000

Estimated tax benefit = $8,000

Excess = $2,000 (APIC)

Example 2: Expected DTA is less than the actual tax benefit

NQ granted for 5,000 shares, price = $3.00

Expense = $4.00 per share × 5000 shares = $20,000

DTA = 40% × $20,000 = $8,000

Shares exercised when market value = $5

Tax deduction = 5,000 shares × $2 gain per share = $10,000

Actual tax benefit = $10,000 × 40% = $4,000

Estimated tax benefit = $8,000

Shortfall = $4,000

In summary, when one is reconciling the estimated to actual tax benefit, two conditions can exist. The first exists when the estimated amount is equal to the DTA. Here we book the DTA as an expense. So, the booked amount will be the FAS 123(R) expense times the corporate tax rate. The other condition is when there is an excess or shortfall. The recognition for this condition is made at the taxable event. The actual tax benefit is calculated using the applicable corporate tax rate. The excess or shortfall is reconciled with the APIC pool. Excesses increase the APIC pool and shortfalls are offset against the existing APIC pool. If the amount needed exceeds remaining APIC pool, an additional expense is recorded.

International Tax Implications of Share-Based Employee Compensation Plans

With the growth in the globalization of business, there has been an increase in the prevalence of global employee compensation programs. Compensation programs now have to be designed for employees on worldwide basis. Therefore, we are also witnessing a growing trend in cross-border employee stock option plans. These plans must then comply with the tax laws and regulations in a wide variety of tax jurisdictions.

Stock Options

The basic tax principle affecting stock option plans is the same principle that exists for any other compensation program: The employee should be taxed when the compensation is received. In the case of options, this event occurs when the option is granted.

However, international tax policy, rules, and practice are not uniform when it comes to the policy of taxed when granted. Tax liability may arise at varying points of time, depending on the specific tax jurisdiction. The variation in practice may be guided by a particular government's desire to tax compensation at the earliest point in time.

The taxing jurisdiction becomes a major determining factor for tax liabilities in the international arena. And the tax jurisdiction mainly depends on the country of employment. Cash compensation is normally taxed by the country in which the employee is employed. However, tax treaties often dictate that capital gain income should be taxed in the country in which the employee resides. So, conflicting practice can hinder effective decision making. An employee may be granted an equity award in one country, vest that award in another country, exercise that award in yet another country, and finally sell that award in a fourth country. Employer withholdings and even individual tax implications can differ in each jurisdiction in which the company operates and distributes shares under various employee stock-based compensation plans.

With regard to share-based employee stock plans, corporate taxpayers want to focus on the following:

- Ensure that sufficient income is earned and taxed in each tax jurisdiction so that the company can utilize all available tax credits.
- Decide whether to have maximum compliance and adhere to reporting and withholding requirements in most if not all tax jurisdictions.
- Conduct an annual review of plans for compliance with local tax laws and rules.
- Determine whether granting awards in a particular country constitutes a public offering, which might require various detailed prospectus filings.

The other international tax issues with regard to international taxation of employee share plans for U.S. multinational corporations include the following:

- U.S. multinationals must expense stock awards even if those grants are made to their non-U.S. employees working abroad.

- If the foreign operation is a branch operation of the U.S. parent, generally any income tax deduction may be taken by the parent and can also possibly be claimed as a local deduction. If the foreign operation is not a "pass-through" operation, only the local jurisdiction gets the deduction if it is allowed in that jurisdiction.

- That entity that has the most likelihood of claiming a deduction can record a DTA based on the applicable effective tax rate. And then the entity that actually claims the deduction calculates any shortfall or excess against the DTA accrued. The timing of when the ultimate tax deduction can be taken varies by local jurisdiction.

- Very few tax jurisdictions allow a tax deduction without that jurisdiction's local entity bearing the actual cost related to the employee stock plan. So, a tax deduction strategy has to be developed. A common approach for companies is to establish intercompany chargebacks. The steps in executing global intercompany stock chargebacks are as follows:

  1. The parent company delivers stock to the employee.
  2. The employee pays the exercise price to the parent company.
  3. The employee provides services to the foreign operation.
  4. The foreign operation reimburses the parent company for the spread (the current market price minus exercise price) pursuant to a reimbursement agreement.

Other requirements might exist, too, such as documentation of a contractual obligation prior to the grant date before chargeback practices can be implemented.

IFRS Versus GAAP: Differences in Employee Stock Plan Accounting

This section examines the differences between U.S. *Generally Accepted Accounting Principles* (GAAP) and *International Financial Reporting Standards* (IFRS) with regard to employee stock option plans. This is important because of the impending convergence between U.S. GAAP and IFRS.

In Income Tax Accounting

U.S. GAAP dictates that a DTA for a stock option should be based on the options fair value (FAS 123(R)) on the date the option is granted. A DTA is still recorded irrespective of whether the option is "out of the money." No adjustments are made to the fair value of the underlining stock prior to the exercise or expiration date. Under IFRS, the DTA is based on the tax deduction available based on the current market price of the underlying share at each reporting date. Therefore, DTA is recognized only when the option is "in the money." Under IFRS, in most tax jurisdictions the tax deduction is based on the *intrinsic value* of the stock option at exercise. This is the excess of the stock value over of the stock option exercise price. So, where exercise price equals fair value, no DTA is recognized under IFRS at the time of the grant. Tax benefits are recognized only if the fair value exceeds the exercise price. This happens as the stock price rises. Often, the tax benefit recognition trails the recorded compensation expense.

Under IFRS, because of remeasurement each reporting period caused by fair value fluctuations, the effective tax rate is subject to change. This results in volatility in the effective tax rate and the deferred accounts over the life of the stock options. This is because of the stock price changes at each recording period. And under IFRS, these changes are reported in the operating section of the statement of cash flows.

Under IFRS, the tax effect of any excess in the estimated tax deduction over the recorded compensation expense is recorded in the equity section of the balance sheet and also as a DTA. Under U.S. GAAP, only excess tax benefit recognized at the time the exercise is credited to equity in the APIC account. IFRS does not apply the U.S. GAAP concept of an APIC pool, which enables tax benefit shortfalls to be offset against aggregated prior windfalls.

The difference in the calculation of the DTA under U.S. GAAP and IFRS is demonstrated in the following example.

Let's assume that on January 1, 2013, ABC Corporation grants 5,000 options with a grant date fair value of $20. The awards vest after five years of service. The exercise price is $33. And the share price at the end of the first year, 2013, is $35. The company's tax rate is 30%.

The DTA under U.S. GAAP is as follows:

$$5,000 \text{ options} \times \$20 \times 1/5 \text{ vesting} \times 30\% = \$6,000$$

Under IFRS, the company calculates the DTA based on the current market share price as the reporting date of December 31, 2013:

$$5,000 \text{ options} \times (\$35 - \$33) \times 1/5 \text{ vesting} \times 30\% = \$600$$

Under IFRS, the tax benefit is considerably lower than under U.S. GAAP.

In Valuation and Expense Recognition

Although both IFRS and U.S. GAAP require compensation expense determination using value pricing models, the accounting for tiered options differs. IFRS requires each vesting tranche of an option to be valued using different fair values, whereas U.S. GAAP allows aggregate estimation or each tranche can be valued separately.

The amortization of the expenses under IFRS needs to be commenced on the grant date. Under U.S. GAAP, amortization can be straight-line or accelerated for awards that vest after the required service period.

For Payroll Tax Accounting

Under U.S. GAAP, a company recognizes a payroll tax liability for employee stock plans when the liability arises (that is, when the options are exercised). Under IFRS, companies can recognize an accrued payroll tax liability when the options vest. Under IFRS, Social

Security taxes related to employee share plans are accrued at each reporting date. This can require payroll process changes and thus create a lot more administrative work.

Employee Share Purchase Plans

Employee share purchase plans (ESPPs) or 423 Plans generally permit employees to purchase stock at a discount or favorable terms through payroll deductions. The primary objective of these plans is to encourage employee ownership of companies. Also, these plans allow employees to purchase shares without incurring brokerage fees. Some companies, to encourage employee participation, match or partially match employee purchases.

A qualified 423 ESPP allows employees under U.S. tax law to purchase stock at a discount from fair market value without any taxes owed on the discount at the time of purchase. In some cases, a holding period is required for the purchased stock to receive favorable long-term capital gains tax treatment on a portion of your gains when the shares are sold.

A nonqualified ESPP usually is structured like qualified 423 Plan, but without the preferred tax treatment for employees.

ESPPs can be considered compensation expenses unless three conditions are satisfied:

- All employees have to be eligible to participate. No restrictions can be placed on employee participation.
- The discount provided has to be small, less than 5%. If the amount is 5% or less, no compensation needs to be recorded. Many plans have had discount percentages of 15% or more. These plans are considered compensation for tax purposes.
- The plan cannot have an option feature.

Plans that are considered compensatory should record the compensation expense over the employment service life of participating employees.

If all employees can participate and employees have no more than one month after the price is fixed to enroll and the discount is no greater than 5%, the accounting for these plans is straightforward. The company just records the sale of shares as the employee buys the shares.

If the discount is more than 5%, the plan is considered compensation, and an expense has to be recorded. Suppose, for instance, that an employee purchases shares under the plan for $4,250 (15% discount) rather than the current market price of $5,000. The $750 discount is recorded as a compensation expense:

Cash (discounted price)	4,250	
Compensation expense ($5,000 × 15%)	750	
Common stock (at market value)		5,000

Stock Appreciation Rights

Stock appreciation rights (SARs) allow employees who are granted stock options to receive a cash or stock payment upon the exercise of the option. The payment of stock or cash is based on the difference between a predetermined price (usually the market price on the date of the grant) and the market price on the date of exercise. This overcomes a major disadvantage of stock option plans where the employees are required to buy the shares at the exercise price. Upon exercising his or her options, the employee has to come up with the cash. If the employee received a large grant, the cash outlay can be quite onerous. Note that the payment can be made either in cash or shares. The participant has the choice. The granting of SARs mitigates the cash-outlay disadvantage.

If an employer decides to settle the SAR with stock, the transaction becomes an equity transaction. If the employee elects to receive a cash settlement or has the option to elect a cash settlement, the award is then considered a liability transaction. This definition is based on the definition of liabilities under SFAS No. 6. Because a cash-settled SAR requires the transfer of an asset (cash), it is considered a liability. And if a SAR award requires the transfer of stock (equity), it is considered an equity transaction.

SARs Payable in Shares

When a SAR is considered an equity exchange (because the employer can settle the claim in stock rather than cash), the fair value of the SAR is estimated on the grant date. The compensation expense is accrued over the employment period of the employee. The fair value of the SAR is the same as that of a stock option, developed using an appropriate pricing model. The same fair value determination method is used and the compensation expense is accrued over the service life. No adjustments are made based on future changes in the stock price.

SARs Payable in Cash

For cash-settled SARs, which is a liability as stated previously, a fair value estimation is done, and a compensation expense is taken over the service period in the same way as done for options and other share-based plans. Because these plans are considered a liability, however, the fair value must be reestimated over time to continually readjust the fair value and corresponding compensation expense until it is paid.

The period's expense is that portion of the total compensation expense earned to date by SAR participants based on the fraction of the employment term that has elapsed. This amount is reduced by any already expensed amounts for past periods.

Suppose, for instance, that the fair value of the SAR at the end of a period is $10. The total compensation would be $10 million if one million SARs were to vest. Let's assume that one million SARs were granted on January 1, 2013, and that these are five-year grants. So, the compensation expense for each year is $2,000,000 if SARs are considered to be equity. This is because the company can settle in shares at exercise. The SARs can also be considered to be a liability because there can be an election made to settle in cash. The journal entries for both these transactions are shown here.

Journal entries for SARs that are considered equity transactions

For the years, 2013, 2014, 2015, 2016, 2017

Compensation expense ($10,000,00/5 years)	2,000,000	
Paid-in capital – SAR plan		2,000,000

Journal entries for SARs considered a liability

January 1, 2013 – no entries made.

December 31, 2013

Compensation expense	2,200,000	
($11 fair value estimate on 12/31/13) × (1,000,000 × 1/5)		
Liability – SAR plan		2, 200, 000

December 31, 2014

Compensation expense	1,800,000	
[($10 (fair value estimate on 12/31/14) × (1,000,000 × 2/5) – 2,200,000]		
Liability – SAR plan		1,800,000

December 31, 2015

Compensation expense	800,000	
[($8 (fair value estimate on 12/31/15) × (1,000,000 × 3/5) – 4,000,000]		
Liability – SAR plan		800,000

December 31, 2016

Compensation expense	4,800,000	
[($12 (fair value estimate 12/31/16) × (1,000,000 × 4/5) – 4,800,000]		
Liability – SAR plan		4,800,000

December 31, 2017

Liability – SAR plan	5,600,000	
Compensation expense		5,600,000
[($4 (fair value estimate on 12/31/17) × (1,000,000 × 5/5) – 9,600,000]		

The variability occurs in this example because of the changing market price of the stock.

December 31, 2018

Compensation expense [($7 (fair value estimate 12/31/18) × 1,000,000) – 9,600,000 + 5,600,000]	3,000,000	
Liability – SAR plan		3,000,000

We continue to adjust both the expense and liability until the SARs are exercised or they expire. Let's assume that in this example the SARs are exercised on September 14, 2019, when the fair value is $6.00 and the earn-out is in cash.

Liability – SAR plan	1,000,000	
Compensation expense[($6.00 (fair value estimate on 12/31/18) × 1,000,000) – $7,000,000 ($12,600,000 – $5,600,000)]		1,000,000
Liability – SAR plan ($7,000,000 - $1,000,000)	6,000,000	
Cash		6,000,000

Exhibit 5-6 demonstrates the numbers for each year.

Exhibit 5-6 Demonstrating the Numbers with a T-account

Liability – SAR Plan

		2.2	2013
		1.8	2014
		.8	2015
		4.8	2016
2017	5.6	3.0	2018
2019	1.0		
2019	6.0		

All SARS Exercised on September 14, 2019

As you have seen in this chapter, share-based compensation has been gaining in popularity across the world. But this is an area rife with accounting, finance, and tax issues. It is a fairly technical topic. And it is imperative that compensation and benefits professional (and HR professionals) have an in-depth understanding of the accounting and finance principles behind share-based compensation. Relying exclusively on consultants is not a very good idea.

Key Concepts in This Chapter

- Restricted stock plans
- SFAS 123(R)
- Stock option expensing
- Stock plans with contingencies
- Tax implications of stock plans
- Deferred tax assets
- APIC pool
- Stock purchase plans
- Stock appreciation rights
- Incentive stock plans
- Nonqualified stock plans
- Accounting for stock options
- Option pricing theory
- International tax implications of share-based employee compensation plans
- IFRS versus U.S. GAAP with respect to share-based compensation

Appendix: Stock Options and Earnings per Share

An important accounting issue with regard to employee share plans is their effect on the key accounting indicator of business success: *earnings per share ratio.* Stakeholders use many financial indicators to evaluate the success or failure of companies. No one indicator can be claimed to be the most important. Many believe that the *earnings per share* (EPS) indicator comes closest to being the most important. Because of the importance of EPS, we need to analyze how employee share-based compensation plans can affect the calculation of the EPS.

There are two ways in which the EPS indicator is presented in financial statements.

First, the basic earnings per share calculation:

$$\text{Earnings per share} = \frac{\text{Net Income} - \text{Preferred Dividends}}{\text{Weighted} - \text{Number of Shares Outstanding}}$$

To calculate the weighted average number of shares, companies must weigh the shares by the fraction of the period they are outstanding. A weighted average is used because the number of outstanding shares can fluctuate during a reporting period.

But there is second aspect to the EPS calculation. This involves complex capital structures. Companies with "complex capital structures"—those with a potential common stock impact—must also report diluted EPS.

Potentially, common stock options when exercised can increase the number of common shares, which will result in decreasing the EPS; therefore, it constitutes a complex capital structure.

Both the basic EPS and diluted EPS reflect the current earning power of a company's common stock. But diluted EPS measures how the exercise of stock options would affect EPS in the event that all options were exercised.

Employee share-based plans like stock options are in a category of instruments that may become common stock once they are exercised. They will then dilute (reduce) earnings and are therefore called potential common shares. A company is said to have a complex capital structure if there are potential common shares involved from exercising stock options or from earning out stock awards.

For stock options, an assumption is made that the options have been exercised. Another assumption is also made that the options were exercised at the beginning of the reporting period or when the options were issued, whichever is later.

The treasury stock method is now used, which assumes that the cash proceeds from selling the new shares at the exercise price is used to buy back as many shares as possible at the stock's average market price during the reporting year.

In the treasury stock method, an assumption is made that the options will be exercised; then, the numerator of the EPS equation increases. However, this cannot be the only assumption that is being made. If the options were exercised, that would generate cash for the company. The cash can be used in wide variety of different ways. As a matter of fact, each and every company might have a different way to use the cash, depending on their needs and desires. However, this use of cash will certainly also have an effect on the numerator (that is, net income). Under GAAP, a uniform application is applied to the EPS calculation, in the interest of intercompany comparability. So in GAAP, an assumption is made that the funds received upon exercise will be used by companies to buy back the stock of their companies at the average market price during the reporting period. Consequently, the weighted average number of shares in the denominator are increased by the difference in the number of shares exercised versus the number of shares the company buys back.

This is called the treasury stock method, based on the assumption that treasury shares are being purchased with the cash generated by the exercising of options. This treasury method, under GAAP, is an effort to create intercompany comparability.

But, two scenarios can exist when the treasury stock method is applied. If the exercise price of the option is lower than the average market price, the shares are added to the denominator (dilution occurs). If the exercise price of the option is higher than the market price of the stock, this effect reduces the number of shares in the denominator. In this case, the options are antidilutive.

Now, let's look at the calculations assuming that there are 2,000 options granted at an average market price of $40 per share at a point in time. The treasury method would consider that there are only 1,000 incremental shares outstanding.

Proceeds 2000 options @ $20 a share	40,000
Shares issued upon exercise	2,000
Treasury shares ($40,000 / $40)	1,000
Incremental shares	1,000

Or

$$\frac{\text{Market price} - \text{Option price} \times \text{Number of options}}{\text{Number of shares}} =$$

$$\frac{\$40 - \$20 \times 2000}{\$40} = 1000 \text{ shares}$$

The impact of employee share plans on EPS depends on the plan type. For purposes of diluted EPS, accounting needs to be maintained as to when the options are being exercised so that the flow through of the effect on the numerator of the EPS equation can be updated at the EPS calculation point.

Effect of Restricted Stock

Awards of restricted stock are treated like options for EPS purposes. In most cases, unvested awards are excluded from basic EPS and are included in diluted EPS. Once vested, these awards are included in basic EPS—even if the shares haven't actually been issued.

For purposes of computing diluted EPS, restricted stock are also considered outstanding at the beginning of a reporting period, even though they are contingent on an employee's continued service. However, performance-based awards that are contingent on earnings or stock price targets are not included in diluted EPS unless those targets are being met as of the end of the reporting period.

6

International and Expatriate Compensation

Aims and objectives of this chapter

- Explain theoretical and structural concepts in international and expatriate compensation systems
- Explain the balance sheet system for expatriate compensation.
- Discuss the allowance structure within the balance sheet system
- Review the concepts underlying the expatriate income tax system
- Explain the methodologies used to calculate the cost-differential allowance
- Examine the issues surrounding the global payroll system
- Discuss the main challenges in establishing international employee pension plans
- Set overall framework for the design of global stock option plans

International and expatriate compensation is one of the most technically involved aspects of *human resource* (HR) management. The technical issues involved with design, development, implementation, and administration of such systems require expertise of accounting, finance, statistics, law, and taxes. These technical issues are interwoven into the various facts of international and expatriate compensation programs.

This chapter discusses international and expatriate compensation, with the technical issues as the focus. But, first we review the theoretical and structural basis for the programs. Our discussions, true to the purpose of this book, will stay focused on the technical accounting, finance, and statistical issues.

The topics in international and expatriate compensation that have a significant finance, accounting, and statistical content are as follows:

- Expatriate taxes
- Cost-differential allowance calculations (has more of a statistical focus)
- Costing expatriate assignments
- International and expatriate payroll and payment processing
- International pensions
- Global stock option plans

In this chapter, we go through these topics in some detail, from a theoretical and structural point of view as well as from an accounting, finance, and statistics angle. Before we do so, some theoretical and structural issues need to be dealt with.

The Background to International and Expatriate Compensation

When we talk about the overseas staff of a company doing business outside of the country in which their headquarters is located, the composition of the staff can be quite diverse. This company could have

- Headquarters country nationals working in another country, sent from the headquarters country to work there. The employee can be on a temporary or a permanent assignment in the foreign country. Let's say that the home country is Country A and a Country A employee is being sent to work in Country B. This type of staff in normally called headquarters staff or home-country employees.

- A company could hire an employee from Country C and send that employee to a different foreign country to work. This type of employee will normally be called a *third-country national* (TCN).

- The company that is setting up operations in a foreign country can hire local nationals in that country. So, if a company is setting up operations in Country B, and if they hire employees who are nationals of Country B (and most certainly they will), these staff members will be called local staff.

These distinctions are critical to the flow of expenses through the accounting system. Clearly, defining the intent of the assignment within the context of the definitions provided here will reduce foreign assignment complications.

Before we go further, it is important to state that in international compensation, the word *expatriate* refers to employees who are being sent to a different country only for a temporary period of time (and temporary, by its very nature, indicates that it is short term; one to five years). In HR management, the concept of a permanent expatriate is a misnomer. In current practice, this word is often misused, creating confusion and increased expenses.

In expatriate compensation, those employees being sent on an assignment by the company are provided additional (additional to base) allowances, premiums, and payments. All these payments are designed to mitigate the discomforts of uprooting home-country roots and family life temporarily. If an expatriate being paid like an expatriate continues to stay in a foreign location indefinitely, the costs of that assignment will rise, creating a very expensive proposition.

Now let's set the stage for a detailed analysis of the topics to be discussed. Most companies today do business in countries outside of their home base country or outside the country in which their headquarters is located (that is, outside their country or origin).

The main objective of a global compensation program is the attraction and retention of employees who are qualified for foreign assignments. Then there is the facilitation of the transfer between foreign affiliates, between foreign affiliates and the parent company, and between the parent company and the foreign affiliate. Companies attempt to establish and maintain a consistent and reasonable relationship between the compensation of employees of all affiliates, both at home and abroad. They also have to be concerned with the maintenance of a compensation program that is reasonable in relation to the practices of competitors. This has to be accomplished at optimal costs.

To achieve the objectives stated, additional compensation is provided to employees being sent by the company to work in a different country. The major elements of the additional compensation are as follows:

- Providing an incentive to leave the home country for a foreign assignment.

- The ability to maintain a standard of living that the employee and his/her family are used to in their home country or permanent resident location.

- Consideration is given to career and family requirements that, because of the temporary nature of the assignment, need to be maintained in the home-country location. The idea is that the employee and his or her family will return to the home country when the assignment is completed. The compensation structure is designed to facilitate reentry into the home country at the end of the assignment.

To fulfill these objectives, the determination of individual and organizational pay and benefits on a global basis can become extremely complex. There are many dimensions to consider. The complexities are based on the varying compensation structures from country to country. Salary levels and benefit provisions differ among countries. Complicating the situation further are the issues surrounding multiple currencies and multiple tax laws, processes, and procedures.

Currently, the systems being used in practice are as follows:

- **Balance sheet:** The balance sheet system is the most prevalent system in use and is discussed in some detail in the next section.

- **Lump sum:** This system uses the home country's system for determining base salary. In addition to the base salary, the expatriate is offered a lump sum of money to apply toward the foreign-service expenditures. In this system, it is up to the expatriate to use the lump sum to meet various expenses without intruding on the individual expatriates' specific expenses.

- **Cafeteria:** Similar to the lump-sum method, but instead of offering a single sum of money for the foreign assignment, the expatriate is offered a selection of options to choose from. The expatriate can choose which option he or she wants. Options might include a company car, children's education expenses paid by the company, relocation expenses for household goods, or a country club membership. Limits are imposed on the expenses for each option.

- **Negotiation:** In this plan, each expatriate employee's package is negotiated on a one-to-one basis. Companies want to keep things simple. The terms negotiated should be mutually agreeable.

- **Regional:** Similar terms and conditions offered to expatriates assigned to particular regions. Regional terms and conditions vary from region to region.

- **Global pay system:** Standardized worldwide terms and conditions are used. No variation exists in the terms and conditions. This system does not allow for much flexibility. Worldwide pay systems, such as job evaluation and performance evaluation, are in use.

- **Localization:** In this method, the expatriate is essentially paid under the same terms and conditions that exist for local nationals who occupy the same job or position as the expatriate will occupy. This is an appropriate system if the expatriate is being permanently transferred to that location and very little probability of mobility exists for this particular expatriate.

These systems have been widely used in expatriate compensation program planning and administration for many years.

U.S.-based companies use the balance sheet system extensively. There are a very large number of U.S. expatriates working abroad, and because U.S.-based companies prefer to use the balance sheet system, it can be inferred that this system is the most common system.

The Balance Sheet System

The balance sheet system is an effort to ensure that the expatriate employee is "made whole." That is at a minimum, the expatriate should be no worse off or even better off for accepting an overseas assignment with respect to his or her compensation and benefit terms (see Exhibits 6-1 and 6-2).

The balance sheet approach consists of making a balance sheet for the assignment before the assignment begins. This is the approach followed by most U.S. multinationals and is used mostly for senior and middle-level management expatriate employees. The main reason for such an approach is that firms seek to standardize the process. Policies are developed that delineate what is covered and what is not.

We now turn our attention to the incentive and allowance payments normally provided under a balance sheet system.

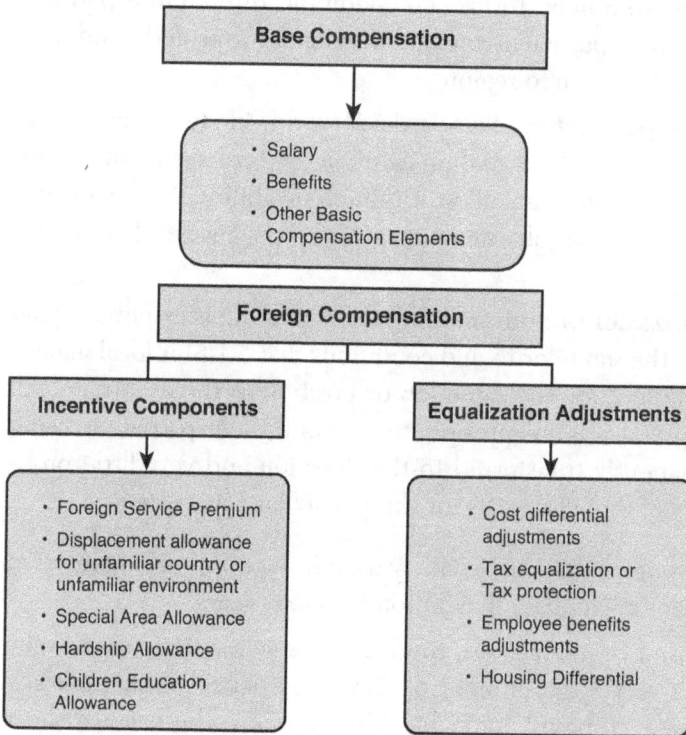

```
                    ┌──────────────────────────┐
                    │     Base Compensation     │
                    └──────────────────────────┘
                                 │
                                 ▼
                    ╭──────────────────────────╮
                    │  • Salary                 │
                    │  • Benefits               │
                    │  • Other Basic            │
                    │    Compensation Elements  │
                    ╰──────────────────────────╯

                    ┌──────────────────────────┐
                    │    Foreign Compensation   │
                    └──────────────────────────┘
```

Base Compensation

- Salary
- Benefits
- Other Basic Compensation Elements

Foreign Compensation

Incentive Components

- Foreign Service Premium
- Displacement allowance for unfamiliar country or unfamiliar environment
- Special Area Allowance
- Hardship Allowance
- Children Education Allowance

Equalization Adjustments

- Cost differential adjustments
- Tax equalization or Tax protection
- Employee benefits adjustments
- Housing Differential

Exhibit 6-1 The Total Compensation Structure for Expatriate Compensation

Incentive Components

- Overseas / foreign service premium
- Compensation for life adjustments (displacement allowances: unfamiliar country, uncomfortable / harsh / dangerous environment)
- Relocation / travel expenses; house – hunting expenses; shipment and storage of household goods; furnishings for foreign housing; home sale protection or rental assistance; automobile shipping or sale protection
- Settling – in allowance
- Temporary living expenses
- Education allowance (self, children, spouse); language and cultural training allowance
- Spousal / husband support: education, income replacement, employments services and career planning
- Perquisites, e.g. club memberships, home leave, R&R leave, company car and driver
- Tax preparation assistance
- Financial advice
- Expatriation counseling
- Home – country career support and counseling
- Repatriation assistance planning

Equalization Adjustments

- Cost-differential adjustments
- Reimbursement for payments into host – country welfare plans
- Income taxes – withheld for home taxes, local taxes; equalization or protection
- Protection for fluctuation in exchange rates
- Employee benefits adjustments (pension, retirements saving plan, health care)
- Housing allowances: comparable to original home; comparable to foreign peers; utilities allowance

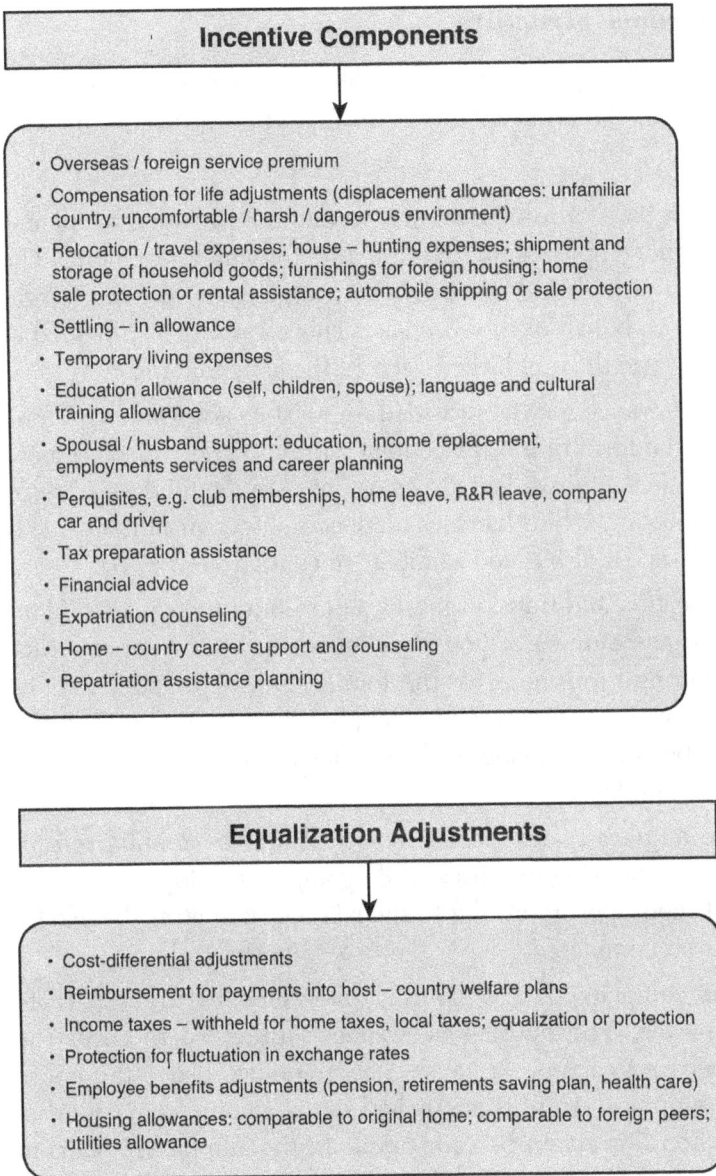

Exhibit 6-2 A comprehensive list of the possible components is shown.

The Allowance Structure

Not every company provides all these components of expatriate compensation. But what follows is a description of all the possible components:

- An overseas or foreign service premium is provided to encourage the employee to take on the foreign assignment. The employee is being asked by the company to take the assignment on behalf of the company. This allowance is provided to encourage the employee to accept the assignment.

  An allowance may be provided for lifestyle adjustments. These take the form of a displacement allowance. The displacement allowance is provided for living in an unfamiliar country or in uncomfortable, harsh, and dangerous environments. This allowance is also called a mobility incentive allowance.

- Relocation and travel expenses, house-hunting expenses, shipment and storage of household goods expenses, expenses for acquiring furnishings for the foreign house, temporary rental assistance, and automobile shipping or sale expenses are all reimbursements made by the employing company to the expatriate employee.

  The employee and the family would also be reimbursed for temporary living expenses while going to the foreign location and then upon returning to their home base after the assignment is completed.

- The company pays a housing allowance to the expatriate employee. The housing allowance is provided to cover the expenses to acquire a house that is comparable to the house the employee and his family had in their home country. Also, the house needs to be comparable to the employee's peers in the foreign location. The allowance may also include a utilities allowance.

- An education allowance may also be provided. The education allowance can be for the accompanying spouse and/or children. The education allowance would also include expense reimbursement for language and cultural training for all family members. Other perquisites (for example, club memberships, home leave, R&R leave, company car and driver) are also normally provided.

- Miscellaneous other services are also paid for by the company. These services include tax-preparation assistance, financial advice, expatriation counseling, home-country career support and counseling, and repatriation assistance planning.
- Settling-in allowance is paid to compensate for costs of small items when the expatriate and his/her family relocate, at the beginning and at the end of an assignment. This payment can be made as a fixed payment or as a percentage of home-country gross pay and as a percentage of home-country net pay.

In addition to allowance and incentives, employees being sent to a different country are usually compensated with equalization payments. These payments are designed to ensure that the expatriate employee neither gains nor loses monetarily from the overseas assignment:

- The first equalization payment that is normally provided is a cost-differential adjustment or allowance. This is not a *cost-of-living adjustment* (COLA). It is a cost-differential allowance. The cost-differential allowance is based on a consulting company's table. The cost-differential index is applied to a spendable income amount to derive the cost-differential allowance. The calculation of this amount can be quite involved, so we look at its computational details later in the chapter.
- Another equalization payment is the reimbursement for the payments for host or assignment country government-mandated health and welfare plans.
- Yet another equalization payment that has accounting implications is income taxes. These are amounts withheld for home-country taxes and local taxes. The tax obligations are then equalized through either of two methods: tax protection or tax equalization. This topic is further explored later in this chapter.
- Then there are payments for protection against the fluctuation in exchange rates between the two countries (the home country and the assignment country).
- Finally, there is the complex issue of a pension benefit equalization arrangement. This topic is also discussed later.

Looking at the list of compensation payments, you can understand that these amounts can easily add up, creating a large financial burden for the employer. Therefore, it is a very important exercise to budget these expenses carefully before the assignment starts. The budgeting exercise is one of the more important accounting tasks that needs to be undertaken by the HR department. We look at the budgeting exercise in a later section of this chapter.

Note here that the payments and expenses listed and described earlier are not all used in every cross-country assignment. The payments and allowances should be provided only to employees who are being sent by the company for a fixed duration and not for those being hired on a regular or long-term basis. The cross-border transfer is undertaken because there is a specific skill shortage in the country to which the employee is being sent. The employee could also be sent abroad for a fixed duration for training purposes. Payments and allowances are not provided for short-term (less than a year) assignments. Nor are they provided for extended business trips.

Finally, a foreign national employee could be hired or and sent by an employer for regular employment to a different country (direct or regular hires). Those employees are hired for the foreign country operation from a different country on a regular long-term basis. These hires might be provided some temporary payments and allowances for a short while, but they should not be provided all the expatriate allowances and payments described so far.

The Balance Sheet System Explained

A sound expatriate compensation system uses the balance sheet approach. The balance sheet structure is built on the principle that the employee (and his family) being assigned to the foreign assignment should neither gain nor lose financially from the assignment. It also allows planners to design a system that is financially sound from the point of view of managing the expenses within the operational budget guidelines.

The process begins with the employee's existing compensation in the home country (salary, benefits, and other monetary and nonmonetary remuneration regularly received). Then the two components of

(1) the incentives provided to attract and retain employees for the foreign assignment and (2) the equalization components that ensure the expatriate does not suffer from the foreign-country differences in salary and benefits, are added to establish the desired total compensation package for the foreign assignment, as shown in Exhibit 6-3.

Exhibit 6-3 Example of a Compensation Package for an Expatriate Relocation from New Jersey to Paris, First Year in US Dollars

Basic Compensation	
Salary	$100,000.00
Bonuses	20,000.00
Stock options	0.00
Miscellaneous salary adjustments	0.00
Employer pension contribution	20,000.00
Total Basic Compensation	***$140,000.00***
Allowances	
Cost differential	$35,000.00
Housing allowance	$35,000.00
Automobile	4,500.00
Moving expenses reimbursement	10,000.00
Home leave	15,000.00
Children (two) / Spouse education allowance	25,000.00
Cultural / Language training allowance	5,000.00
Expatriate premium	12,000.00
Hardship premium	0.00
Danger premium	0.00
Home management / maintenance	0.00
Club memberships / fees	5000.00
Tax services provided	0.00
Other allowances	0.00
Mobility premium	0.00
Relocation allowance, first year only	5,000.00
Other earned income	0.00
Loan bonus interest	0.00
Nontaxable assignments costs	0.00
Other adjustments to salary / allowance detail	0.00
Total Allowances	***$ 151,500.00***

Exhibit 6-3 Continued

Total Cost	
Actual Tax Liabilities	
US Federal	$3,713.00
US FICA	8,034.00
New Jersey	552.00
France Income tax	101,150.00
France social insurance tax	0.00
Total Actual Tax	*$113,449.00*
Less Hypothetical tax	
US Federal	($23,834.00)
US FICA	(5,580.00)
New Jersey	(3,374.00)
Total Hypothetical Tax	*($32,788.00)*
Other Employer Taxes	
Employer's social insurance, US	$8,034.00
Employer's social insurance, France	0.00
Other corporate taxes	0.00
Total Other Employer Taxes	*$8,034.00*
Tax Cost to Company	*$88,695.00*
Total Cost	*$380,195.00*

From this example, an employee who was earning $140,000 at the home location will be earning $380,195 in the foreign location. This is an escalation factor of almost 3. It can get expensive!

Multinational employers also need to address these additional questions when designing global compensation programs:

- Under which country compensation and benefit programs should the employees be covered?
- How will potential gaps in pension and health be covered?
- Is the benefit coverage adequate for all employees?
- Is the benefit package equitable when compared with the benefits of peers in the country of assignment?
- Can coverage under employees' home-country social programs be maintained as the employee moves around?

During the recent past, with the threats of global economic crisis looming large, companies have had more difficulty ensuring that expatriate employees are paid fair salaries. The achievement of this objective has been made more difficult by rapid currency and inflationary fluctuations. These conditions have created the need to constantly review expatriate salaries. Fluctuating currencies and a wide variety of inflationary patterns across different countries can create differences in the amount of salary received and thus impact the expatriate employee's purchasing power (positively or negatively) within very short time periods. One way to approach this challenge is to convert a spendable percentage (typically 60%) of the expatriate's salary into the host-country currency on a monthly basis. The other way is to provide direct reimbursements for benefits such as accommodation, transportation, and the education of children.

The spendable percentage leads to a spendable income. This is the amount that the expatriate's counterpart in the same location at the same salary level and family size spends for goods and services in their home country. This is the portion of base salary that is typically spent on goods and services on a daily basis. This amount varies by family size and income level.

A concluding point with respect to the balance sheet system is the issue of stated and paid amounts. In many cases, the pay terms and conditions are stated in a certain currency, but actual payment occurs with another currency. Sometimes total payment is split into two payrolls: one payment coming from the home-country payroll, and another portion being paid by the host-country payroll system. Therefore, it is critical that the pay method be clearly understood and accepted by all parties involved. Actual practice with regard to the quotation and delivery of pay varies.

Some companies quote net assignment cash pay to the expatriate. Others deliver home gross pay plus allowances with a guarantee of net pay. Yet others quote gross assignment pay, and in a small percentage of companies the approach varies from country to country.

Expatriate Taxes

Now let's look at the tax accounting issues affecting expatriate employment. Two structural policy formulations exist: tax equalization and tax protection.

Tax Protection

If additional taxes result from the foreign assignment, the employee is "protected" from those additional taxes. And if the taxes are lower than what the employee paid at home, the expatriate employee can take that benefit as a windfall. This might happen if the employee goes from a high-tax country to a low-tax country or a no-tax country. So, employees might' pay less in tax than what they were paying but never more than what they paid in their home country. Tax protection is not a common policy.

Tax Equalization

In this policy, expatriates are "equalized" so that they pay the same amount of tax as they paid in their home country before their departure to the foreign assignment. They pay no more or no less in taxes from what they would have paid if they were still in their home-country assignment. If there are additional taxes as a result of the foreign assignment the employing company pays. At the same time, the company also benefits if the foreign assignment taxes are less than what the employee had to pay at home. It is believed that this policy is fair to everyone concerned because the employee's obligation remains the same as they were before the foreign assignment–that is the same amount of tax as if they were still in their home-country assignment.

Tax Equalization Explained

Tax equalization is applied when employees are transferred to a country outside of their home country. Again, the basic concept of the policy is that an individual employee will pay no more or no less taxes than he or she would have paid if they had not been sent on the expatriate assignment.

A tax equalization policy must initially take into account what income will be covered. An expatriate policy normally indicates whether (in addition to salary and bonuses) stock option exercises, restricted stock earn outs, interest, dividends, capital gains, and the spouse's income will be equalized.

Personal exemptions and deductions are taken into account, even if they differ from home-country deductions. This can get tricky. Suppose while at home an expatriate was taking a mortgage and other principal residence-allowable deductions. Because of the expatriation, the employee sold his home. So would the tax equalization policy take into account the fact that the expatriate's home-country taxes were significantly reduced before the assignment because of the principal residence deductions and now they are not going to be able to take these deductions? Because of this contingency, most companies require employees to maintain their home-country principal residence and rent it out during their expatriate assignment. The company might also pay property-management fees to facilitate renting of the home. But the question still remains if the employee does sell the house whether the tax equalization policy calculates home-country tax obligation with or without the principal residence deductions. The expatriate tax policy for most companies would clearly address these and other issues. Therefore, the tax equalization policy can be lengthy, because it must attempt to account for every contingency that could be encountered in the foreign assignment.

At the planning stages of an assignment, a tax specialist, whether internal or external, computes the amount of tax an individual would have paid had he or she not been sent on the expatriate foreign assignment. This is a hypothetical calculation, and as such it is commonly referred to as the hypothetical tax or hypo tax.

Let's take an example of a married couple, where the husband is the employee and is an engineer. The couple has no children, and they currently live and work in San Francisco. Let's say they rent an apartment in downtown San Francisco at a cost of $3,000 a month. The engineer's current compensation is $150,000, and the employer has asked him to relocate to Abu Dhabi on January 1, 2014. Note that according to the expatriate policy the spouse's income is being excluded from the hypothetical calculation. For this example, we are assuming that the spouse is a working professional and is not planning to accompany her husband because she does not want to give up her job. Also note that the company will use the standard tax deduction for one individual and calculate the hypothetical tax based on a filing status of a single tax payer. The specific path chosen for this situation is simply because of the facts for this expatriate employee.

The employee is being sent on a single-status assignment because of the spouse's employment situation. The hypothetical tax would be as shown in Exhibit 6-4.

Exhibit 6-4 Hypothetical Tax Calculation

United States	
Federal income tax	$32,957
State income tax	10,714
Social Security tax	4,486
Social Security tax	2,035
Total	**$50,192**

The $50,192 will be deducted from the employee's gross compensation, and the employee will receive a net compensation of $99,208 plus allowances such as housing, cost-differential allowance, home leave, and so on based on the terms of the overseas assignment. The employer now is responsible for paying all U.S. and foreign income and social taxes on behalf of the employee. In this case, the employer might gain because the U.S. taxes on $99,208 will be lower and because there are no Abu Dhabi taxes. The matter is slightly more complex than stated so far. This is because the employee's actual tax obligation will be based on a married filing jointly status. So, the company most likely will pay a tax consultant to prepare and file the couple's actual taxes. When the tax consultant calculates the actual married filing jointly obligation, the consultant will do resolution calculation as shown here.

Married filing jointly obligation minus tax obligation on single status income of $99,208 equals additional (if any) employee required payment. In this case, the company might actually pay the taxing authorities the married filing jointly obligation and require the employee to reimburse the company if there is any difference.

Tax Protection Explained

Only a few differences exist between tax protection and tax equalization policies.

The first difference is that if the actual tax burden of the expatriate employee on a worldwide basis is less than the tax obligation the expatriate employee had in his or her home country before the assignment started, the employee can retain that benefit.

The second difference is that under tax protection, no hypothetical tax withholding is taken from the expatriate employee's pay.

The third difference is that unlike tax equalization the expatriate employees will themselves pay both their home-country tax obligations and the country-of-assignment tax obligations.

After the expatriate employee tax obligations are paid, the company makes a tax protection calculation. If the tax obligation both to their home countries and their destination country paid directly by the employees is more than what they would have paid before the assignment started in their home country, the employing company reimburses the employee directly for that amount. This might create a tax windfall for the employee.

For various reasons, tax protection policies are not very common. The major reason is that the expatriate employees would not want to pay the tax obligations directly and have a major impact on their personal cash flow situations.

Tax Gross-Up

As indicated under a tax protection policy, the company reimburses the employee the difference between what they pay in taxes during the foreign assignment and what they would have paid had they not gone abroad. However, that amount now becomes income to the employee, which then becomes taxable income to the employee. We then have a tax-on-tax situation. This is where the tax gross-up calculations come in.

The gross-up calculation will become an iterative calculation to determine the amount needed to be paid to the employee so that in effect the expatriate employee will receive the tax protection payment on a tax-free basis. The gross-up calculation is not limited to the tax protection payment; it also applies to all other tax payments the company makes on behalf of the expatriate employee while he or she is on the foreign assignment.

The Actual Tax Calculation

When the expatriate's actual tax return has to be prepared and filed, the company will engage a tax consultant or a tax specialist to complete and file the return on behalf of the employee. When the expatriate is sent to a country where there is a local country tax obligation, the company will usually engage a tax consulting company with multicountry operations so that both the home country and the local tax obligations are properly calculated and proper tax credits are taken. (Often there are tax agreements between countries stipulating tax credits.)

The Applicable Tax Provisions

Next we provide a summary of the tax provisions that apply to U.S. citizens and permanent residents living and working in a foreign country.

A U.S. expatriate policy applies to a citizen or resident of the United States who lives outside the United States for more than one year. U.S. citizens or permanent residents on business trips lasting up to one year or more must also consider the U.S. and foreign tax consequences related to that long-duration business trip.

U.S. citizens and residents must report 100% of their worldwide income on their U.S. individual income tax return, regardless of where they live and regardless of where the income is paid. Therefore, U.S. expatriates must continue to file U.S. tax returns and in many cases owe U.S. tax during their foreign assignments. U.S. expatriates take advantage of two special tax provisions to reduce their federal income tax liability while on a foreign assignment. These provisions are: foreign tax credit and exclusions from income.

Foreign Tax Credit

The foreign tax credit can reduce U.S. federal and the state individual income tax. The foreign tax credit is designed to help reduce the double taxation of income. So, if the expatriate has a foreign tax obligation for income earned in that foreign country, the amount paid to that foreign tax jurisdiction offsets the U.S. income subject to U.S. tax. This is called the foreign tax credit.

Exclusions from Income

A U.S. citizen or resident who establishes a tax residence in a foreign country and who meets either the bona fide residence test or the physical presence test may elect to exclude two items from gross income:

- Foreign earned income exclusion in 2011 is up to $92,900. This is a straight exclusion of foreign source income in the determination of taxable income.

And

- For the foreign housing exclusion, the current IRS regulation states,[1]

> The housing exclusion applies only to amounts considered paid for with employer-provided amounts, which includes any amounts paid to you or paid or incurred on your behalf by your employer that are taxable foreign earned income to you for the year (without regard to the foreign earned income exclusion). The housing deduction applies only to amounts paid for with self-employment earnings.
>
> Your housing amount is the total of your housing expenses for the year minus the base housing amount. The computation of the base housing amount (line 32 of Form 2555) is tied to the maximum foreign earned income exclusion. The amount is 16% of the maximum exclusion amount (computed on a daily basis), multiplied by the number of days in your qualifying period that fall within your tax year.
>
> Housing expenses include your reasonable expenses actually paid or incurred for housing in a foreign country for you and (if they lived with you) for your spouse and dependents. Consider only housing expenses for the part of the year that you qualify for the foreign earned income

[1] From the IRS Web site, we quote this section from the IRS regulation for clarity of understanding.

exclusion. Housing expenses do not include expenses that are lavish or extravagant under the circumstances, the cost of buying property, purchased furniture or accessories, and improvements and other expenses that increase the value or appreciably prolong the life of your property. You also cannot include in housing expenses the value of meals or lodging that you exclude from gross income (under the rules for the exclusion of meals and lodging), or that you deduct as moving expenses.

Also, for purposes of determining the foreign housing exclusion or deduction, your housing expenses eligible to be considered in calculating the housing cost amount may not exceed a certain limit. The limit on housing expenses is generally 30% of the maximum foreign earned income exclusion, but it may vary depending upon the location in which you incur housing expenses. The limit on housing expenses is computed using the company's worksheet.

Additionally, foreign housing expenses may not exceed your total foreign earned income for the taxable year. Your foreign housing deduction cannot be more than your foreign earned income less the total of your (1) foreign earned income exclusion, plus (2) your housing exclusion.

Other U.S. Tax Issues

In addition to the special tax provisions that apply to U.S. expatriates, an expatriate is still subject to the normal U.S. tax laws with respect to all other items of income, expenses, and credits. Other common federal tax issues that arise due to a foreign assignment include the following:

- Treatment of employer-provided allowances and reimbursements
- Moving expenses
- Rental of principal residence
- Sale of principal residence

- Exchange gains and losses
- Short-term versus long-term assignments
- Social Security taxes

This review has provided an overview of the tax calculation structures of U.S. citizens living and working abroad. The actual specifics of each taxpayer will vary based on each individual's tax filing status, exemptions, and standard or itemized deductions. Other implications on an individual tax obligation will be determined by that individual expatriate's investments and many other tax factors.

The Cost-Differential Allowance

Of the many allowances that expatriate employees are provided while on a foreign assignment, the allowance that requires the most technical understanding is the cost-differential allowance.

In practice, the cost-differential allowance is called by various names: goods and services differential, commodities and services allowance, cost-of-living index, and COLA (cost-of-living allowance). The last two designations are not quite correct, as you will understand from this discussion. The meaning of all these terms is the additional money needed to maintain a similar standard of living as was enjoyed by expatriates and their families in the home location. This difference may arise because of cost differences and living-pattern changes between the home and the foreign locations. This is not a cost-of-living allowance. It is a cost-differential allowance. The cost-of-living allowance is based on a time period-to-time period index. The time-to-time index is one of the measures that are normally used to calculate the inflation rate in macroeconomics. The cost-differential allowance is based on a place-to-place index. The basic idea is that the expatriate and his or her family enjoyed a certain market basket of goods and services in his or her home-country location. This market basket of goods and services cost the expatriate employees a certain percentage of their income (called spendable income). Under the balance sheet philosophy of compensation, the company wants the expatriate employee to neither gain nor lose from accepting the company-initiated assignment. So, the company relies on a place-to-place price-differential index for the same market basket of goods and services that the expatriate employee was using while in his or her home location. Then the company applies that index to a spendable income, which results in a cost-differential allowance amount. The cost-differential allowance is then paid to the employee on a regular basis. With this allowance, the employee and his or her family can buy and enjoy the same market basket of goods and services in the foreign location. So, they neither gain nor lose vis-à-vis their home-country standard of living.

Of course, all these calculations are based on average prices. Because there is no "average expatriate employee," the cost-differential allowance in reality can be either sufficient or not for any particular expatriate employee.

Let's look at the cost-differential allowance calculation methodologies.

Various data services companies (Organization Resources' Council, AIRINC, and INCOMP) research and compute the place-to-place indices. In addition to the consulting companies, the U.S. State Department also calculates and publishes cost-differential indices covering various cities around the world. The State Department does these computations for the use of its various foreign stations to adequately compensate foreign-service employees.

The consulting companies normally conduct a consumer income and expenditure survey every few years. These surveys result in a series of data tables (that is, spendable income in different cities around the world sorted by base salary levels). The spendable income is a number that includes all costs for food at home, food away from home, tobacco and alcohol, clothing, medical expenses, transportation (excluding car-purchase payments), recreation, personal care, household furnishings and operation, domestic services, and miscellaneous expenses. This data is collected from expatriates or their sponsor (if located in the foreign jurisdiction).

The surveys indicate that for a given income level, the percentage spent by a standard family for goods and services may vary depending on the local conditions.

The consulting companies in this manner calculate the spendable income and spendable income percentages for a variety of cities around the world. The collected data also determines the spending situation (availability and ease of purchase) in that particular city. In some cities, most goods and services are readily available, and in others they are not. The survey delineates the ease of purchase in each of the cities surveyed. In London, it is possible to buy nearly anything at a comparatively reasonable price. So, the percentage of income spent locally for goods and services is relatively high in London and in similar cities having well-established and well-stocked markets. In remote areas, however, the availability of clothing, medical care, recreation, and so on is quite limited. The expatriate employees will tend to defer these purchases until they go on home leave. Therefore, they spend a higher percentage of income in the United States, and they spend a smaller amount in the foreign location.

The consulting companies, after establishing the spendable income levels for various cities, then assign them to one of three categories: maximum loading, standard loading, and minimum loading. The designation depends on the availability of goods and services and the estimated required expenditures in that city.

From the results of the consumer income and expenditure survey, the consulting companies report spendable income levels separated into the three different loading levels. In other words, they average out the data from the survey into the three categories (maximum, standard, minimum). After that, further sorting of the data occurs. The spendable income level is then reported by family size. Finally, the data is reported to clients, by loading factors, by six family sizes, and by income level.

Cost-differential indices assume the home country has an index of 100. All foreign-assignment locations are measured relative to this base. An index above 100 indicates that the cost of living in the foreign-assignment country is higher than the cost of living in the home country. If the index is below 100, the cost of living in the foreign location country is lower. If the foreign-assignment location city has an index of 110, this means the relative cost of living in that city is 10% more expensive than the home location. In contrast, an index of 95 implies that the host city is 5% cheaper than the home location.

Then, the calculated index is multiplied into the spendable income level for a particular city and by the indicated loading factor assigned to that foreign location.

If the spendable income is $60,000 a year and the index is 110, the allowance is computed as $0.1 \times \$60,000 = \$6,000$. The expatriate employee will be given an allowance of $6,000 a year to cover the additional costs for goods and services in that foreign location.[2]

Exhibit 6-5 gives an example of the survey data presentation.

Exhibit 6-5 Survey data presentation

Monthly Base Salary	S	HW	HW+1	HW+2	HW+3	HW+3 Over
$7,500 - $7,600	2632	2968	3325	3710	4123	4571

The consulting companies report the collected data in the format shown.

So, let's say the cost-differential index for this location is 111.25 and the expatriate employee is on an HW +2 family assignment and the expatriate employee's monthly base salary is $7,545. In that case, the employee's monthly cost-differential allowance is $3,710 \times .1125 = \$417.37$.

Currency Fluctuations

Expatriate employees are also faced with the challenge of managing multiple currencies. Currency fluctuation can have an impact on the buying power of the expatriate's income. The expatriate faces two challenges: transferring money from home base to the foreign assignment location and paying required bills across countries. Remember that the expatriate employee invariably needs to pay bills in the home country, to continue a lifestyle that will allow the expatriate to return home after the assignment without having to start all over again.

To mitigate the currency-fluctuation issues, companies usually take the following actions:

- **Split-payment arrangements:** Many companies pay the employee a certain percentage of income in the host country itself (and in the host country's currency). The rest of the income is paid in the home-country currency. This way the

---

[2] www.expatica.com./hr/story/cost-of-living-allowances-basics-16245.html.

expatriate has appropriate currency funds in both home and host countries without experiencing currency fluctuations. In actuality, the corporate practice in this regard varies. Surveys indicate that the practice is distributed among (1) payment in home country, (2) host-country currency, (3) depends on the home and host location, (4) paying everything in a reference currency and (5) paying part of the salary in a reference currency.

In companies that engage in split-payment policies, the split formula becomes important. Surveys indicate that actual practice involves (1) paying a savings part in home-country currency, (2) leaving the choice up to the expatriate, and (3) paying a certain percentage of the host-country salary in the host-country currency.

Companies also employ a policy to adjust the expatriate's salary to mitigate the effects of currency fluctuations. Practice among companies here is also varied. Company policy in this regard includes (1) no adjustments for currency fluctuations during assignment, (2) making an adjustment every year, (3) making adjustments every six months, (4) making an adjustment when the currency devaluates by more than a certain percentage, and (5) making adjustments on a case-by-case basis.

- **Adjust the cost-differential allowance for currency fluctuations:** We have explained in the cost-differential section of this chapter how the cost-differential allowance is calculated. We have shown that the various consulting companies establish spendable income levels by family size and income levels in various countries. We have also shown that the spendable income levels are modified by a goods and services loading factor. Now we show that the cost differential can be further adjusted for currency fluctuations. To demonstrate this adjustment calculation, let's use an example of an expatriate with a spouse and two children moving from New York to Mumbai, India.

The company expatriating this employee will complete the calculation shown in Exhibit 6-6.

Using this calculation, the company ensures that the expatriate and his/her family moving from New York to Mumbai is kept whole for (1) purchasing power and (2) a cost-differential allowance that is stable in the host location (Mumbai) for a currency fluctuation.

Exhibit 6-6 Currency Adjustments to the Cost-Differential Allowance

Date of Adjustment	Annual Spendable Income $	Cost-differential Index	Exchange Rate $ 1 = Rupees	Annual Spendable Income Adjusted for Cost-differential Index ($)	Annual Spendable Income Adjusted for Currency Fluctuation (Rupees)
June 2011	108,000	108.0	48.5	116,640	5,657,040
June 2012	108,000	108.5	49.6	117,180	5,812,128

Global Payroll Systems

The laws that regulate HR labor practices and payroll procedures vary from country to country. There are specific requirements to comply with, pay-frequency timings, pay and work rules, and tax. For example, in Italy, taxes must be paid at the country, regional, and local levels and need to be submitted by the deadlines as established by the law. It does not matter how many employees are employed; compliance with the laws is mandatory. In addition, different data privacy and cross-border data-transfer laws further complicate the implementation.

Payroll is not only affected by local laws but also by languages, currencies, and time zones. A U.K. company based in China cannot provide its Chinese employees with pay notices in English or pay them in British pound sterling. Chinese employees must be paid on time, in the local currency, and documented in Chinese.

Cultural differences exist, as well. In different countries, employees are accustomed to different payment methods. For example, although employees in many countries expect direct deposit, those in the Netherlands might prefer paper verification, whereas employees in the Middle East might prefer electronic verification. In Russia, Mexico, and Brazil, paper pay notices are customary.

In other cases, past practices create precedents that cannot easily be changed. For example, German Works Councils maintain great influence over the payroll process and other aspects of labor and personnel practices on job sites. And the Works Council has to be consulted on any and every HR and payroll policy and practice issue.

Global payroll systems will need to cover different country-of-origin expatriate employees and local national employees. In large global construction projects, like those undertaken in the Middle East, employees are sourced from as many as 30 countries. The payroll system has to work with the specific tax-related compensation policies from all these separate employment entities. It also has to cope with the movement of salaries and tax distributions across the world in different currencies. There are also country-specific payroll regulations that need to be adhered to. Accounts with reputable international banks need to be managed to make rapid, mistake-free funds transfers and payments.

In many European countries, vacation and sick leave must be tracked as part of the payroll process. In France, failure to do so will likely mean that upon termination the labor courts will rule that no vacation has been taken, and a full payout to compensate may be required. In Italy, it is necessary to accrue a mandatory severance payment each month, which can create challenges in payroll accounting. In many countries, the additional 13th- and 14th-month holiday payments or bonuses have to be paid at certain times within the year. In the Netherlands, it is necessary to account for mandatory medical insurance contributions through the payroll process.

Payroll processes also have to contend with other forms of compensation, such as stock-based compensation schemes, stock options, and stock grants. These programs require coordination between the parent and local entity to ensure that grants/exercises are correctly captured for reporting purposes and that any taxation related to the compensation is correctly withheld and within required time frames. Sometimes employees will want their salaries adjusted to take into account these country-specific transactions, which means finance and HR professionals should be clear on the payroll processes. Proper payroll accounting and processing becomes crucial in the effort to reduce employee complaints and disputes. Operational logistics that span many locations, cultures, currencies, languages, and laws can add levels of complication. Fortunately, these can be addressed and streamlined.

Therefore, global HR and payroll professionals need to be skilled enough to understand and manage the many vagaries of an international payroll system.

With payroll processes so complex and country specific, U.S.-based companies first turn to their U.S. payroll provider for advice and assistance. Some of these providers can offer services in certain countries, but not all countries. Many of these providers are not willing to provide such services unless the number of employees is large enough for them to make the financial commitment to provide the services.

Other companies attempt to manage global payroll in-house. This will require that the staff in both IT and payroll departments need to be experts who understand the complexities associated with all the company's various locations. Hiring the right skilled staff might prove very difficult. When implemented completely in-house, solutions can lead to an increased risk of error. In-house solutions and implementations can lead to employee dissatisfaction and possible legal problems.

More commonly attempted is a local solution, where payroll is managed with different vendors in each country. Although this method helps address concerns surrounding local cultures, languages, currencies, and regulations, it can prove costly and difficult to manage. In this solution, local employees are tasked with managing the individual vendors. Because payroll systems are maintained within each country, consolidations are time-consuming, with information generated by the various local payroll systems not being consistent in many ways. This makes consolidated payroll and accounting reporting an onerous task.

The most effective alternative then becomes using a consolidated global payroll platform. A global software-based payroll platform can reduce costs, automate reporting, facilitate compliance, and improve financial control. However, it can also be intimidating. The answer lies in selecting the right technology and the right vendor.

For companies where the *return on investment* (ROI) in these complex software-based platforms is not justifiable, the viable option is outsourcing to a reputable third-party administrator. Whether acquired for in-house use or for use by a third-party administrator, the global software platform should have modules that include payroll accounting, social insurance, travel-expenses administration, incentive compensation, posting to accounting ledgers and journals, entity funding mechanisms, statutory (compulsory) benefits, and tax withholding and reporting requirements. Note that these provisions will vary widely from one country to another. The chosen software must also assist the company to track complicated leave formulas and understand local employment requirements and expectations. They must also be able to file health and welfare documentation.

In addition to an adequate software platform, the international payroll provider who uses the chosen software platform should be able to advise and assist with all the mandatory activities that go along with supporting international and local payrolls, including the following:

- **Entity setup:** The payroll provider should be able to advice which entity type is best for the specific company and assist with the setup of the entity.

- **Registration of tax and social programs:** Once the appropriate entity has been identified and the registration setup completed, there could be follow-on registrations required to support a locally compliant payroll.

- **Benefits:** The provider should be able to advice on structuring mandatory benefits and health and welfare programs. The provider should also advice as to the best way to accrue and account for leaves and vacations in accordance with the country's rules and regulations, commensurate with the company's accounting procedures and processes.

International Pensions

As you have seen in this chapter, the expatriation of employees abroad is a fairly complex matter. The assignment comes entangled with accounting, finance, legal, tax, and HR issues. You have seen that many issues need to be resolved:

- Which Social Security system will the expatriate remain in?
- Where will the Social Security contributions be made?

- Where, when, and how the tax obligations of the expatriate will be dispensed.

The answers to these questions depend on specific terms and intentions of the assignment.

But still remaining is the very important question as to the status of the employee with respect to the company's pension benefits. There are legal and tax concerns attached to the issue.

Under these circumstances, organizations have various paths that they can take with respect to the expatriate's pension benefits. (We are assuming here that the employee was participating in the company's defined-benefit pension plan before the expatriate assignment commenced.) Note that we devote an entire chapter on pension accounting. Here we are simply talking about ensuring the protection of the expatriate's pension rights while on a foreign assignment.

Companies have four options:

- Keep the expatriate in the home country's defined benefit pension plan.

- Switch and enroll the expatriate into the host-country pension scheme while he or she is on the foreign assignment.

- Established a top-up pension arrangement that is run in conjunction with the home-country or host-country pension plan.

- Set up a completely separate offshore pension plan. The participants of this plan will be expatriates. The assumption here is that the organization setting up such a plan has a cadre of internationally mobile expatriates who will continue on an expatriate career path for long periods. Companies setting up such a plan are those that deal with expatriates who are regarded as permanent transferees who are unwilling to move to their home-country pension plans.

A PricewaterhouseCoopers survey in 1999 found that 85% of permanent expatriates join the host-country pension plan. And 90% of fixed period expatriates remain in the home-country pension plan. Top-up offshore plans are rare.[3]

---

[3] *Investment & Pensions Europe Magazine*, December 1999, www.ipe.com/magazine/.

Companies setting up top-up offshore plans should be aware of the following issues:[4]

- Compliance with home-country and host-country employment laws and regulations.
- Coordination of benefits between home and host plans that the expatriate has participated and will participate in. These terms can be vesting requirements, integration of defined pension formulas, and government-sponsored Social Security plans (offsets) the expatriate has contributed to.
- Government-dictated pension guarantees triggers in case of plan dissolution. Unfunded top-up plans usually do not provide the participant any guarantees.
- Currency fluctuations.
- Impact of benefit taxation and the deductibility of employer contributions.

All of these complex issues make a top-up offshore unfunded pension plan for permanent expatriates and third-country nationals highly infeasible.

Global Stock Option Plans

The worldwide business community is recognizing the advantages of sharing equity with employees. Rewarding employees with stock options or other equity-based compensation is a common practice in the United States. Emulating this practice, multinational corporations are increasingly extending these plans to employees in other countries. Companies that want to expand these programs to other countries must understand that they face unfamiliar securities, tax, and accounting laws.[5]

---

[4] Internationally Mobile Employees and Pensions, Swiss Life Network from Employee Benefits.co.uk., www.employeebenefits.co.uk.

[5] Landua, S.E., and Benedict, B.A., "Going Global with U.S. Employee Stock Plans," Pillsbury Winthrop Shaw Pittman LLP Advisory, Executive Compensation and Benefits, May 2011.

There are various forms of stock-based compensation programs: stock options, restricted stock, restricted stock units, stock appreciation rights, performance shares, and stock purchase plans. The type of award offered and the way the stock plan is designed are two primary factors that affect legal compliance issues in different countries.

Local tax laws dictate the form of equity compensation to be used in a country. For example, restricted stock awards have become popular in the United States. In other countries, restricted stock awards are not as common. In countries where such awards are taxed at the time of grant, there can be an unfavorable tax outcome. Restricted stock units may be a better choice under those circumstances. Other foreign tax laws may also result in awards being taxed prior to the employee's receipt of all or a portion of the award. It is important to understand the international tax implications for all aspects of proposed stock-based plan awards.

Tax rules in some countries provide tax advantages for certain qualifying stock-based arrangements. These arrangements are subject to restrictions as to eligibility, holding requirements, and grant limitations. The tax benefits offered will ultimately have to be judged based on other mitigating factors.

The country-specific securities laws are another complicating factor in the selection of the appropriate stock-based compensation program. Stock registration and the publication of prospectus may apply when stock-based plans are implemented. This might require that the proposed plan be customized to qualify for an exemption. In the absence of an exemption, publishing the required prospectus can be time-consuming and cost prohibitive.

Implementing equity-based incentive plans in countries with strict exchange-control regulations can be especially challenging and will often require customizing a plan for use in the country. In addition, employment law considerations might apply, and these might include (1) taking steps to reduce the risk that equity compensation will be regarded as a part of contractually promised compensation and (2) understanding the impact of awards on employees' compensation with respect to governmental requirements and other employee benefit programs.

Another issue is the enforceability of the award agreement provisions. Two areas to highlight in this regard are restrictive covenants (such as noncompetition and nonsolicitation clauses) and recoupment (or clawback) provisions.

Plan administrative practices need to be considered prior to the issuing of awards in each jurisdiction. And these practices are (1) tax-withholding requirements, (2) filing and reporting obligations, (3) payroll and accounting information flow, and (4) data-privacy compliance.

Cross-border equity grants give rise to special administrative issues. For example, plans having a sell-to-cover feature for tax withholding (where a portion of the shares issued are sold to cover the employer's withholding obligation) in foreign jurisdictions can be complicated by fluctuating currency exchange rates and sales restrictions under local securities laws.

Other considerations are the proper allocation of equity plan expenses and the availability of corresponding deductions between the parent issuing company and the local subsidiary employer. Chargeback agreements are often used to deal with expense allocation, exchange control, and stamp-duty matters.

The mobility of today's workforce across international boundaries raises further issues for the design and administration of stock-based compensation plans. As individuals transfer from one tax regime to another, they may be at risk of incurring double taxation or other adverse consequences. Implementing effective monitoring procedures, whether managed internally or in coordination with third-party service providers, can help companies meet these challenges. It is important to keep up-to-date on developments in the relevant laws in each jurisdiction in which awards are or may be granted. Regular compliance reviews are an important responsibility of global equity plan sponsors.

Companies also face nonlegal challenges when expanding their equity-based compensation plans to employees overseas. Finding appropriate compensation surveys to benchmark per person award grants can be difficult. Reliable surveys with comparison data on which to base these decisions are not readily available. Compensation comparisons across jurisdictions are complicated by fluctuating exchange rates and disparate wage and cost-of-living rates.

Cultural factors should also be considered. Employees in countries where equity-based compensation is rare may be uncomfortable or suspicious of noncash remuneration. A clear communication program is key to successful introduction of a plan granting unfamiliar types of awards or having complicated design features. Note also that translation of some plan-related documents may be required.

Key Concepts in This Chapter

- Expatriate compensation systems
- The balance sheet system
- Foreign service premium
- Housing allowance
- Education allowance
- Cost-differential allowance
- Expatriate taxes
- Tax equalization
- Tax protection
- Tax gross-up calculation
- Foreign Tax Credit
- Spendable income
- Global payroll systems
- International pensions
- Global stock option plans

7

Sales Compensation Accounting

Aims and objectives of this chapter

- Review various accounting and finance issues that affect the design of sales compensation and sales/commission programs
- Describe general accounting practices as they relate to sales compensation programs
- Explore the design implications, using a hypothetical base and sales commission program
- Examine the various components of a sales compensation program
- Review the accounting control and audit triggers for a sales compensation program
- Identify the various sales compensation allowances paid to a typical salesperson
- Review IRS rules and regulations that relate to sales compensation allowances
- Examine commission accounting processes using commission accounting software

Sales compensation is another important component of a total compensation system. There are many financial and accounting dimensions to the design, implementation, and administration of sales compensation plans. The design dimension that has significant financial and accounting implication is the concept of sales commissions. Commission accounting is also an important consideration. This chapter analyzes all these accounting and finance dimensions as they affect commission program design, implementation, and administration.

General Accounting Practices

Sales compensation plans are specifically designed to compensate sales personnel. Sales compensation is paid to sales professionals to generate revenue for the company. Sales compensation, especially sales commission plans, is therefore directly tied to the fluctuations in sales revenue. That is, as more revenues are generated, the more sales commission is earned by sales professionals, (and vice versa). So, the variable portion of sales compensation directly correlates with sales revenue. So variable sales compensation can be considered a direct cost (that is, one directly traced to a specific cost object). It can be considered a part of absorption costing.

In cost accounting, the cost designations are as follows:

- Direct costs
- Indirect costs
- Fixed manufacturing overhead
- Variable manufacturing overhead
- Selling, general, and administrative expenses

In managerial accounting, when specific product costs need to be calculated, different methods are available for use: absorption costing (job-order costing and process costing) and variable costing. In absorption costing, all manufacturing costs are absorbed into the product cost, whether they are variable or fixed. Not so in variable costing, where only manufacturing costs that vary with output are absorbed into the product cost.

Within this context, the variable costs for sales compensation (that varies with the number of units sold) can be considered a direct product cost. But under current *Generally Accepted Accounting Principles* (GAAP) accounting, the variable portion of sales compensation is considered a *selling, general, and administrative* (SG&A) expense, which is recognized in the current period. Note all managerial accounting-based costing systems (job-order, process, variable) categorize the variable portion of sales compensation as an SG&A expense. This is in contrast to a factory manager's salary, which currently is a fixed manufacturing overhead expense. In absorption costing, the factory manager's salary is classified and absorbed into the product's cost.

This is not the case under variable costing. In variable costing, the factory manager's salary would be included in the SG&A expense. This is the case even though both the factory manager's salary and the salesperson's variable compensation have a somewhat similar contribution to the product's cost. This issue remains unresolved.

The sales commission expense is reported when the company has incurred the expense and a liability. This is also when the sales commission is earned by the salesperson. Commission expense is reported as a selling expense along with other selling and administrative expenses.

Another sales compensation accounting issue should be noted here. Some organizations believe that separating fixed and variable costs can better assist in forecasting and controlling costs. Therefore, some organizations use the contribution format income statement. In the contribution approach, the objective is to determine the contribution margin (the amount remaining from sales revenues after variable expenses are deducted). The contribution margin determines the amount contributed toward covering fixed expenses and then profit.

In the contribution margin approach, sales compensation is divided into a variable portion, which goes toward calculating the contribution margin, and a fixed portion, which is deducted after the contribution margin is calculated. Exhibit 7-1 shows an example.

Exhibit 7-1 Contribution Approach

Sales		$24,000
Variable Expenses:		
Variable production	$4,000	
Variable selling	3,000	
Variable administrative	1,500	8,500
Contribution Margin		15,500
Fixed Expenses:		
Fixed production	6,000	
Fixed selling	5,000	
Fixed administrative	2,500	13,500
Net Operating Income		**2,000**

Organizations that use activity-based costing as an internal decision-making tool define five levels of activity:

- Unit
- Batch
- Product
- Customer
- Organization sustaining

Sales compensation costs in an ABC system will normally fit under two activity pools: customer orders and customer relations. These costs are regarded as selling expenses. The activity measures used are usually the number of customer orders (for customer orders) and the number of active customers (for customer relations).

Having described the current general accounting practice for variable sales compensation or sales commission plans, we now look at specific accounting and finance issues that determine the structure of a typical sales compensation plan. Then we go on to the issues specific to commission accounting.

Sales Compensation Plans

Sales compensation plans can be structured as follows:

- A base, commission, and bonus plan
- A base and bonus plan
- A base-only plan
- A commission-only plan

The structure that a company adopts is based on the sales strategy of the company and the desired salesperson behavior. Other triggers are intended to direct salesperson actions toward achieving specific sales goals and targets. Our main concern here is to analyze the accounting and finance issues that are a part of the sales compensation plan design and administration. In this context, we look at a base, commission, and bonus plan, which by its very nature has more accounting and finance issues than the other sales compensation structures.

Before analyzing the base, commission, and bonus sales compensation plan, let's first define the sales commission payment. BusinessDictionary.com defines the *sales commission payment* as follows:

> The amount of money that an individual receives based on the level of sales he or she has obtained. The sales person is provided a certain amount of money in addition to his/her standard salary based on the amount of sales obtained.[1]

The main element of any sales compensation plan is the use of variable pay. The objective is to align the sales and marketing objectives of the organization with the specific objectives of the salesperson. The sales targets or quota targets that can be used in establishing the "right" sales compensation incentives include the following:

- **Sales volume:** The number of sales volume over a specified time period.
- **New business:** Sales to new customers. This may require a great deal of cold-calling, prospecting, converting, and closing.
- **Retaining sales:** Keeping customers from one sales time period to another.
- **Product mix:** The organization might want to sell a predetermined mix of products. This will help the competitiveness of the company by selling the whole product line, upselling and cross-selling up and down the product line.
- **Win-back sales:** This is a sale made to old customers who are being regained as customers.
- **New product sales to existing customers:** This is sales of new products to existing customers.
- **Selling across the company's product lines:** Cross-selling and upselling.

---

[1] www.businessdictionary.com.definition/sales-commission.html#ixzz1oDlkCaOh.

A Cautionary Note on Using Sales as a Commission Trigger

When deciding on targets or measures to trigger sales commission payouts, consider this: If sales volume is used as the exclusive triggering measure, this could lead to a reduction in profit. Let's demonstrate this with an example (see Exhibit 7-2). Suppose, for instance, that a company has two products in its portfolio, Product A and Product B.

Exhibit 7-2 Analyzing The Effects of Sales as a Commission Trigger

	Product A	Product B
Selling Price	$525	$825
Variable Expenses	$255	$650
Margin	$270	$175

If the sales personnel were paid a 15% commission on sales, they would clearly focus their efforts on selling Product B, although Product A has a greater contribution margin. Focusing on Product B will give the salesperson a higher commission payout. As far as the company is concerned, however, selling more of Product A will give the company a higher profit from which they could cover their fixed expenses and generate a higher net income.

So, if the company sets commissions on the contribution margin or a combination of factors, the likelihood is greater that the salespeople will be encouraged to sell a mix of Products A and B. If fixed costs are not affected by the sales mix, the company can achieve a higher level of profitability if the salesperson is encouraged to sell a mix of products and not just the product with the highest commission potential.

The base, commission, and bonus structure is by far the most common sales compensation structure used by organizations that engage salespeople to generate revenue. Several advantages are associated with compensation plans that combine base salaries with commissions, including the following:

- The plans motivate the sales force to produce greater effort and results.

- The plans enable companies to provide additional rewards to superior salespeople.
- The structure of these plans facilitates the close correlation of compensation with sales performance.
- The plans are generally fairly easy to administer.

Note that in addition to commissions, compensation paid to sales personnel may include expense accounts, automobile leases, advances against future commission earnings (called draws), and sales contests.

Expense accounts are common in many industries. Salespeople routinely use business lunches, dinners, and other networking occasions to close deals. Salespeople often use their own vehicles to travel long distances to meet with customers, and so they expect the company to cover their vehicle expenses (as a business requirement). Providing these compensation elements in the sales compensation package is a competitive requirement if the company intends to hire and retain the highest-caliber sales professionals. You will learn more about these elements of a sales compensation plan later in this chapter.

Sales contests are another compensation element organizations use to motivate sales personnel. Under these programs, sales personnel who beat their annual sales targets or quotas are rewarded with a company-paid trip to an exotic location (or any other reward that has a prestige factor attractive to high-achieving sales personnel). Sales contests can be highly motivational.

Because of these reasons, the company might establish quota clubs. Quota club memberships are reserved for sales personnel who on a year-to-year basis continue to beat their target achievement numbers. As indicated, the annual quota club event often takes place in an exotic location. During these quotas club events, organizations celebrate the top performers, who are thus motivated and encouraged to outdo their current-year performance during the next sales cycle.

Now let's analyze in detail a hypothetical sales compensation plan with a base, commission, and bonus structure from a finance and accounting perspective. Using this plan, we will discuss both the relevant potential and actual accounting and finance issues.

Accounting Issues Impacting Sales Compensation Program Design

A number of specific accounting and finance issues impact the design of sales compensation plans, as follows:

- **Quota-based plans:** In these plans, there is usually an *order quota* and a *booking quota*. The order quota usually serves as the basis for determining commission earnings. And the booking quota usually serves as the basis for the eligibility for non-cash incentives, such as the quota club.

  A commission factor can then be determined. The following is an example of the calculation of a commission factor:

  Commission Factor =

  $$\frac{\text{Target Commission Earning @ 100 Order Quota}}{\text{Order Quota Dollars}}$$

  Commission credit can be granted only for firm purchase orders procured by the sale representative and accepted by the company. The criteria for the acceptance of purchase orders is usually determined on a year-to-year basis.

  Now that the commission formula is established, the commission payment structure can be triggered. Commission earnings are based on the order dollars generated by the salesperson's efforts.

  If the commission factor were calculated to be (using formula) 8%, then if an order is received for $10,000, the commission earned would be $800. Some organizations might set up a sliding scale to determine the payout commission amount, as demonstrated in Exhibit 7-3.

Exhibit 7-3 The Commission Earned Sliding Scale

$1 sales to $X dollars sold	4% commission factor
$X sales to X_1 dollars sold	5% commission factor
$X_{1.1}$ sales to X_2 dollars sold	6% commission factor
$X_{2.1}$ sales to X_3 dollars sold	7% commission factor
X_3 sales to quota dollars	8% commission factor
Quota dollars + $Y dollars sold	10% commission factors
$Y_{1.1}$ + Y_n dollars	12% commission factors

The commission formula scheme is an escalating scheme geared to motivate the salesperson to increase sales order dollars to as high as possible.

Sales personnel are also assigned an individual booking quota. The booking quota can be the prime determinant for quota club participation and for any other noncash recognition awards. Booking quota credit can be given for the total contract quantity for the first 12 months of the contract.

- **New customer/new product bonus plans:** Because the generation of new business is important to the company, a bonus for new customers and new products sold to existing customers can be made whenever certain criteria are met within a specific time period. The bonus quantity might need to be shipped to qualify for the new account/new product bonuses.

A schedule for the bonus element can be laid out as shown in Exhibit 7-4.

Exhibit 7-4 A Sales Bonus Schedule

#Customer/New Product	Bonus
1	$5,000
2	6,250
3	7,500
4	8,750

A stipulation might apply as to which new product qualifies for this bonus.

- **Shipment commission:** An additional shipment commission can also be provided for a revenue-recognized shipment of product and spare parts per a predetermined schedule, as shown in Exhibit 7-5.

Exhibit 7-5 A Shipment Bonus Schedule

Revenue Amount	Commission
$0 - $5,000, 000	.5 (1/2 of 1%)
$5,000,001 and above	.3

Shipment commissions are paid for shipments within a given yearly period.

- **Split commissions:** If the orders are booked in one territory and shipped from outside that territory, a formula can be set up to split the commissions. For example:
  - One-third commission to salesperson in territory where order is placed.
  - One-third commission to salesperson in territory into which product is shipped.
  - One-third or any partial one-third commission to wherever the approval, sales liaison, or sales effort was made. The adjudication of this commission is usually left up to management.

- **Draws:** When circumstances warrant, a draw against future commissions may be approved by management. The draw is often set for a fixed period at a particular level, but usually at no more than 50% of year-to-date quota performance. The maximum level of the draw balance that will be permitted in the draw account is specified as to amount and length of time the draw can be outstanding. Then a stipulation can be made saying that the draw balance can be recovered based on a percentage of commission credits per month until 100% of the draw is recovered.

- **Reserves:** During any particular month, if the net commission results in a negative amount, the negative balance can be placed in a reserve account. Recovery is made at a certain percentage of the subsequent month's commission until the reserve balance has been reduced to zero.

- **Price changes and adjustments:** If the price for any product units ordered by the customer changes, a quota and commission credit adjustment can be charged or credited to the sales representative who originally received quota credit.

- **Commission recovery:** If the customer or the company cancels any part of an accepted purchase order, the quota and commission and any bonuses for units not yet shipped can be charged back to the sales representative who originally received quota credit. Also, if a receivable on an account goes beyond 60 days (for example), a straight chargeback can be applied to the commission on those accounts.

- **Exceptions:** Sales and revenue resulting from accounts designated "house accounts" may not qualify for commission purposes. Each house account can be treated on an individual basis, with an appropriate sales bonus associated with it. Plan conditions, might state, for example, that house accounts cannot be included in quota assignments for certain specific accounts.

Accounting Control and Audit Issues

From an accounting control point of view, the following potential provisions of sales commission plans are important to understand:

- Commissions and bonuses will be paid upon the firm acceptance of a purchase order and revenue shipments.
- Commissions and bonuses can be paid in advance of the company's anticipated receipt of revenue. Advanced commissions and bonuses are considered earned and vested only upon receipt of full payment of revenue on which they are based. Commissions and bonuses not earned as a result of an order cancellation, returned shipment, or billing adjustment must be refunded to the company.
- Commissions and bonuses can be calculated and paid monthly. Each month's commissions are normally calculated monthly even if payment is not made. Each calendar month's net commissions and bonuses can be paid by the end of the following month.
- The net dollar amount paid during a particular month can be (1) the sum of the positive commission and bonus dollars calculated for the previous month minus any negative commission or bonus dollars owed pursuant to the plan provisions and not previously deducted, (2) and/or minus any draw recovery, and (3) any amount recovered as an offset to a negative reserve balance. (A maximum incentive dollar amount payable under the plan can normally be stipulated in the plan.)

- As an accounting control, companies can reserve the right, in sales compensation plans, to make a fair and equitable adjustment to quota, commission, and bonuses where business clearly has been lost because of nonperformance outside the control of the direct sales employee. This is in spite of the best efforts of the direct sales representative to manage the situation.

- Under certain circumstances, the company can reserve the right, at its discretion, to reduce quota achievement or commission and bonus dollars below levels set forth in this plan. These circumstances might include but are not limited to the following transactions:
  - Where profitability has been affected adversely by concessions
  - Where normally required sales effort was not expended
  - Where unusual assistance has been provided to the salesperson
  - Where violations of good business practices or professional ethics occurred

- Each sales representative can be provided with a copy of the plan. The sales representative is expected to acknowledge receipt of the plan, read the plan, confirm his/her understanding by signing the plan, and then return it to their managers (all before any commission can be paid by the accounting department). Of course, the accounting department can make payment only subject to plan provisions.

- Contracts and purchase orders: A duly executed contract is often required for the acceptance of a purchase order. The contract should be referenced in each purchase order. A contract, even if a quantity over time is indicated, does not normally represent a purchase order. No quota credit is usually granted against contracts for purposes of determining commission payment amounts. Purchase orders need to be firm and in writing. If electronic media is used to transmit a purchase order, a written confirmation within 30 days (for example) might be required. In addition, for a purchase order to be accepted, it must specify the product, the quantity, the unit price, the extended price, and the requested delivery schedule. All these stipulations will need to be consistent with the terms of the underlying contract. Also, a provision can be included that if delivery on a purchase order extends beyond 14 months the commission credit will be granted only for units to be delivered within 14 months.

Other Salient Elements of a Sales Compensation Plan

Expense Allowances

Sales personnel are often required to travel as a part of their jobs. This travel might be part of their daily work routine or might cover longer distances that require them to be "on the road" for considerable periods of time. Per the U.S. tax code, this is a tax-deductible expense for the employee, if there is no employer reimbursement. But, most organizations reimburse the employee for these expenses.

Accountable and Nonaccountable Plans

If the employer reimburses employee business expenses, how the employer treats this reimbursement on the employee's Form W-2 depends in part on whether the employer has an accountable plan.[2] Reimbursements treated as paid under an accountable plan are not reported as pay. Reimbursements treated as paid under nonaccountable plans are reported as pay.

To be an accountable plan, the employer's reimbursement or allowance arrangement must meet all the following conditions:

- Expenses must have a business connection; that is, the employee must have paid or incurred deductible expenses while performing services as an employee of the employer.
- The employee must provide adequate accounting for these expenses within a reasonable period of time.

---

[2] This section was adapted from IRS publications at www.irs.gov and http://irs.gov/ publications/.

- The employee must return any excess reimbursement or allow-ance within a reasonable period of time. An excess reimburse-ment or allowance is any amount that the employer paid the employee that is more than the business-related expenses that the employee adequately accounted for to the employer.

The definition of *reasonable period of time* depends on the facts and circumstances of the employee's situation. However, regardless of the facts and circumstances of the situation, actions that take place within the times specified in the following are treated as taking place within a reasonable period of time:

- The employee received an advance within 30 days of the time the employee incurred the expense.

- The employee adequately accounts for the expenses within 60 days after they were paid or incurred.

- The employee returns any excess reimbursement within 120 days after the expense was paid or incurred.

- The employee is given a periodic statement (at least quarterly) that asks the employee to either return or adequately account for outstanding advances and to comply within 120 days of the statement.

If the employee meets the three conditions for accountable plans, the employer should not include any reimbursements in the employ-ee's income in box 1 of the Form W-2. If the expenses are equal to the reimbursement, the employee does not have to complete Form 2106. The employee has no deduction because the expenses and reimburse-ments are equal.

If the employer includes the reimbursements in box 1 of the Form W-2 and the rules for accountable plans are met, the employee should ask for a corrected Form W-2.

Even though the employee is reimbursed under an accountable plan, some of the expenses may not meet all three conditions. All reimbursements that fail to meet all three conditions for accountable plans are generally treated as having been reimbursed under a nonac-countable plan.

If the employee is reimbursed under an accountable plan, but the employee fails to return, within a reasonable time, any amounts in excess of the substantiated amounts, the amounts paid in excess of the substantiated expenses are treated as paid under a nonaccountable plan.

The employee may be reimbursed under an employer's accountable plan for expenses related to that employer's business, some of which are deductible as employee business expenses and some of which are not deductible. If the reimbursements the employee receives for the nondeductible expenses do not meet the first condition for accountable plans, they are treated as paid under a nonaccountable plan.

The deductibility for the company as a business expense depends chiefly on whether the payment is made under an accountable plan. There is a definite advantage from a tax perspective, for both the organization and the employee, to seeing that reimbursements are made under an accountable plan.

If the organization's plan does not meet these conditions, as listed earlier, the plan is not an *accountable plan*. If it is not, the company has to pay FICA taxes on the reimbursement amounts paid to employees. For employees, the difficulty is having the reimbursements considered wages and then having to deduct them from their own tax returns.[3]

Travel Allowances

In practice, three main types of travel allowances are used: automobile allowances, company vehicles, and per diems.

Automobile Allowances

There are three basic types of reimbursement plans used for the accounting of automobile expenses:

---

[3] This section was adapted from IRS publications at www.irs.gov and http://irs.gov/publications/p463/ch06.html.

- **Actual expense method:** In this method, employees are required to keep track of all expenditures related to their automobile and to report them periodically to their employer for reimbursement. This includes all the items mentioned earlier with regard to accountable plans. The items can include fixed expenses such as registration fees and variable items such as gasoline and oil. The total costs then have to be divided by the percentage of total usage of the automobile for business purpose versus usage of the automobile for personal purposes.

  The advantage to this method is that it reflects the actual costs rather than estimated costs. The disadvantage of the method is that it is time-consuming and can be quite involved to keep such a complete record of expenses. Because the employee keeps these records, there may be a tendency to inflate the figures.

- **Standard mileage method:** The simplest and most common way to reimburse employees for their automobile expenses is to pay them a mileage allowance based on the number of business-related miles they drive.

  Ordinarily, the employer uses the standard mileage rate established by the IRS each year (.555 cent a mile in 2012). However, the organization might pay employees a higher rate, so long as the rate is reasonably designed not to exceed the employee's actual or anticipated expenses. In this case, the amount of expense the organization can deduct is the lesser of:

  - The amount the organization paid under its own mileage allowance
  - The government's standard mileage rate multiplied by the number of business miles substantiated by the employee

  The standard mileage rate is reviewed and changed each year by the IRS. You can find this information at www.irs.gov.

  The main advantage to using the standard mileage method is clearly its simplicity. The record keeping is limited. Further simplification is provided in that the mileage rate is not subject to dollar caps or the special rules that apply if qualified business use does exceed 50% of total use. The major disadvantage to the standard mileage method is that it might not cover all the costs of driving the automobile. Fixed costs such as depreciation are not taken into account. The employee may be able to calculate these additional costs and deduct them as expenses from their taxes separately.

- **Fixed and variable rate (FAVR):** This is an allowance the employer may use to reimburse the employee's car expenses. Under this method, the employer pays an allowance that includes a combination of payments covering fixed and variable costs. For example, a cents-per-mile rate may be provided to cover the employee's variable operating costs (such as gas, oil, and so on). A flat amount to cover your fixed costs (such as depreciation, lease payments, insurance, and so on) can also be added on. If the employer chooses to use this method, the employer must request the necessary records from the employee.

Use of Company Vehicles

Some companies provide their sales personnel with company vehicles. If the company vehicle is used entirely for business purposes, the employer might be able to deduct the costs of the vehicle as a business expense. If the employee also uses the company-owned vehicle for personal use, however, the accounting treatment differs. The employee personal use portion of the vehicle's operational costs becomes a benefit to the employee and is considered income and is taxable. This will increase the record-keeping requirements, in that the employee will have to maintain a log of all travel in the company vehicle indicating whether each trip was for a business or personal reason.

For company-owned vehicles, the personal-use portion is calculated via one of three methods: cents-per-mile rule, commuting rule, and lease-value rule.

Cents-Per-Mile Rule

Under the cents-per-mile method, you multiply the current mileage rate ($.51 for January through June 2011; $.555 for July through

December 2011) and .555 per mile in 2012 times the personal-use mileage. To use this method, you must, among other requirements, use the vehicle more than 10,000 miles per year, and the vehicle must be valued at less than the maximum permitted value when placed in service ($15,300 autos, $16,000 truck or van for 2010) and also meet the regular use requirements.

Commuting Rule

Valuation for the commuting rule is based on $1.50 per one-way commute (per employee). To qualify for this method, the employer must (1) provide the vehicle for bona-fide business purposes and require the employees to commute in the vehicle and (2) establish a written policy stating that the employer does not allow the vehicle to be used for personal purposes other than for commuting.

Lease-Value Rule

Most employees can qualify under the lease-value rule based on the fair market value of the vehicle. The fair value is equal to what it would cost to lease a similar vehicle from a third party, known as the annual lease value. To make this calculation easy, the IRS provides an annual lease value for vehicles based on the vehicle's fair market value. The vehicle's fair market value can be determined from any number of Web sites or automobile appraisers. The best source is Kelley Blue Book's Web site: www.kbb.com. Once the vehicle's fair market value is determined, the employer can use the annual lease value table provided by the IRS in Publication 15-B.

After the personal-use percentage and the annual lease value have been determined, the two items are multiplied together to determine the taxable value of the benefit. The taxable value of the benefit is subject to both income and payroll taxes. The value of the benefit must be increased to cover the payroll tax liabilities. This increased value should be shown on the employee's Form W-2 at the end of the year, because the employee will be subject to taxes on the value of the benefit. It is advisable that these calculations be done in advance so that additional income tax withholding can be taken out of the employee's regular pay.

The key thing is good record keeping, and it is essential to avoid understating or overstating the employee's tax liability.

Per Diems

A per diem allowance is a fixed amount of daily reimbursement the employer pays the employee for lodging, meals, and incidental expenses. Federal government per diem rates can be figured by using one of the following methods:

- **The regular federal per diem rate:** This rate varies by location. It includes all the lodging, meals, and incidental expenses. You can find these per diem rates online at www.gsa.gov/portal/catagory/100120.
- **The standard meal allowance:** The standard meal allowance alternative is used when the employee does not have any lodging expense, such as when the employee stays in a company-owned accommodation or with relatives. It covers only meals and incidental expenses. You can find calculations for this category of expenses at the IRS Web site.
- **The high-low rate:** A simplified computation with one rate for high-cost cities and another for regular locations. The amount changes each year. You can find the current amounts and cities in IRS Publication 1542 (www.irs.gov/pub/irs-pdf/p1542.pdf).

Commission Accounting

We now turn our attention to commission accounting.

Usually, commission accounting activities are performed with add-on commission accounting software, many of which are available. Examples include the following:

- QCommission
- Glocent
- Sales Wand (for SAP only)
- Account Pro
- Actek ACom

- APPX
- Maestro
- TrueComp
- CompensationMaster Commission Planner
- Exaxe
- planIT Sales Compensation
- GreenWave

This is just a partial list; many others are available.

These applications improve sales productivity by centralizing and automating commission-based sales compensation plans. The commission accounting applications allow performance tracking, reporting, and the calculation of commission compensation based on performance variables and also the management of key dates in the company's sales/compensation cycles. Software applications can also assist in the management of regulatory requirements as it pertains to the sales compensation programs. The primary advantages of these applications are accounting integration, commission calculations, commission splits, quota management, and chargebacks.

The main operational functions of the software applications are transaction processing, file maintenance, reporting and inquiry, and time-bound processing.

The commission accounting applications should include commission compensation administration features such as the following:

- Commission posting from accounts receivables and order entry into the commission accounting software
- Transfers of sales commissions to accounts payable and the payment of sales commissions through accounts payable
- Options for transferring summary or detail information to accounts payable

This chapter focused on just the accounting-related and finance-related issues of sales compensation program design. We used a hypothetical sales compensation plan to discuss the key financial and accounting issues. We also looked at various IRS rules and regulations with respect to factors that affect the design of sales compensation programs. This chapter also described commission accounting systems and various sales compensation payment types (allowances).

In sales compensation program design, another key implication is equally important: The program needs to be aligned with the organization's overall strategy, and especially the sales and marketing strategies.

Key Concepts in This Chapter

- Quota-based plans
- Base, bonus, and commission plans
- Commission factor
- Expense allowances for sales personnel
- Automobile allowance reimbursement plans
- New customer/product bonus plans
- Shipment commission
- Split commission
- Quota clubs
- Draws
- Reserves
- Commission accounting
- Gross margin versus revenue as a triggering mechanism

8

Employee Benefit Accounting

Aims and objectives of this chapter

- Review specific accounting issues related to health and welfare employee benefit programs
- Discuss the standards framework for the accounting and reporting of employee benefit programs
- Establish the difference between defined contribution and defined benefit programs within a health and welfare employee benefit structure
- Discuss the relevant points of FASB 965 – Employee Benefits
- Discuss the concept of claims incurred but not reported
- Review the reporting requirements for postretirement health plans
- Discuss the concept of self-funding of health and welfare plans
- Explain self-funding within the ERISA structure
- Review reporting standards for health and welfare plans under IFRS – IAS 19 standards
- Explain the financial reporting requirements for employee benefit plans, focusing on health and welfare plans

Employee benefit programs are a crucial element of the total compensation system for any organization. Normally, the employee benefit element of the total compensation structure makes up about a third of the average total compensation. Within the employee benefit structure, the healthcare benefit element is experiencing ever-increasing cost inflation. Because of healthcare costs, the total benefit component can create significant cost exposure for most organizations. This makes the review and comprehensive analysis of employee benefits very important. The next three chapters cover the employee benefit component of the total compensation system.

We now turn our attention to the accounting and finance issues related to employee benefit programs as a whole.

Before 1980, U.S. *Generally Accepted Accounting Principles* (GAAP) had not issued any guidelines for the accounting treatment of employee benefit plans. So before 1980, in actual practice the principles used for the accounting of employee benefits was widely divergent. In March 1980, the *Financial Accounting Standards Board* (FASB) issued the *Statement of Financial Accounting Standards* (SFAS) No. 35, Accounting and Reporting by Defined Benefit Plans. Because these standards addressed only defined-benefit plans, the *American Institute of Certified Public Accountants* (AICPA) issued guidelines for the accounting of defined-contribution and health and welfare plans. The guidance was incorporated in AICPA's Audit and Accounting Guide: Audits of Employee Benefit Plans. The Audit and Accounting guide document was issued in 1983. Since then, the guidance has been updated quite a few times. In August 1992, FASB issued its Statement of Financial Standards No. 110, Reporting by Defined Benefit Pension Plans of Investment Contracts, which extended the fair value accounting to certain insurance contracts.

Specialized accounting and reporting guidance for employee benefit plans is now included in the FASB ASC 900s[1] topics. FASB ASC 960 addresses defined benefit pension plan accounting and reporting, FASB ASC 962 addresses defined contribution pension plan accounting and reporting, and FASB ASC 965 addresses health and welfare benefit plan accounting and reporting.

Employee benefit programs can be generally classified into three categories:

- Risk benefits (covering medical, disability, and life insurance benefits)

---

[1] Financial Accounting Standards Board (FASB) – Accounting Standard Codification (ASC).

- Time-away-from-work benefits
- Savings and retirement benefits (sometimes also called wealth-accumulation programs)

This chapter and Chapter 9, "Healthcare Benefits Cost Management," discuss the accounting and finance implications of the first category of benefits. In this chapter, we focus on the accounting and financial reporting issues connected to health and welfare plans. Chapter 9 is devoted to the important issues of controlling and managing healthcare costs. Chapter 10, "The Accounting and Financing of Retirement Plans," then discusses the third category of employee benefits: retirement benefits. Retirement benefits entail many accounting and finance implications (and so require a more comprehensive analysis).

The Standards Framework

Health and welfare program accounting in the United States is influenced by two significant guiding principles as codified in the U.S. GAAP (FASB) and the *Employee Retirement Security Act* (ERISA). Internationally, the guiding principle is the *International Financial Reporting Standards* (IFRS). In the U.S. GAAP, the accounting for health and welfare plans is codified in FASB ASC regulation 965, and the IFRS standard is in IAS 19.

Guiding our discussions throughout this chapter are the rules, regulations, and principles for the accounting of health and welfare benefit plans both under the U.S. GAAP and the IFRS (that is, FAS 965 and IAS 19, respectively). We discuss relevant elements of the accounting requirements under both codes. If you want a detailed analysis and understanding of the codes, you can review the complete codes at the respective Web sites (www.fasb.org and www.ifrs.org).

Companies in the United States have been analyzing the differences between the IFRS and the U.S. GAAP in anticipation of the convergence of the standards. All parties are waiting to find out when a requirement will be imposed by rule-making bodies requiring U.S. companies to adopt IFRS standards. The *Securities and Exchange*

Commission (SEC) had stated that they would evaluate the feasibility of requiring IFRS conversion in 2011. The convergence time-line indicates that the earliest years the SEC would require U.S. IFRS conversion is 2014 to 2016.

Analyzing, interpreting, and understanding the FASB standards with respect to employee benefit accounting is a worthwhile exercise. However, we also need to do the same analysis with the IFRS standards in mind. This is needed because U.S. companies will face convergence in the near future. Looking at the accounting principles under both the standards will assist in the execution of the convergence effort if and when it is needed. Later in this chapter, we look at IFRS regulations as they pertain to health and welfare plans. The discussion that follows is based on a direct analysis, interpretation, and discussion of the standards.[2]

Defined Contribution Versus Defined Benefit Plans

Defined contribution health and welfare plans differ from defined benefit health and welfare plans. A defined contribution health and welfare plan keeps a record of each individual plan participant's account. Records are kept of each participant's contribution and the employer's contribution attributable to that employee.

A defined benefit health and welfare plan[3] specifies a defined benefit, which may be a reimbursement to the covered plan participant or a direct payment to providers or third-party insurers for the cost of stipulated services on behalf of the participating employee. Defined benefit plans provide participants with a specifically determined benefit based on a formula provided in the plans, whereas defined contribution plans provide benefits based on amounts contributed to an employee's individual account.

---

[2] FASB 965 Plan Accounting–Health and Welfare Plans (based on an analysis of FASB 965).

[3] Hicks, S.W., "Accounting and Reporting by Health and Welfare Plans," *Journal of Accounting*, Vol. 174, Issue 6, 1992.

Both the types adjust values based on the following:[4]

- Forfeitures
- Investment experience
- Administrative expenses

Each type of plan provides a benefit that has value. Therefore, the defined benefit health and welfare plan's financial statements need to provide financial information that will aid in understanding and assessing the plan's present and future ability to pay its benefit obligations when they become payable. To meet this objective, a plan's financial statements should provide information about the plan assets and its benefit obligations, the results of transactions or events affecting the plan's assets and liabilities, and any other pertinent information necessary for users to analyze the information provided.

The different types of defined benefit health and welfare plans (multiemployer and single employer) should separately report benefit obligations, including postretirement benefit obligations.

Section 965 Explained[5]

Benefit Payments – 965-30-25-1: Health and welfare plans are able to process benefit payments directly, or the employer may retain a *third-party administrator* (TPA) through an *administrative service arrangement* (ASA). Benefits need to be paid by both fully and partially self-funded plans.

Premiums Due Under Insurance Arrangements – 965-30-25-3: Premiums due but not yet paid should be a part of the accounting of any obligation.

Postemployment Benefits – 965-30-25-3: Plans specially designed to provide postemployment benefits need to recognize a benefit obligation for current plan participants based on amounts that

---

[4] FASB – 965 – 325 – 05 – 2; www.fasb.org.

[5] In this part of the chapter, we are interpreting, adapting, and explaining relevant code sections (stating the relevant section) of FASB 965, www.fasb.org.

will be paid in future periods if certain conditions are met. The conditions are as follows:

- The participant's right to receive the benefit needs to be based on services already provided.
- The participant has a vested benefit.
- There is a high probability of making the payment.
- The amount needs to be estimated in an accurate manner.

The exception to the rule is when all employees are provided the same benefits upon the occurrence of another specific event, such as medical benefits provided under a disability plan. In disability plans, medical benefits are paid regardless of the length of service. These disability plans usually do not have a vesting provision. Disability benefits need to be accrued from the start date of the disability (965-30-25-4).

Obligations for Premium Deficits – 965-30-25-5: In fully insured experience-rated plans, the experience ratings determined directly by insurance companies or estimates developed by those companies can result in deficits. Premium deficits need to be included in the total benefit obligation if both the following criteria are met:

- It is probable that the deficit will be applied against the amounts of future premiums or future experience rated refunds. The determination has to consider both of the following:
  - To what extent the insurance contract requires payment of the deficits
  - The plan's desire to transfer coverage to another insurance company
- And the amount of the deficit can be estimated in a reasonable manner.

Recognition of Employer Contributions – 965-310-25-1: If there is formal commitment to make the employer contribution, there has to be documented evidence of the commitment. Documentary evidence can include the following:

- A resolution of a governing body signing off on this commitment.

- Evidence of a continuing pattern of making payments after the end of a plan year. This payment pattern needs to be made under a funding policy.

- Evidence of a deduction of a contribution taken for federal tax purposes. The deduction should be for periods ending on or before the financial statement date.

- Evidence of an accounting recognition of the contribution as a current expense payment liability. It is just not sufficient to show on the balance sheet that there is accrued liability. It is also insufficient evidence if the statement simply reflects that an accrued liability amount exceeds the plan's assets available to meet the plan's obligations.

Recognition of Premiums Paid to Insurance Companies – 965-310-25-2: This depends on whether a premium was paid to an insurance entity. It also depends on whether the premium payments were for the transfer of risk or merely a deposit. An analysis is required to determine the extent of the risk transfer to the insurance company. To mitigate the risk transfer, insurance companies might require a deposit be placed that can be applied toward possible future losses. The deposits need to be reported as plan assets until the amounts are used to pay premiums. Premium stabilization reserves that are maintained when premiums paid are in excess of claims and other charges paid should also be reported as assets of the plan until the reserves are used to pay premiums. If these reserves are forfeitable when the insurance contract is terminated, this possibility should be considered when calculations are made to determine assets. If experience-rated premium refunds are expected, and if the policy year does not coincide with the plan's financial year, the refunds due should also be reported as plan assets. This is done only when a determination is made that the refund will become due. Finally, it is assumed that all the calculations can be reasonably performed (965-310-25-3).

Calculating Plan Benefit Obligations

965-30-35-1: All benefit obligations for single-employer and multiple-employer defined benefit health and welfare plans should include the actuarial present value of

- Claims payable
- Claims *incurred but not reported* (IBNR)
- Premiums due to insurance companies for accumulated eligibility credits and for postemployment benefits, net of amounts currently payable, and IBNR claims. This should be premiums for retired plan participants, including beneficiaries and covered dependents, for other plan participants eligible for benefits, and for plan participants not yet fully eligible. Information elements need to be in the body of the financial reports and should not be footnote disclosures.

Claims Incurred but Not Reported (IBNR)

An important concept that affects the actuarial valuation of plan assets and liabilities is the IBNR (claims *incurred but not reported*).[6] According to HealthDictionarySeries.com, an IBNR claim signifies healthcare services that have been rendered but not invoiced or recorded by the healthcare provider, clinic, hospital, or any other health service organization. IBNRs are usually an integral part of a risk-adjusted contract between managed care organizations and healthcare providers. An IBNR claim refers to the estimated cost of medical services for which a claim has not been filed. These claims are normally monitored by an IBNR collection system or control sheet.

More formally, IBNR is the financial accounting of all services that have been performed but because of a time element or a "lag" have not been invoiced or recorded as of a specific date. The transactions

---

[6] Adapted from a blog authored by Dr. David Edward Marcinko, "What is an IBNR medical claim?" Blog: Medical Executive Post ... Insider News and Education for Doctors and Their Advisors, October 2008, http://medicalexecutivepost.com/2008/10/07/what-is-an-ibnr-medical-claim/.

covering medical services that were provided should be accounted for using the following IBNR entry:

> Debit—Accrued payments to medical providers or healthcare entity
>
> Credit—IBNR accrual account

An example of an IBNR in a hospital is a coronary artery bypass surgery for a managed care plan member. The surgeon or healthcare organization has to pay for all related services, such as physical and respiratory therapy, rehabilitation services, drugs, and durable medical equipment [DME] out of a future payment fund. These payments are contractual obligations (liabilities).

The health plan might not be completely billed until several weeks, months, or quarters later or even further downstream in the reporting year after the patient is discharged. To accurately project the health plan's financial liability, the health plan and hospital must estimate the cost of care based on past expenses.

Since the identification and control of costs are paramount in financial healthcare management, an IBNR reserve fund (an interest-bearing account) must be set up for claims that reflect services already delivered but, for whatever reason, not yet reimbursed.

From the accounting point of view, the IBNR needs to be accrued as an expense and a short-term liability for each fiscal month or accounting period. Otherwise, the organization may not be able to pay the claim if the associated revenue has already been spent. The proper handling of these "bills in the pipeline" is crucial for proactive providers and health organizations. IBNRs are especially important with newer patients who may be sicker than prior norms. Amounts that hospitals hope to recover (recoverable) are posted as part of their reserve charges. In many cases, these recoverables end up being IBNR losses. They are recorded as IBNR claims on the balance sheet. When these book losses start becoming actual losses, the hospital might look to the insurer to pay a part of the claim. This might end up being a disputable charge.

For self-funded plans, the IBNR cost should be measured at the present value of the plan's estimated ultimate cost of settling the claims. Estimated ultimate costs should reflect the plan's obligation to pay claims to or for participants (for example, continuing health coverage or long-term disability) regardless of employment status and beyond the financial statement date if stipulated (965-30-35-1A).

Other Benefit Obligations

- Administrative expenses incurred by the plan can be recognized by including the estimated administrative expenses in the benefits expected to be paid or by reducing the discount rate (965-30-35-2).

- Postretirement retirement benefit obligations should be measured as the actuarial present value of future benefits that are tied into the participant's service performed as of the cost measurement date. The calculation should be reduced by projected future contributions from plan participants. The determined calculation represents the employer's funding requirement and the accumulated plan assets. This calculation should also consider the following variables:

  - Continuity of the plan.

  - That all assumptions made about future events for the calculation will indeed be met.

  - Any anticipated forfeitures and integration with other plans.

  - The discount rate used assumes a rate of return that matches the rates of return for high-quality fixed-income investments.

- Any insurance premiums paid for plan participants who have accumulated enough eligibility credits or hours of employment. This is usually calculated by multiplying eligibility credits by the current insurance premium and for self-funded plans by using the average of benefits per eligible participant. Mortality, expected employee turnover, and other required assumptions should be considered in the calculation.

- Any additional premiums as a result of the loss ratio exceeding a preset percentage.

- Additional payments to insurance companies resulting from stop-loss arrangements (965-30-35-9 and 965-30-35-12).

Additional Obligations for Postretirement Health Plans

If a benefit is provided for as part of a postretirement health plan, the estimated payments to participants needs to be accounted for. These benefits usually trigger on the retirement date, or sometimes these benefits trigger at a certain age. The calculation of the estimated obligation as of a given date is based on an actuarial present value of all future benefits that can be attributed to the participant's period of employment. Benefit recipients should cover (1) retirees, (2) a terminated employee, if benefits have been earned, (3) a beneficiary or a covered dependent, and (4) and active participants, their beneficiaries, and any covered dependents.

Benefit obligation calculations need to include the following assumptions and calculation elements:

- Appropriate discount rates to account for the time value of money
- Per-capita cost of claims by age
- Healthcare cost trends
- Current Medicare reimbursement rates
- Retirement age
- Dependency status
- Mortality
- Salary progression
- A probability of payment calculation
- Participation rates

Benefit obligations should not include death benefits that might need to be paid during a participant's active service period. This benefit obligation generally is determined by applying current insurance premium rates or, for a self-funded plan, the average cost of benefits per eligible participant. In either case, the calculation should consider assumptions on mortality rates and the probability of employee turnover (965-30-35-15 to 22).

Self-Funding of Health Benefits

One major financial issue of employer-provided health and welfare plans is the self-funding of these plans. In a self-funded health plan, the employer funds the plan from the company's general funds instead of buying an insurance product.

With the cost of healthcare soaring over the past many years, employers look for ways to bring these costs down to ensure corporate profitability. Self-insuring health plans, rather than purchasing them from insurance companies, was recognized as such an opportunity.

Companies can pay the claims submitted under the plan by using a pay-as-you-go process. When employee claims come in and are reviewed and audited as eligible claims under the terms of the health plan, the employer pays the claims from general funds. Or the employer could set aside funds for use by this self-funded health plan and pay eligible claims from the set aside funds.

There is no insurance element here except that this arrangement can be considered as the company insuring itself. By way of contrast, an insured plan is one where the insurance company pays the claims, and the employer regularly pays the premiums to the insurance company. The premiums set by the insurance companies are adjusted each year based on the past-year usage experience of the insurance plan. Note that medical premiums and total healthcare costs have been the highest inflation-affected cost element in the whole market basket of goods and services within the Consumer Price Index sector of the economy.

Another point to note here is that the company will usually engage, on an annual fee basis, a TPA to administer the claims that come in for payment under the company's self-insured employee health plan. The claims processing part can be a time-consuming effort, and so companies often outsource this activity to a knowledgeable external third party.

ERISA and Self-Funding

The *Employee Retirement Income Security Act* (ERISA) encouraged the growth in self-funded plans. ERISA covers all employee benefit plans sponsored by an employer. This includes employee pension plans and employee welfare plans. However, the emphasis of ERISA is on pension plans. Employee welfare plans include any nonpension employee benefit, including health plans, life insurance, and disability plans.

The key provisions of ERISA that relate to health plans are found in Section 514. This is known as the "preemption" clause, which states, "The provisions of this title and Title 4 shall supersede any and all state laws insofar as they now and hereafter relate to any employee benefit plan."

Under Section 514, all private-sector employer-provided health plans are ERISA plans and therefore exempt under the preemption clause from state regulations. ERISA exempts self-insured plans from providing state-mandated benefits and from paying state premium taxes because the employers offering them are not considered to be in the business of insurance. But ERISA does not prevent state regulation of insurance. States therefore can and do regulate health plans covered under insurance contracts. This is one factor that encourages self-insurance.

To avoid state regulations of the employer-provided health plans, a company can set up the plan as a self-funded plan; in other words, they self-insure the plan. The employer now assumes the risks of the health plan. In the insured plan, the insurance company bears the risks of the plan. Bigger companies have the financial resources to take on additional financial risks that comes with self-insurance and at the same retain their capital rather than passing it onto insurance companies by way of premiums.[7] The stable claims experience from year to year, due to the large employment base, also enables large businesses to safely assume the financial risk.[8]

---

[7] Scammon. D.L., "Self-funded health benefit plans: Marketing implications for PPOs and employers." *Journal of Health Care Marketing*, 9 (1): 5-14.

[8] Park, Christina, H., "Prevalence of Employer Self-Insured Health Benefits: National and State Variation," *Medical Care Research and Review*, Vol. 57, No. 3, September 2000, p. 342; Sage Publication, Inc.

So, as indicated, the term *self-funding* can indicate that the employer sets aside the money to pay the claims. Quite often, however, the employer sets up a pay-as-you-go arrangement, funding the claims from general funds. Nevertheless, hybrid arrangements can be set up, with self-funding as a primary feature.[9]

In some cases, the companies might choose to carve out certain elements of the health plan and buy an insurance contract to cover those elements. The other remaining elements would then be paid from general funds, again on a pay-as-you-go basis. Typically, these carved-out elements could be related to mental health or prescription drugs. The carved-out segment then can be regulated by state insurance regulations by those states where the benefits are being paid.

Another funding mechanism is the purchase of stop-loss coverage. This is usually done to provide coverage for catastrophic losses. There are usually two types of stop-loss coverage:

- Insures against the risk that any one claim will exceed a certain amount
- Aggregate stop-loss, which insures against the entire plan's losses exceeding a certain amount

In their 2011 annual report on employer health benefits, the Kaiser Family Foundation and Health Research and Educational Trust provided the data shown in Exhibit 8-1 on the prevalence of self-insured health plans.

---

[9] EBRI Databook on Employee Benefits, Chapter 28, Employee Benefits Research Institute, update March 2008.

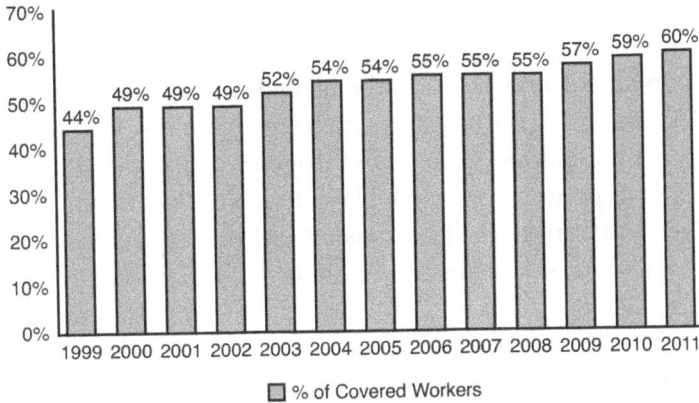

Exhibit 8-1 Percentage of Covered Workers in Partially or Completely Self-Funded Plans, 1999–2011

Source: Employer Health Benefits Survey, 2011, The Henry J. Kaiser Family Foundation and Health Research & Educational Trust, September 2011.

International Financial Reporting Standards and Employee Health and Welfare Plans

In the IFRS, the accounting for employee benefits is addressed in IAS 19, Employee Benefits. This section covers provisions in IAS 19 that affect employee benefits items only. Note that IAS 19 also covers items that are termed employee compensation for the purposes of the book. The main provisions of IAS 19 that affect employee benefits are as follows:

- **Short-term benefits:** Benefits payable within one year. The employee will have to have been provided the services for which required compensation has been earned. These items cover medical benefits provided to regular employees, vacation and sick pay, as they relate to the employee benefit categorization. IAS 19 requires that the undiscounted amount of these benefits expected to be paid, after the service has been rendered, should be recognized in that period.

- **Postemployment benefits:** Benefits that are payable after the employment term is completed. These benefits include pensions, retiree health benefits, life insurance, and the continuation of medical and life benefits after employment. No termination benefits are included in this category. In this category, IAS 19 states that if the benefit program is a defined contribution plan, the costs need to be recognized in the period the contributions are made in exchange for employee services during that period. For defined benefit plans, the amount recognized in the balance sheet needs to be the present value of the defined benefit obligation, as adjusted for unrecognized or actuarial gains or losses. Also included are unrecognized past service cost for pension plans (see Chapter 10). The balance needs to be reduced by the fair value of plan assets at the balance sheet date.

- **Termination Benefits:** Benefits paid upon involuntary termination or a voluntary termination where compensation has been paid for a temporary period.

For termination benefits, IAS 19 specifies that amounts payable should be recognized when the company has made a decision to either terminate the employment of an employee or group of employees before the normal retirement date or provide termination benefits as a result of an offer made to encourage voluntary terminations.

Under IAS 19, the company has to show that the planned termination is being done within the terms and provisions of a formal written plan and that the company does not plan to cancel the plan after the termination action has been taken. IAS also allows discounting of termination action costs when 12 months have expired from the balance sheet date and the benefits are currently being paid.

The Financial Reporting of Employee Benefit Plans

The financial reporting for employee benefit plans cover reporting requirements for defined benefit and defined contribution plans health and welfare plans. The reporting standards for these plans have components that are similar in nature.

ERISA requires many different reports be prepared and filed annually. These reports need to be prepared and filed with the Department of Labor and provided to plan participants, plan beneficiaries, and others. ERISA requires the report filing, but the *Department of Labor* (DOL) regulations define the filing requirements.[10]

DOL requirements stipulate the filing of Form 5500, with attachments, every year. The attachments include financial statements, notes, supporting schedules, and an accountant's report.

SFAS No. 35 requires that every plan issuing financial statements distribute, at the end of each year, a statement of net assets available to pay out plan benefits. A statement of the changes in net assets for the year ended also needs to be developed. Related notes need to be filed, as well, as part of the financial statements.

The financial statements presented need to be a comparative form (that is, a year-to-year comparison). The statements have to be prepared under GAAP principles, which mean the use of accrual accounting. Under the accrual basis, the purchases and sales of securities must be recognized on a trade date basis rather than a settlement date basis.

Statement of Net Assets Available for Plan Benefits

Because plan investments are usually a plan's biggest asset, the valuation of those plan assets is particularly important. Most plan investment assets are reported using a fair value concept.

In accounting, the fair value is usually the value that can be expected in a transaction between a willing buyer and a willing seller. For securities traded on an active market, the fair value is the quoted market price. For assets for which there is no quoted market price, alternative valuation methods need to be used. A commonly used method is the *discounted cash flow* (DFC) method.

Contracts with insurance companies need to be valued differently. Valuation of investment contracts with insurance companies for health and welfare plans and defined-contribution plans is governed

---

[10] Doran, Donald A., and Verrekia, JulieAnn, "Employee Benefit Plan Accounting & Reporting," Chapter 41, *The Handbook of Employee Benefits*, Edited by Larry S. Rosenbloom, 2001, McGraw Hill, New York.

by AICPA's SOP 94 – 4: Reporting of investment contracts held by health and welfare benefit plans and defined contribution pension plans. The AICPA requires that most plan contracts be valued at fair value, except contracts that incorporate mortality and morbidity risk or those that allow for withdrawals for benefits at contract value. In these cases, the contract can be reported at contract value.

It also depends on whether the payment to the insurance company is allocated to purchase insurance or annuities for the individual participants or whether the payments are accumulated in an unallocated fund to be used to pay retirement benefits. These are referred to as allocated and unallocated arrangements.

In allocated funding arrangements, the insurer has a legally enforceable obligation to make benefit payments. The obligations of the plan may have been transferred to the insurer through the payment of premiums. Payment of a premium where the risk is transferred to the insurance company represents a reduction in the net plan assets. So, for plan reporting purposes, the investments in the allocated insurance contract should be excluded from plan assets.

Unallocated funds are included in plan assets.

Premiums paid that represent deposits should be reflected as plan assets until such time as the deposit is refunded or are used to pay claims. Insured plan claims reported and claims incurred are the obligations of the insurance companies and do not therefore need to be reported. However, this is not the case in self-insured plans. So in these plans, the claims need to be reported. The footnotes should disclose significant assumption changes used to determine plan liabilities.

Often, funds for reporting purposes are commingled trust funds, pooled separate accounts of insurance companies, or master trust funds containing assets of two or more plans pooled for investment purposes. Common or commingled funds are generally for two or more companies. Master trusts hold assets for a single employer or for members of a controlled group.

For reporting purposes, the value of funds is based on unit value of the fund or the separate accounts that need to be reported at fair value. The specific portion of interest of the plan in the master trust needs to be reported as a separate line item. The net change in fair value of each significant type of investment of the master trust, the total and net investment income, the method of determining fair value, the general type of investments, the basis used to allocate net assets, gains and losses to participating plans, and the plan's percentage interest in the master trust should all be reported in the footnote.

The general disclosure requirements for the statement are

- Whether fair value was measured using quoted market prices in an active market or an alternative method was used.
- The method of valuation.
- Detail of the investments must be provided either on the face of the statement of net investments or in a footnote.
- Investments must be segregated by types, such stock, bonds, and so on.
- Investments representing 5% or more of net assets available for plan benefits must be reported separately.

Receivables must be reported separately for employer contributions, participant contributions, amount due from brokers for securities sold, and accrued interest and dividends.

Contributions receivable must report only those that are receivables as of the date of the report. Participant contributions are usually those that are payroll withholdings that have yet to be remitted to the plan. Supporting documentary evidence for employer contributions must be provided. Allowances for unaccountable receivables need to be established as per normal accounting practice. This becomes imperative considering that troubled companies might not have the ability to make the necessary contributions to the plan. Under these circumstances, the receivables need to be reduced by the uncollectible offset. Explanation for this probability should be disclosed in the footnotes. Finally, any deficiency in the funding status of the plan should be recognized as a receivable.

Statement of Changes in Net Assets Available for Plan Benefits

Significant changes in net assets during the reporting period need to be disclosed. The net appreciation or depreciation includes realized gains or losses from the sales of investments and unrealized gains. Losses from market appreciation should also be disclosed. The separate disclosure is required by ERISA. But, the realized or unrealized gain or loss needs to be based on the value of the asset at the beginning of the plan year and not the historical cost of the asset.

Additional General Disclosure Requirements

- A description of the plan, including vesting and benefit provisions, significant plan amendments during the year, and the policy regarding forfeitures
- The fund's funding policy along with changes made during the year
- Plan policy regarding the purchase of allocated insurance contracts that are excluded from plan assets
- Actuarial assumptions and any changes made to these assumptions during the year
- The federal tax status of the plan, including any IRS determination letters received
- Significant transactions with interested parties such as plan sponsor, plan administrator, employees, or employee representatives
- Significant events or transactions that happened during the plan year
- Accounting policies that differ from GAAP
- Commitment and contingencies
- Significant risks, uncertainties, and estimates used
- Information on off-balance sheet risks of accounting loss and the significant concentration of credit risk
- Facts on any investments in derivative financial investments
- Differences in amounts reported in financial statements and those reported in DOL Form 5500

Additional General Disclosure Requirements for Health and Welfare Plans

The general disclosure requirement for health and welfare plans are as follows:

- The organization's policy with regard to participant contributions to the plan
- The actuarial assumptions used to calculate plan benefit obligations and actuarial assumptions changed during the current plan year
- The method of funding plan benefits, if there are fund deficits
- The types and extent of insurance coverage that transfers risk from the plan
- The healthcare cost trend rates used to calculate cost of benefits
- For postretirement benefit plans, the effect of a percentage point increase in assumed healthcare cost trend

Key Concepts in This Chapter

- FASB 965 – Employee Benefits
- The standards framework
- Defined-contribution health and welfare plans
- Defined-benefits health and welfare plans
- Claims incurred but not reported
- Postretirement health plans
- Self-funding of health plans
- ERISA and self-funding
- International Financial Reporting Standards – IAS 19
- Financial reporting of employee benefit plans
- Statement of net assets available for plan benefits
- Statement of changes in net assets available for plan benefits

9

Healthcare Benefits Cost Management

Aims and objectives of this chapter

- Discuss healthcare benefits cost containment
- Expose the causes for the escalating costs of healthcare benefit programs
- Consider various healthcare cost management options.
- Review consumer-driven healthcare cost containment initiatives
- Examine health savings accounts
- Discuss health reimbursement accounts
- Examine flexible spending accounts
- Discuss utilization reviews
- Discuss corporate wellness programs
- Model the forecasting of healthcare benefit program costs

This chapter examines healthcare benefits costs for employers only. Because this category of employee benefits is the major component of the total employee benefits program, understanding and forecasting these costs accurately is vital. After all, on average, the cost of a total employee benefit program is about 30% of the total compensation program costs in most organizations. So, in most organizations, this is a big-ticket cost, requiring close analysis and monitoring.

The Background

Any book about financial and accounting aspects of *human resource* (HR) management must examine the escalating costs of employer-sponsored healthcare programs. The cost of this one element of the total compensation system has been continually rising, and so organizations need to exert sufficient analytical rigor and, when possible, implement fairly stringent cost-containment measures. Rising overall costs of doing business and stiff global competition make this even more of a business imperative.

Medical costs, which seem to continually increase, are a hot-button issue. Recent media coverage of the subject has been extensive, fueling emotions and ongoing political debates. With the Affordable Care Act (ObamaCare) signed into law, and the Supreme Court upholding its constitutionality, the issue remains at the forefront of our current societal dialogue and so must also be addressed by decision makers in business organizations.

The overall inflation rate (of all goods and services) has been around 2.3% since the year 2002. In contrast, the average annual premium for family healthcare coverage through an employer-sponsored plan reached $15,073 in 2011, an increase of 9% over the previous year (according to a Kaiser Family Foundation study). The annual growth in premiums has slowed in recent years to 5%, however, rising just 3% in 2010. Double-digit increases in medical premiums were the norm for a long time, so any relief from that is most welcome. Note, however, that overall the cost of family coverage has doubled since 2001, when premiums averaged $7,061, compared with a 34% gain in wages over the same period, according to the *New York Times*.[1] Any moderation in the inflation rate of medical premiums for employers is the result of the slowing down of the economy since 2008 (and the not-so-robust economic recovery since then). Nevertheless, the same *NY Times* article suggests that employers expect to see medical premiums increasing at an annual rate of about 5% over the next few years.

Note, as well, that since the recession of 2008-2009 and the weak recovery thereafter the number of people covered by employer-sponsored healthcare programs has steadily declined. In a comprehensive briefing paper published by the Economic Policy Institute, author Elise Gould provides some interesting statistics derived

---

[1] Data from www.nytimes.com/2011/09/28/business/health-insurance-costs-rise-sharply-this-year-study-shows.

from an analysis from U.S. Census Bureau data.[2] She states that for the entire under-65 population, the number of those covered by employer-sponsored medical benefit coverage fell from about 170 million to about 157 million from 2000/2001 to 2009/2010. This indicates that more and more people are uninsured because they are not in an employer-sponsored plan.

The contributing factor is that over the past four years unemployment has been in the range of 8% to 10%. This is a good and a bad piece of information. Because the number of covered employees has been going down, the total cost of medical coverage has been (most probably) decreasing along with it. However, many people are currently unemployed. During their unemployment period, they could be on COBRA (*Consolidated Omnibus Budget Recovery Act*) coverage for up to 18 months. When their COBRA expires, they often go uninsured. When they need medical care, the uninsured go to the public hospitals and receive care free of charge. However, somebody has to pick up the tab for the uninsured. And most likely, the remaining working employees pick up this tab with higher premiums and with rising doctor fees and hospital costs.

In 2010, 49.1 million people under 65 were uninsured. This is a huge indirect cost, borne by those covered by employer-sponsored medical plans. Therefore, rising medical premiums and unit coverage costs offset any potential savings from fewer persons being covered. So, even as the number of people covered by employer-sponsored medical plans declines, the cost of medical plans continues to climb faster than the overall inflation rate. For example, since 2001, premiums for employer-sponsored health coverage for families have increased by 113%, placing more cost burdens on employers and workers. And health expenditures in the United States neared $2.6 trillion in 2010, more than ten times the $256 billion spent in 1980.[3] According to the Congressional Budget Office, between 1975 and 2005, annual per-person health spending in the United States rose, on average, 2% faster than per-person economic growth.

[2] Gould, Elise, "A Decade of Declines in Employer-Sponsored Health Insurance Coverage," EPI Briefing Paper #337, February 23, 2012.

[3] U.S. Healthcare Costs, Kaiser EDU.org, *Health policy explained*, www.kaiseredu. org/issue-modules/us-health-care-costs/background-brief.aspx.

The Reasons for the Rising Costs

Many factors have contributed to the ever-rising cost of employer-sponsored medical benefit programs (medical premiums), including the following:

- Cost of medical malpractice insurance
- The unusually high increase in hospital costs
- The ever-increasing number of underinsured and uninsured who need care (which adds indirectly to the cost of medical premiums because the payers [hospitals, doctors, and insurance companies] are forced to pass these costs on to regular plan participants)
- The increasing demand for medical services from an expanding population base
- The consumer demand for better medical care and services

This is a plethora of reasons—many factors contributing to increasing costs. Many of these reasons are situational and not necessarily caused by problems within the structures of medical care.

There are other reasons for the rising costs as well. Among these is that for several years spending on prescription drugs has been a primary contributor to the increase in overall healthcare spending. Analysts state that the availability of more expensive prescription drugs, with their high development costs, is contributing to the rising costs.

Similarly, state-of-the-art medical technologies fuel healthcare spending through development costs and the subsequent demand for more costly services. These technologies might be improving quality of diagnosis and care, but they might not necessarily be cost-effective.

People in general are living longer, but they often face severe diseases as they do so. This places a tremendous demand on the healthcare system. Severe chronic diseases account for more than 70% of total healthcare expenses. Treatment of heart disease, obesity, diabetes, and other long-term disease conditions contributes to the rise in healthcare costs. In addition, as the population ages, use of medical care increases, with the cost of care rising with a person's age. Data indicates that in the last two years of a person's life is when the highest healthcare expenses are incurred.

Another reason for the rising costs is the inefficiency and the waste in the system. There is evidence that an excess of 25% of healthcare spending (or more $600 billion) a year can be traced to inefficiency and waste.[4]

Businesses are always scrambling to improve their bottom lines. And because of the increasing pressures from rising costs of medical plans and because of pending regulations (for example, the Affordable Care Act), businesses remain vigilant about this major cost element that can affect their bottom lines directly. All of this evidence suggests that management will continue to challenge the HR and benefits department staff to build various cost-containment measures in to their healthcare plan designs, annual updates, and revisions.

Nevertheless, this is a joint responsibility of the HR staff and the accounting staff. One activity where cooperation is essential is in projecting as accurately as possible the future costs of medical benefit programs. Accurate costs are essential for effective financial planning, budgeting, and overall effective managerial accounting. We discuss the projecting of medical benefit costs later on in this chapter.

Much has been written and published on the subject of healthcare costs and their containment, with entire books and numerous articles devoted to the subject. Even so, the objective of this chapter is to review the issue of healthcare costs from the employer's point of view and to discuss various cost-containment alternatives that can be built in to medical benefit plan designs.

The main objective for the employer in providing employees with a medical plan benefit is to help employees mitigate the financial risks associated with getting sick, both on minor and major illnesses. The mitigation of the risks is done for both the employee and his or her direct family. Major exposure arises when the employee or any member of his or her family becomes severely ill for whatever reason. These can be catastrophic events. Another primary reason that

[4] Chanin, Jeffrey, Parke, Robert, and Mirkin, David, "Insight – Expert Thinking from Milliman," *Want to manage employer healthcare costs? It starts with managing utilization,* March 18, 2010, http://insight.milliman.com/article.php?cntid=7217.

employers provide medical benefits to employees is to ensure that the employee stays physically healthy so that the employee currently is and continues to be productive for the entire duration of the employee's service life within the organization.

So, the medical benefit plan is an important component of the total compensation program. But costs need to be managed by building various cost-containment features into the design of the plan and by systematically forecasting these costs for effective managerial budgeting and control. We now look first at cost-containment ideas and concepts. Then the discussion turns to the issue of forecasting and budgeting medical benefit expenses.

Cost Containment Alternatives

Healthcare benefit is one of the keys to the hiring and retaining of critical employees. So, when this benefit costs the employer large sums of money, it becomes imperative that these costs be analyzed and containment measures be put into place. Many cost-containment ideas and concepts have been floated. This discussion focuses on the most direct and concrete concepts for the cost containment of healthcare expenses.

Consumer-Driven Healthcare

One concrete way to contain costs has been given the broad designation of *consumer-driven healthcare.* The fundamental principle here is that individuals are in control of their health condition—the good and the bad. The individual can direct the medical care expenditure by choosing a healthy lifestyle, by controlling diet, and by exercising. Consumer-driven healthcare advocates that the individual should self-direct these expenditures with monies they directly set aside as a saving for the eventuality of these expenses (with *some* structural facilitation provided by employers and the government). After all, when the employees are spending their own money, it makes them responsible purchasers of healthcare and they create the necessary cost-containment measures by themselves for themselves.

Self-directed healthcare programs that have been introduced in the recent past include

- Health savings accounts
- Health reimbursement accounts
- Flexible spending accounts (not really a consumer-driven cost-containment initiative, but rather a pretax spending provision)

Health Savings Accounts

Health savings accounts (HSAs) were created in 2003 so that individuals covered by high-deductible health plans could receive tax-preferred treatment of money saved for medical expenses. Generally, an adult who is covered by a high-deductible health plan (and has no other first-dollar coverage) may establish an HSA.

The caveat for the establishment of an HSA is that an individual is eligible for an HSA only if he or she is covered by a high-deductible health plan. A *high-deductible health plan* (HDHP) is a health insurance plan with lower premiums and higher deductibles than a traditional health plan. HDHPs are usually for catastrophic coverage, intended to cover specific catastrophic illnesses.

HSAs were established as part of the Medicare Prescription Drug, Improvement, and Modernization Act, which was signed into law by President George W. Bush on December 8, 2003.

A survey conducted by the Kaiser Family Foundation in September 2008 found that 8% of covered workers were enrolled in a consumer-driven health plan (including both HSAs and health reimbursement accounts), up from 4% in 2006. The study found that roughly 10% of firms offered such plans to their workers. Evidence suggests that the vast majority of HSA plans were employer-sponsored plans and about 25% of the total plans were individually set up. Another survey, done by *America's Health Insurance Plans* (AHIP), provides confirming evidence. They reported that the number of Americans covered by HSA-qualified plans had grown to 6.1 million as of January 2008 (4.6 million through employer-sponsored plans and 1.5 million covered by individually purchased HSA-qualified plans).

Evidence gleaned from various data sources on the use of HSAs since inception finds that contributions to these plans far outstrip the withdrawals. Contributions are normally almost double the withdrawals.

Contributions to an HSA may be made by any individual member of an HSA-eligible high-deductible health plan or by their employer, or by any other person. If the employer makes a contribution to such a plan, the plan is considered the same as any other *Employee Retirement Income Security Act* (ERISA) qualified plan, and nondiscrimination rules become effective. If contributions are made through a Section 125 plan, however, nondiscrimination rules do not apply.

Employers have flexibility in the design of the plans in that they may treat full-time and part-time employees differently. Employers may also treat individual and family participants differently.

Contributions from an employer or employee may be made on a pretax basis through an employer. In the absence of employer contributions, contributions may be made on a post-tax basis and then used to decrease gross taxable income the following year.

The main advantage of making pretax contributions is the ability to avoid the FICA and the Medicare tax deduction, which amounts to a savings of 7.65%. Because of the temporary Social Security tax rate holiday, the 7.65% number may be different for employees. The stated percentage applies to employer and employee (subject to limits of the Social Security Wage Base). Regardless of the method or tax savings associated with the deposit, the deposits may only be made for persons covered under an HSA-eligible high-deductible plan.

Initially, the annual maximum deposit to an HSA was the lesser of the actual deductible or specified *Internal Revenue Service* (IRS) limits. Congress later abolished the limit based on the deductible and set statutory limits for maximum contributions. All contributions to an HSA, regardless of source, count toward the annual maximum. A catch-up provision also applies for plan participants who are age 55 or older, allowing the IRS limit to be increased.

All deposits to an HSA become the property of the policyholder, regardless of the source of the deposit. Funds deposited but not withdrawn each year carry over into the next year. Policyholders who end their HSA-eligible insurance coverage lose eligibility to deposit further funds, but funds already in the HSA remain available for use.

The Tax Relief and Health Care Act of 2006, signed into law on December 20, 2006, added a provision allowing a one-time rollover of *Individual Retirement Account* (IRA) assets to be used to fund up to one year's maximum HSA contribution. State tax treatment of HSAs varies. According to IRS Publication 969: Health Savings Accounts and Other Tax-Favored Health Plans, an individual can generally make contributions to an HSA for a given tax year until the deadline for filing income tax returns for that year, which is typically April 15.

IRS-stipulated contributions for the years 2012 and 2013 are as follows, respectively:

- **Single**: $3,100 and $3,250
- **Family**: $6,250 and $6,450

Funds in an HSA can be invested in investments similar to the investments made in IRA funds. Investment earnings are sheltered from taxation until the money is withdrawn.

HSAs funds can be "rolled over" from fund to fund. However, an HSA cannot be rolled into an IRA or a 401(k), and funds from IRAs and similar investments cannot be rolled into an HSA, except for the one-time IRA transfer mentioned earlier.

Unlike some employer contributions to a 401(k) plan, all HSA contributions belong to the participant immediately, regardless of the deposit source. HSA participants do not have to obtain advance approval from their HSA trustee or their medical insurer to withdraw funds, and the funds are not subject to income tax if made for qualified medical expenses. These include costs for services and items covered by the health plan but subject to cost sharing, such as a deductible and coinsurance or copayments. Funds can be withdrawn for expenses not covered under medical plans (such as dental, vision, and chiropractic care; durable medical equipment such as eyeglasses and hearing aids; and transportation expenses related to medical care). Through December 31, 2010, nonprescription over-the-counter medications were also eligible. Beginning January 1, 2011, the Patient Protection and Affordable Care Act, also known as Health Care Reform, stipulates HSA funds can no longer be used to buy over-the-counter drugs without a doctor's prescription.

There are several ways that funds in an HSA can be withdrawn, such as through a debit card, personal checks, and a reimbursement process similar to medical insurance. Funds can be withdrawn for any reason, but withdrawals that are not for documented qualified medical expenses are subject to income taxes and a 20% penalty. The 20% tax penalty is waived for persons who have reached the age of 65 or have become disabled at the time of the withdrawal. Then, only income tax is paid on the withdrawal, and in effect the account has grown tax deferred (similar to an IRA). Medical expenses continue to be tax free. Prior to January 1, 2011, when new rules governing HSAs in the Patient Protection and Affordable Care Act went in to effect, the penalty for nonqualified withdrawals was 10%.

Account holders are required to retain documentation for their qualified medical expenses. Failure to retain and provide documentation could cause the IRS to rule withdrawals were not for qualified medical expenses and subject the taxpayer to additional penalties.

The HSA plan is an innovation whose primary objective was to contain healthcare costs for employers. It is believed that HSAs should reduce the growth of healthcare costs and increase the efficiency of the healthcare system. When individuals spend their own money, it makes them responsible purchasers of healthcare. They pursue cost-effective choices. Many believe that individuals who see that they are having to pay the medical expenses themselves will consume less medical care, ask the doctors more questions about tests and medical exams, shop for lower-cost options, and be more vigilant against excess and fraud in the healthcare industry. For all these reasons, the HSA program has great value as a cost-containment measure.

Two other plans fall within the genre of consumer-driven health plans. These plans have similar objectives but differ in structure.

Health Reimbursement Arrangement

Health reimbursement accounts or *health reimbursement arrangements* (HRAs) are IRS-approved programs that allow an employer to set aside funds to reimburse medical expenses that have been paid by employees. HRA programs have tax advantages for both employees and employers.

An HRA is an account offered to employees or retirees that the employee can use to pay for deductible and co-insurance amounts or covered medical expenses. Like an HSA, leftover dollars generally can be used from year to year, as long as the employee continues to be a member of the plan. Also, the money is contributed by the employer and doesn't count as income, saving valuable tax dollars.

Employers set up HRA programs and then engage a third-party administrator to manage the program. A feature of this plan can be that participants would be allowed to roll over plan balances from one year to the next. However, the employer needs to decide how much can be rolled over from one year to the next. This can be stipulated as a percentage or a flat amount.

According to the IRS, an HRA "must be funded solely by an employer," and contributions cannot be paid through a voluntary salary-reduction agreement. No limit applies to the employer's contributions, which are excluded from an employee's income.

Per the IRS regulations documented in IRS Publication 96, "Employees are reimbursed tax free for qualified medical expenses up to a maximum dollar amount for a coverage period." HRAs reimburse only those items (copays, coinsurance, deductibles, and services) agreed to by the employer that are not covered by the company's standard insurance plan. With an HRA, employers fund individual reimbursement accounts for their employees and define what those funds can be used for.

Before a plan is implemented, qualified claims must be described in the HRA plan document. Approved reimbursements could be for medical services, dental services, copays, coinsurance, and deductibles. But these reimbursement guidelines can vary from plan to plan. The employer is not required to prepay into a fund for reimbursements. Instead, the employer can reimburse employee claims as they occur.

Reimbursements under an HRA can be made for current and former employees, spouses, and any person the employee could have claimed as a dependent on the employee's tax return (with stipulated exceptions).

The biggest cost-containment advantage of an HRA plan is that employers will have predictability regarding their expenses in providing attractive healthcare benefits for their employees. Employers will know their maximum expense liabilities.

Flexible Spending Accounts

As indicated earlier, *flexible spending accounts* (FSAs) cannot be classified as a cost-containment device for the employer. Instead, an FSA is more of a program that facilitates employees spending their own money on healthcare and dependent care expenses. In such programs, an individual can set aside a certain percentage of earnings to pay for qualified expenses, mostly medical expenses and dependent care expenses. The money set aside by the individual is not subject to payroll taxes. A major disadvantage of an FSA is that funds not used in an FSA by the end of the year are lost to the employee. This is not the case with an HSA.

The most common type of FSA is a medical-expense FSA. HSAs and FSAs are similar in nature. The main difference is that an HSA is offered as a component of a consumer-driven healthcare plan, whereas an FSA can also be offered with a traditional health benefit plan.

An FSA plan can have two components; one is for qualified medical expenses, and the other is for dependent care expenses.

Medical-Expense FSA

The most common type of FSA is used to pay for medical expenses not paid for by insurance, usually deductibles, copayments, and coinsurance amounts. As of January 1, 2011, over-the-counter medications are allowed only when purchased with a doctor's prescription, with the exception of insulin. Over-the-counter medical devices, such as bandages, crutches, and eyeglass repair kits, are covered.

Prior to the enactment of the Patient Protection and Affordable Care Act, the IRS permitted employers to set any maximum annual amount for their employees. The Patient Protection and Affordable Care Act amended Section 125 such that FSAs cannot allow employees to choose an annual election in excess of a limit determined by the

IRS. The annual limit will be $2,500 for the first plan year beginning after December 31, 2012. The IRS will index subsequent plan years' limits for cost-of-living adjustments. Employers have the option to limit their employees' annual elections further. This change starts in plan years that begin after December 31, 2012. The limit is applied to each employee, without regard to whether the employee has a spouse or children. Nonelective contributions made by the employer that are not deducted from the employee's wages are not counted against the limit. An employee employed by multiple unrelated employers may elect an amount up to the limit under each employer's plan. The limit does not apply to HSAs, HRAs, or the employee's share of the cost of employer-sponsored health insurance coverage.[5]

Dependent Care FSA

FSAs can also be established to pay for certain expenses to care for dependents who live with someone while that person is at work. The dependent care FSA is federally capped at $5,000 per year, per household. Married spouses can each elect an FSA, but their total combined elections cannot exceed $5,000. At tax time, all withdrawals in excess of $5,000 are taxed.

Other FSA Provisions

An FSA's coverage period ends either at the time the plan year ends or at the time when coverage under the plan ends.

In recent years, the FSA debit card was developed to allow employees to access the FSA directly. It also simplified the substantiation requirement, which required labor-intensive claims processing.

A drawback to the FSA program is that the money set aside must be spent "within the coverage period" as defined by the benefits plan coverage definition. The *plan year* is commonly defined as the calendar year. Monies left unspent at the end of the coverage period are forfeited. These funds can be used for administrative costs or can be equally distributed as taxable income among all plan participants. The

---

[5] All the provisions stated have been derived from http://healthcare.gov and from the IRS Web site http://irs.gov.

coverage period ceases with the termination of employment, whether the employee or the employer initiated the termination. The exception to the rule is when the employee continues coverage with the company under COBRA or another arrangement.

The next most direct and concrete way to contain healthcare expenses are utilization reviews.

Utilization Reviews

The utilization review process has been used for awhile now. It is a process that determines whether medical services are appropriate and necessary. The process helps the organization minimize costs. Utilization reviews take various forms, including the following:

- Preadmission review for scheduled hospitalization (precertification review)
- Admission review for unscheduled hospitalization (precertification review)
- Second opinions for elective surgeries (precertification reviews)
- Concurrent reviews
- Individual case retrospective reviews
- Aggregate plan retrospective reviews

Insurance companies engage doctors and other healthcare professionals to perform these reviews. The reviews could also be conducted by independent agencies. In utilization reviews, there is a need to balance the desire to directly reduce the volume of services provided and the desire to increase the quality of care.

There are various types of utilization reviews. First is the precertification review. This is the preapproval process for treatments that the insurance companies have designated require precertification before the medical care is provided. Most precertification lists include non-emergency hospitalizations, outpatient surgery, skilled nursing and rehabilitation services, home care services, and some home medical equipment. The review and approval involves determining whether the requested service is medically necessary.

Most insurance plans have predetermined criteria or clinical guidelines of care for a given condition. Once the precertification request is submitted to the insurance company, a committee reviews these guidelines and determines whether the particular case meets the criteria for precertification coverage. If necessary, the committee may contact the healthcare provider. The process begins with data collection, including the symptoms, diagnosis, results of any lab tests, and a list of required services. The committee then reviews the submitted case against the criteria for the given condition. It may compare the medical information provided to the health plan's medical-necessity benchmarks.

The second type of a review is the concurrent review. Concurrent reviews are used for approval of medically necessary treatments or services. Concurrent reviews are conducted during active management of a condition. This could be inpatient or ongoing outpatient care. The main objective of a concurrent review is to make sure that the patient is getting the right care in a timely and cost-effective way. After the physician has started a specific course of medical treatment, any new treatments found on the insurance companies' preapproval list are submitted to the insurance company for approval. Information is collected on the care provided up to that point in time. Information on clinical status and any progress or lack thereof is collected. Once the insurance company or an independent review organization reviews the information, the physician and other providers are informed as to the insurance company's position with respect to the particular case.

An important part of concurrent review is the assessment of the need for continued hospitalization. This is because a primary objective of the concurrent review is to decrease the amount of time the patient remains in the hospital. Often, the concurrent review feedback includes a specific discharge plan. This plan can include transfers to rehabilitation, hospice, or nursing facilities. Although discharge plans often change due to complications or abnormal test results, it is very important to minimize length of hospital stays to contain costs.

The final type of utilization review is the retrospective review. In this review, medical records are audited on the particular case after the treatment is completed. The retrospective review takes two forms.

One reviews a particular plan's aggregate utilization statistics, and the other deals with individual cases.

The insurance company can use the results to approve or deny coverage an individual has already received. The particulars of individual cases are compared to those of other patients with the same condition. Based on the retrospective review of the individual cases, the insurance company may revise treatment guidelines and criteria for that specific condition.

The other function of an individual case retrospective review is the after-the-fact approval of treatments that were conducted without precertification approvals. This can happen if a particular case was an extreme medical emergency and so time prevented the parties involved from securing precertification approvals. Emergency acute care surgeries often result in requesting eligibility for this type of review. The review takes place before any payment is made to the provider or hospital.

The second type of retrospective utilization reviews is the aggregate group review done by the insurance company for the plan sponsor. The plan sponsor, because of confidentiality laws, cannot be shown review results for individual cases. So, they need statistical data in aggregates. Here, average statistics on incident experience is provided for that particular plan sponsor compared to appropriate benchmarks. The health insurance company, an independent review organization, or the hospital involved in the treatment can conduct retrospective reviews.

The term *utilization management* is often used interchangeably with the term *utilization review*. Because the plan sponsor has to foot the bill for all medical costs in an employer-sponsored healthcare plan, they demonstrate the most concern as to how these expenses are being managed. Now, because of advances in information technology, plan sponsors require intermediaries (brokers and insurance companies) to provide them with empirical data about plan utilization. They are also requesting that this data be analyzed to provide them appropriate benchmark studies. Employers believe these studies can help them with their cost-containment efforts by showing them areas for utilization improvement, better waste management potential, and improved ways to adhere to evidence-based medical practices.

Corporate Wellness Programs

Another much discussed healthcare cost containment concept is to encourage and motivate employees to stay healthy. These programs usually fall under the generic title *corporate wellness programs.*

Proponents of this concept contend that there are many hidden costs of poor health. In a U.S. Chamber of Commerce innovative publication, Leading by Example,[6] Dan Ustian, president and CEO of Lincoln Plating, suggests that the main hidden costs of an unhealthy employee population base are (1) higher direct healthcare costs, (2) lower worker output, (3) higher rates of disability, (4) higher rates of absenteeism, (5) higher rates of injury, and (6) more workers' compensation claims. So, according to Mr. Ustian, it is important to understand the factors that are connecting the health of the organization's employees and the corporate performance.

In the U.S. Chamber of Commerce study, a new concept was introduced with regard to corporate health: *presenteeism.* It suggests that there are instances of diminished worker productivity on the job attributable to employee poor health conditions. This leads to an increased concern that unmanaged health conditions such as diabetes, migraine headaches, or asthma attacks can affect on-the-job productivity of workers. Thus, negative employee health factors are of concern to many companies.

The saying "an ounce of prevention is worth a pound of cure" suggests that preventive services under the title *wellness programs* should be implemented as a cost-containment measure. As mentioned in the U.S. Chamber of Commerce study, Intel's president and CEO, Paul Otellini,[7] talks about a landmark study done by the Partnership for Prevention. In the study, they assessed the impact of 25 preventive

---

[6] Leading by Example, Leading Practices for Employee Health Management, U.S. Chamber of Commerce and the Partnership for Prevention, 2007.

[7] Ibid.

health services recommended by the U.S. Preventive Services Task Force and the Advisory Committee on Immunization Practices.[8] Preventive services recommended included

- Tobacco-use screening/brief intervention
- Colorectal cancer screening
- Hypertension screening
- Influenza immunization
- Problem drinking screening/brief counseling
- Cervical cancer screening
- Cholesterol screening

The report suggests that companies that are instituting healthcare cost-containment measures should examine their current healthcare benefit programs and determine whether coverage gaps exist with respect to preventive services. If the gaps do exist, they should fill the gaps with the addition of the highest-priority preventive services. They should also consider providing incentives for preventive healthcare by reducing out-of-pocket costs for preventive services. They should also educate employees proactively on the value of preventive services and the resources provided under the company-sponsored healthcare plan.

It has also been suggested that companies need to add a health-promotion program as part of their healthcare cost-containment efforts. "The main goals of health promotion are to reduce health risks and optimize health and productivity while lowering total health-related costs," says Andrew N. Liveris, chairman and CEO of Erickson Retirement Communities in the same U.S. Chamber of Commerce and Partnership for Prevention report.[9] A health-promotion program includes

---

[8] Maciosek, M.V., Coffield, A.B., Edwards, N.M., Goodman, M.J., Flottemesch, T.J., and Solberg, L.I., "Priorities among effective clinical preventive services: Results of a systematic review and analysis," *American Journal Preventive Medicine,* Vol. 31, No. 1, 2006, pp. 52–56, http://www.prevent.org/data/files/initiatives/prioritiesamongeffectiveclinicalpreventivesvcsresultsofreviewandanalysis.pdf

[9] Ibid.

- Health education
- Supportive environments
- Integration with the company's ongoing programs and structures
- Health screening

In an effort to promote wellness, companies provide employees with health coaches and risk assessments. Individuals who meet wellness goals are rewarded with discounts off annual premiums. Firms also sponsor wellness committees whose job is to create awareness and to develop promotional and competitive activities. The idea is to engage employees by encouraging each other to stay healthy in an effort to contain the costs as well as increase employee engagement and at the same time increase productivity.

Finally, proponents of organizational wellness programs suggest that return on investment on dollars spent for wellness programs can be much above 100%. It is better to pay for preventive medicine than to spend large sums of money on catastrophic illnesses. That argument is hard to refute.

Other Cost Containment Alternatives

In addition to the core concepts that have been reviewed so far, other healthcare cost-containment measures include the following:

- **Discount drug programs:** Many large retailers (for instance, Wal-Mart) have deep-discount prescription drug programs. Companies should offer the programs to employees and then encourage employees to use the programs. A significant employee participation in such programs can assist organizations with their healthcare costs-containment programs.

- **Spousal coverage:** An employee's spouse can often secure coverage at his or her own place of employment. In these cases, organizations have a provision in their plans stating that if an employee's spouse has comparable coverage available at their place of employment the employee's employer will not cover the spouse. Some companies impose a surcharge in these situations.

- **Self-funding:** With the costs rising and with uncertainties of the new healthcare reform, organizations are considering self-funding as a real cost-containment alternative.

Forecasting Healthcare Benefit Costs

The final topic this chapter covers is forecasting the cost of healthcare benefit programs for budgeting purposes. After all, if we want to contain costs for this ever-increasing component of the total compensation system, we need to develop accurate forecasts and budgets so that the actual expenses can be compared to the forecasts and budgets and then managed with clarity.

A macro goal for most organizations is that the overall benefit program (including costs of the healthcare benefits) should account for approximately 30% of total compensation costs. This will provide an overall total benefits cost target.

Historical data collection on the breakdown of each benefit line item should be undertaken. Here is a comprehensive list of all the benefit components:

- Legally required benefits mandated by various laws
- Medical benefits
- Disability benefits (mandatory and supplementary)
- Group life insurance (company provided and supplementary)
- Accidental death and dismemberment insurance
- Defined benefit pension plan (if the organization has one)
- Defined contribution pension plan (404(k))
- Vision and dental care plans
- Employee service plans
- Employee advisory services

Here is a step-by-step process to develop a fairly accurate forecast for the healthcare benefit program for an upcoming budget year:

1. Collect data on the historical expenditures for each of the line items listed here. Collect data on as many years as possible (from a data-retrievable-ease point of view).

2. After collecting the data, calculate an average dollar cost across the years.

3. An average dollar cost weighted by the total employee population is desirable.

4. Calculate a total dollar cost for all benefit line items.

5. Calculate a percentage for each line item cost of the total weighted average cost.

6. Determine the 30% total benefits cost target with the assistance of the accounting department for the budget year. This measure is usually called–the benefit burden rate.

7. After deriving the 30% total dollar number, apply the percentage numbers calculated in a previous step to the forecasted 30% budgeted total benefits number to determine the budgeted dollar number for each line item benefit budgeted cost.

Using this method, organizations can determine the total budgeted cost for the healthcare benefit plan for the upcoming year, as shown in Exhibit 9-1.

The budgeted healthcare benefits for the upcoming year in this example are $1,960,895. As shown in this exhibit, healthcare benefit costs are the largest line item benefit cost in most organizations. This budgeted healthcare cost number should be used to develop the specifics of the healthcare program next year.

As a final point about healthcare cost containment, most organizations should shop around every year for a better deal for their healthcare dollar. Those who shop may find opportunities to change carriers for better rates. Just because an employer receives a small rate increase from their existing carrier does not mean that all other carriers will charge the same rates. Of course, you must watch out for loss-leading practices. Remember, insurance companies pay benefit brokers, and their motivations are not directed toward earning a lower commission for the benefit of their clients. Instead, they seek to maximize their commission earnings. So, buyer beware!

Exhibit 9-1 Benefit Cost Forecasting

Line Item Benefit	Weighted Historical Average	Percentage (%)	Total Budget Cost	Budgeted Line Item Cost
Legal	$565,000	13.3		$605,102
Medical	1,833,000	43.1		1,960,895
Disability	326,000	7.7		350,322
Life insurance	254,000	6.0		272,978
AD&D	153,000	3.6		163,787
401(k)	655,500	15.4		700,645
Vision	115,000	2.7		122,840
Employee services	226,000	5.3		241,131
Employee advisory	125,000	2.9		131,940
Total weighted average cost	$4,252,500			$4,549,640
Total budget 30% cost			$4,549,640	

Key Concepts in This Chapter

- Consumer-driven healthcare
- Health savings accounts
- Health reimbursement accounts
- Flexible spending accounts
- Utilization reviews
- Utilization management
- Healthcare cost-containment challenges
- Corporate wellness programs
- Forecasting healthcare benefit programs
- Precertification reviews
- Concurrent reviews
- Retrospective reviews

10

The Accounting and Financing of Retirement Plans

Aims and objectives of this chapter

- Establish a framework for employer-sponsored pension plans
- Further explain the difference between defined-benefit and defined-contribution pension plans
- Discuss the accounting for pension plans
- Review the accounting of defined contribution pension plans
- Explain accounting issues surrounding loans under defined contribution pension plans
- Discuss the accounting of defined benefit pension plans
- Explain the concept of income-replacement ratio
- Explain the reasons for the decrease in the use of defined benefit pension plans
- Explain the role of the actuary in the determination of defined benefit plan costs
- Discuss all the components involved in the accounting of defined-benefit pension plans
- Explain all elements of the pension benefit obligation
- Explain the accumulated benefit obligation
- Explain the vested benefit obligation
- Explain the projected benefit obligation
- Discuss the role of Pension Benefit Guarantee Corporation
- Examine the elements involved in accounting for the PBO changes

- Discuss the elements involved in the accounting for pension plan assets
- Explain the reasons for underfunding of defined benefit pension plans
- Explain the elements involved in the accounting for the annual pension expense
- Explore the components of the pension expense
- Review pension plan journal entries and financial statement requirements
- Review the accounting standards governing pension plan accounting

Pension funds in the United States are the largest source of accumulated investment funds. These pension funds control about one fourth of the stock market. Pension costs of an organization constitute one of the largest expenditures of any organization. The organizational liability to provide benefits is huge. Therefore, accounting for these expenditures is a very important organizational responsibility. The responsibility is normally shared between the *human resource* (HR) department and the accounting department.

The Background

So, pension plans are employer-sponsored programs providing benefits to retired employees for services provided to the employer during working years. From an accounting point of view, there are two entities here: the sponsoring employer and the pension plan itself. The pension plan's role is to receive contributions from employers, administer the pension plan assets, and make payments to retired employees. When employers contribute to the pension plan, they are funding the plan. Some pension plans are contributory, where an employee bears some of costs of the plan. Other plans are noncontributory, where the employer bears the entire cost of the plan. Note that the pension plan is a separate legal and accounting entity from the sponsoring company.

Individuals accumulate pension funds in an attempt to ensure old-age financial security, when that person will not be able to continue with gainful economic employment. Therefore, the goal is to collect funds so that when the retirement comes around there will be enough of a passive income that will enable retirees and their partners to live a risk-free and comfortable life, without financial concerns. The idea is to replace earned wages with this source of income at retirement.

Living costs do not have to continue at the preretirement levels; pension planners usually target an income-replacement ratio at retirement of around 70% to 80% of the preretirement income. To achieve that goal, individuals save and invest in stocks, bonds, *certificates of deposit* (CDs), and so on for the sole purpose of saving for retirement.

From an individual's point of view, because of many uncontrollable factors, effective retirement planning suggests a three-prong approach to old-age income security: private savings and investments, government Social Security (less secure day by day), and employer-provided retirement programs.

This is where employer-sponsored retirement plans come in. Companies sponsor retirement programs to provide employees with a sense of security, to create a satisfied and motivated workforce. Sometimes, based on collective bargaining agreements, employers are obligated to provide retirement benefits.

Employers also are motivated to sponsor retirement programs because of specific tax advantages derived from such programs. Employer-sponsored retirement programs that comply with the *Employee Retirement Income Security Act* (ERISA) are called qualified plans because they qualify for tax advantages for the employer. An employer is allowed to take an immediate tax deduction for contributions made into a pension fund within specified limits.

There is also a tax benefit because pension fund assets are accumulated on a tax-free basis. The employee is not taxed on a current basis for contributions they make or are made on their behalf by their employers until they retire and start receiving the retirement benefits. The earnings of the pension funds are also not taxed until benefits are received, which is usually after retirement age. *Individual retirement accounts* (IRAs), Roth IRAs, and company-sponsored 401(k) plans all are tax-advantaged plans. In other words, contributions to these plans are made with before-tax dollars.

For all these reasons, understanding the accounting, finance, and tax aspects of these programs is a must for all those involved in these plans (that is, those who are responsible for the design, development, and administration of the plans), irrespective of their functional designations or their core competencies.

Participation in employer-sponsored retirement plans in the United States grew from 43 million in 1997 to 86 million in 2007.[1] This growth in participation in employer-sponsored retirement plans is directly correlated with the expansion of workers who participated in defined contribution plans (for example, 401(k) plans). Between calendar years 1977 and 2007, the number of participants in defined contribution plans increased 358% compared to a 31% decrease in defined benefit plans. More than two-thirds of workers covered by pension plans are covered by defined-contribution pension plans now. Note, however, that in the United States, 88% of public employees are still covered by a defined-benefit pension plan.[2]

In the private sector, defined benefit plans are certainly on a downward trend with respect to the number of these plans. The reasons are as follows:

- Governmental regulations make defined benefit pension plans administratively complicated.
- Employers do not want the risk of the future with respect to defined-benefit pension plans.
- Long-term "one-employer" employment is not the norm any more.

Although decreasing in numbers, the understanding of the accounting and financing implications of defined benefit pension plans remains an important area of study.

---

[1] Treasury Inspector General for Tax Administration, Statistical Trends in Retirement Plans, August 9, 2010, Reference Number: 2010-10-097.

[2] "City employees' golden years start too soon." Opinion editorial. Statesman.com. May 7, 2009.

Defined Contribution and Defined Benefit Pension Plans "Defined"

Before we go any further, let's define the concepts of defined contribution and defined benefit pension plans, which have also been discussed in the previous chapters.

Defined Contribution Pension Plans

In a defined contribution pension plan, the employee contributes an amount voluntarily and regularly on a before-tax basis. The contributions are then invested, based on the employee's choice, usually in various company-approved investment instruments. There is an annual limit for employee contributions imposed by the government. The limit for employee contributions to a defined contribution plan for the year 2013 is $17,500, up from $17,000 in 2012. The employer normally agrees to match the employee's contribution by a fixed matching contribution amount. The retirement distributions, upon reaching retirement age, then depend on the size of the accumulated funds in the defined contribution plan.

Defined Benefit Pension Plans

Defined benefit plans promise participants a fixed retirement benefit established by a predefined formula. Factors that are considered in the equation include:

- Years of service
- A compensation amount (either final career average pay or the pay level in the year immediately before retirement)
- Age

Such pension plans have to ensure sufficient funds are available to pay out the defined benefit when disbursement of funds to participants is required.

The Accounting of the Plans

Currently, the basic accounting standards requires that the cost of providing postemployment retirement benefits be recognized when the employee is in active service, rather than when the company actually pays those benefits.[3]

The Accounting for Defined Contribution Plans

Employers offering defined contribution plans may promise the participant a fixed matching contribution based on the contribution made by the employee. The employer may agree to match each year and deposit the employee contribution into a trust fund based on a formula. The formula might consider factors such as age, length of employee service, and the compensation level of the employee. There are several variations of defined contribution plans, such as money purchase plans, thrift plans, and 401(k) plans. Over 70% of American workers participate in 401(k) plans, with over $2 trillion invested in 401(k) plans. 401(k) plans are now the most commonly used form for the accumulation of retirement savings.

Defined contribution plans can also be tied into company performance, as in profit-sharing plans, 401(k) profit-sharing plans, and incentive savings plans. The retirement benefits that an employee finally collects under a defined contribution plan depend on the amounts contributed to the plan over the years and the investment performance of the funds.

Accounting for defined contribution plans is fairly straightforward. Each year, the employer records a pension expense equal to the amount the organization contributes to the plan. On the income statement, the amount of the contribution is recorded as an operating expense (typically under Selling, General, and Administrative Expenses) in the period the employee provides the employment services to have earned the contribution.

Suppose that a defined contribution plan promises an annual contribution of 5% of the employee's salary. If the total employee base payroll of those who have elected to participate in the company sponsored 401(k) plan is $10 million, the accounting entry is as follows:

---

[3] Most Intermediate Accounting books cover the subject of pension plan accounting. The explanation in this book relies primarily, but not exclusively, on material from: Spiceland, J. David, James Sepe, Mark Nelson, and Lawrence Tomassini, *Intermediate Accounting, 5th Edition*, McGraw-Hill Irwin, New York, 2009.

| Pension Expense | 500,000 | |
| Cash ($10,000,000 × 5%) | | 500,000 |

If the employer recognizes and records pension expense on a monthly basis (a more likely scenario), the monthly journal entry will be as follows:

| Pension Expense | 41,667 | |
| Cash | | 41,667 |

In most companies, the contribution is "matched" with the employee's base salary. Including the many other elements of cash compensation for matching purposes will introduce too much variability to the pension expense.

In some instances, if the employer chooses to contribute less than the contracted amount to the plan, a pension liability is accrued for these expenses. However, when the employer pays more than the obligated amount to the plan, the employer records a pension asset. On the balance sheet, if the contribution is paid in the same period as the employee earns the benefit, no entries are necessary. If service-related benefits are earned in one period but are expensed in the next, however, the company must record a liability for the amount of the contribution until it is expensed in the income statement. This amount typically falls under Accrued Salary or Other Accrued Expenses.

If the company has recorded a pension payable and makes the contribution at the end of a year, the company then debits Pension Payable (that is, decreases liability) and credits Cash.

Note also that these accounting entries need to be made as and when the employee earns the company contributions by completing the requisite service period. If the plan contract indicates that the company will match up to a certain percentage of employee salary as and when the employee makes his or her contribution, it can be assumed that the service period has been completed. It is important to note that the accounting record keeping is different from the vesting of the employer contributions, which in most plans happens only after the employee has completed a specific employment period. This period in most defined contribution plans is usually three to five years.

Also note that under a defined contribution plan the amount of the employee's retirement income depends on how well the funds in the employee's account do over time. The employee bears all the risk of uncertain investment returns. Therefore, investment portfolio strategic choice becomes critical.

Loans under the Plan

IRS regulations allow loans to be taken out from one's 401(k) accounts. The plan document has to have a provision for such loans. A loan will not be taxable if certain conditions are met.

Generally, a participant may borrow up to 50% of the vested account balance. The loan has to be repaid to the plan within five years, unless the loan was to buy the principal home of the 401(k) account holder. Loans need to be repaid regularly, at least quarterly, over the life of the loan. 401(k) account balances are lowered for loans if there was already a loan outstanding during previous one year before the new loan. Certain participant loans can be considered taxable distributions.

Prior to September 2010, *Financial Accounting Standards Board* (FASB) guidance allowed participant loans to be classified as plan investments as per 962-325-45-10. Subtopic 962-325 stated that these loans be generally measured at fair value. In practice, though, most participant loans were carried at their unpaid principal balance plus any accrued but unpaid interest, which was considered a good faith approximation of fair value. And because some parties raised issues with the fair value determination, the standard was revised as of September 2010. These parties questioned whether the standard as written conformed to the requirement to use observable inputs, such as market interest rates, borrower's credit risk, and historical default rates, to estimate the fair value of participant loans.

So, the current revised standard and guidance indicates that loans to participants be classified as notes receivable from participants. FASB suggested that the guidance now would reduce the amount of time that plan administrators spend on estimating the fair value of participant loans using observable inputs. The classification of participant loans as notes receivable from participants acknowledges that participant loans are unique from other investments in that a participant taking out such a loan essentially borrows against his or her own individual vested benefit account balance.

Also in the discussion about the revised standard it was concluded that it is more meaningful to measure participant loans at their unpaid principal balance plus any accrued but unpaid interest rather than at fair value. Participant loans cannot be sold by the plan. Furthermore, if a participant were to default, the unpaid balance of the loan would reduce the participant's account, and there would be no effect on the plan's investment returns or any other participant's account balance.[4]

401(k) plan's distribution rules are well-defined in IRS regulations. There are specific rules for hardship withdrawals also.

The Accounting for Defined Benefit Pension Plans

Defined benefit plans are based on a predetermined benefit formula. These benefits usually depend on the employee's years of service and on the compensation level of the employees close to retirement. The company has to determine what they should contribute today using the time value of money. The funding method used should ensure that sufficient funds are available in the plan to pay the required benefit when the need arises.

In a defined benefit plan, the employees receive the specified benefits when they retire and they are the beneficiaries of the defined benefit trust. The trust's main objective is the safeguard and proper investment of the accumulated funds so that there is enough to cover the obligations to pay the retirement benefits. Although the pension trust is a separate entity from the employer, the trust assets belong to the employer, and the employer is responsible to pay the defined benefits no matter what the financial position of the trust when benefits have to be paid. So, the employer has to make up any deficiencies in the trust and make up any shortfalls when needed. When there are excesses in the trust, the employer can recapture those excesses either by reducing future funding or taking the excess funds out for

---

[4] Adapted from Financial Accounting Series, Accounting Standards update, No. 2010, September 25, 2010, Plan Accounting–Defined Contribution Pension Plans (Topic 962), Reporting Loans to Participants by Defined Contribution Pension Plans, a consensus of the FASB Emerging Issue Task Force.

other uses. Thus, the employer is at risk with the defined benefit plan because it is their responsibility to ensure that sufficient funds have been accumulated in the defined benefit trust to pay employees' retirement benefits based on the predetermined formula when needed.

The annual predetermined benefit formula normally starts off with an acceptable income replacement ratio (percentage of preretirement income that will be replaced after retirement).[5] The conceptual reasoning behind the income-replacement percentage factor is the percentage of preretirement income the retired person needs to sustain the same standard of living he or she enjoyed before retiring. Logic suggests that the percentage needed is something below 100%. This is because the retired person does not have same types of expenditures in retirement (for example, employment expenses, commuting expenses, child-rearing expenses, and food expenses for a family with children). Therefore, this is usually a policy decision, and in a unionized organization it is often a matter of bargaining negotiations.

The annual benefit pension formula consists of various factors: an average employee salary (either final year, or career average salary, or final five- or ten-year salary), years of credited service, and a preestablished percentage factor such as 1.0%, or 1.5%, or 2.5%. The acceptable formula for any organization needs to be derived using an iterative calculation method with the ultimate goal of achieving the policy-driven income-replacement ratio. Additional factors that go into the calculation are mortality estimates and the estimated number of retirement years before the employee dies.

An example of a derived annual defined benefit formula is shown here.

2.5% × final five year average salary × years of credited service = the retirement benefit lump sum amount.

---

[5] The theory behind the income-replacement ratio is that a retiring employee can sufficiently manage to live the preretirement standard of living at less than 100% of preretirement income because their living expenses are not as high as they were in their earlier years (no children at home, no employment-related expenses, and so forth).

So, an employee who retires after 35 years of credited service and whose final five-year average salary is $150,000 would receive an annual retirement benefit of

$$2.5\% \times 35 \times \$150,000 = \$131,250$$

This works out to be an income-replacement ratio of 87.5%, which is an acceptable income-replacement ratio. Sometimes the calculated lump-sum retirement benefit is (in the preceding example, $ 131,250) distributed via an annuity.

Note that as a result of union negotiations, organizations have inserted different twists to the income-replacement percentage factor. Here is how the *California State Teachers' Retirement System* (CalSTRS) describes this income-replacement factor:

> The age factor is the percent of final compensation to which you are entitled for each year of service credit, determined by your age on the last day of the month in which your retirement is effective. It is set at 2% at age 60. The age factor is decreased if you retire before age 60 and increased to a maximum of 2.4% if you retire later than age 60. If you retire with at least 30 years of earned service credit, a 0.2% career factor will be added to your age factor, up to a maximum age factor of 2.4%.[6]

Some organizations call this income-replacement factor a retirement factor; others call it the age factor. Conceptually and theoretically, however, the need for this factor in the defined benefit pension formula is as what has been proposed here: an income replacement percentage (a percentage of preretirement income needed by the retiree to live at the same standard of living he or she enjoyed before retiring). Manipulating this factor to fit self-serving needs just increases the costs of these programs. No wonder private employers are moving away from defined benefit pension plans. This manipulation of the income replacement ratios adds to the "black box" nature of defined benefit pension plans.

---

[6] California Teachers' Association Retirement Employee Web site: http://ctainvest. org/home/CalSTRS-CalPERS/about-calstrs/calstrs-retirement-benefit.aspx.

Note that in plans where the defined benefit formula uses the final average pay it is possible to make the final average pay artificially high, thus deriving a retirement income level that is higher than pre-retirement income. One can add overtime pay, accumulated vacation pay, expense reimbursements, and other items to make final pay very high. This results in a high level of defined benefit formula generated retirement income. In these situations, the retiree ends up at an income level that is higher than his or her employment period income level. In essence, they get paid more for not working. The logic of such expenditures is really hard to comprehend. This is an issue that is generating a lot public displeasure with the California Public Service employee defined benefit retirement programs.

But more assumptions, covered with uncertainties, have to be made to accumulate enough funds to be able to distribute the promised benefits using the predetermined formula. Also note that these defined benefits are contractually promised to the retiring employee. The assumptions cover the rate of return on plan assets, employee turnover impacting the number of eligible employees, the actual retirement age when the employee retires (which will impact the length of the retirement period benefits will need to be paid out), inflation rates, salary-increase trends resulting in future salary levels, and interest rates.

All of these unknowns, assumptions, calculations, and the use of a fairly arbitrary defined benefit formula can make defined benefit plans a complicated, uncertain, and very expensive black box.

Defined benefit pension plans have suffered from many structural issues. Because many assumptions are used in the calculations, these assumptions need to be continually adjusted for changing financial conditions. In addition, pension investment targets have not been met regularly. Pension liabilities have increased, but pension assets have not kept pace. All of these factors and many others have caused the decrease in the incidence of defined benefit pension plans, at least in the private sector. Nevertheless, as long as these plans exist, there is a need to study the structure from a finance and accounting perspective.

The calculation of the retirement benefit expenses, obligations, liabilities, and the determination of the formula is the responsibility of an actuary. An actuary is professionally trained and certified in a particular branch of mathematics and statistics. They assign probabilities to future events and calculate the organization's defined benefits plan assets and liabilities. Employers depend on actuaries for assistance with developing, implementing, and funding of pension plans. However, these calculations involve a lot of subjectivity. Therefore, the actual numbers end up deviating from calculated figures. This necessitates a lot of adjustments to assumptions to ensure that there are sufficient accumulated funds to pay the promised benefits. The actuary works in a challenging environment, in that the accounting estimates of liabilities and expenses need to be created for cash payments that may occur years in the future. Forecasting has many perils.

The risk of the pension-obligation amount increasing from amounts previously calculated is borne by the employer because in a defined benefit plan a fixed predetermined formula is used. Over the years, the uncertainties of the economic environment and the volatility in the financial markets have resulted in changing pension asset balances. Pension investments have not performed as well as expected. The employer's financial inability to fund the plan regularly has prevented plans from making up funding deficiencies. The shareholders have been confronted with large amounts of unfunded pension liabilities. This has often resulted in weak balance sheets.

Also, falling interest rates and bear markets have wreaked havoc with pension plans, creating a "pensions crisis." The pension plans of many companies have been severely underfunded, as a result companies, such as United Airlines, have had to file for bankruptcy, stating that it is not possible for them to meet their pension obligations. For all these reasons, FASB reformed pension accounting and in 2006 passed a new standard (SFAS 158), in part to fix the problems with pension accounting. The scene has not been pretty! We discuss the FASB standards governing defined benefit pension plans later in the chapter.

The Accounting for Defined Benefit Plans Explained

From an accounting point of view, the key elements to consider in defined benefit plan accounting are as follows:

- The obligation of the employer to pay the retirement benefit when the employee retires at a future date
- The accumulation of assets in the pension plan to pay retirement benefits from, as, and when the participating employee retires
- The periodic expense of offering and maintaining a pension plan

Currently, the expense items are not reported individually in the financial statements, but the pension obligation is netted against pension assets, and the net amount has to be shown as a line item on the balance sheet. The individual balances are reported separately in the footnote disclosures. Also, a calculated pension expense needs to be shown as an operating expense on the income statement. The expense is a composite of the periodic changes in both the plan obligations and the plan assets. The components of the pension expense are as follows:

- The service cost related to employee service during a specific period.
- The interest accrued on the pension liability during a given period.
- The impact of the return on plan assets, on the balances. If this is negative, it reduces the pension expense. The opposite is true if the returns are positive.
- The increased impact of the amortization of prior service cost attributed to employee service.
- Either the positive or negative impact of the losses or gains from revisions in the pension liability or from investing the plan assets.

We now take a closer look at the pension obligation and the pension asset. Then we review the components of the pension expense.

The Pension Benefit Obligation

The employer's pension obligation is the deferred obligation the employer has to its employees for the service they have rendered satisfying the terms of the pension plan. There are various ways of measuring that obligation.

The different measurement methods for the benefit obligations are as follows:

- **The vested benefit obligation (VBO):** This is the amount of the accumulated benefit obligation that plan participants are entitled to receive regardless of whether they discontinue their current employment with their present employer or not (the vested pension benefits). Pension plans usually require a minimum years of service before the employee attains the vested benefits status. The calculation is made at the current salary levels. Since 1989, the plan provisions should indicate that benefits must vest (1) completely within five years or (2) 20% within three years with another 20% vesting each subsequent year until full vesting within seven years.

- **The accumulated benefit obligation (ABO):** This is the amount estimated by the actuary of the discounted present value of the retirement benefits earned by employees as of the valuation date, using the current compensation level of those employees and the plan's pension formula. The measurement here is based on both the vested and nonvested years of service. The current salaries are used in this calculation.

- **The projected benefit obligation (PBO):** The amount the actuary calculates as the present value of vested and nonvested benefits accrued to date based on all the employees' projected salaries at retirement. The accounting profession has adopted the *projected benefit obligation* (PBO) as the measure for overall pension liability of an organization.

  Another way of looking at the projected benefit obligation is the build-up method. Three components form the total pension benefit obligation. The summary given in Exhibit 10-1 should further clarify the three elements of the total pension benefit obligation.

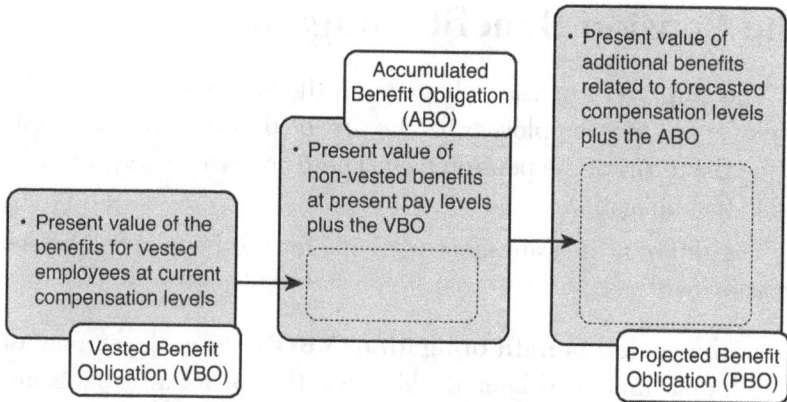

Exhibit 10-1 The Build-up Method for the PBO

A Note about the Pension Benefit Guarantee Corporation

The *Pension Benefit Guarantee Corporation* (PBGC) was established under the ERISA legislation as a governmental insurance entity to which qualified plans pay a premium for each participant enrolled in a plan. The role of the PBGC was to serve as a payer of last resort for retirement benefits in case of a plan default due to a bankruptcy. The maximum pension benefit guaranteed by PBGC is set by law and adjusted yearly. For plans that end in 2011, under PBGC's insurance program for single-employer plans, workers who retire at age 65 can receive up to $4,500 per month (or $54,000 per year).[7] PBGC's role is similar to the role that the *Federal Deposit Insurance Corporation* (FDIC) plays in the banking sector. For 2011, the premium rate is $9 per participant for multiemployer plans; single-employer plans pay $35 per participant plus $9 for each $1,000 of unfunded vested benefits. The per-participant rates are indexed for inflation.[8]

Note that during fiscal year 2010 the PBGC paid $5.6 billion in benefits to participants of failed pension plans. That year, 147 pension plans failed, and the PBGC's deficit increased 4.5% to $23 billion. The PBGC has a total of $102.5 billion in obligations and $79.5 billion in assets.[9] Not a pretty picture!

[7] "Maximum monthly guarantee tables." Pension Benefit Guaranty Corporation.
[8] Federal Register, Vol. 72, No. 230, November 30, 2007, Notices 67765.000.
[9] "Insurer reports wider annual deficit," *Washington Post,* November 16, 2010.

The Projected Benefit Obligation

Note the defined benefit formula might indicate that the final average salary or the final-year salary needs to be used. To calculate the projected benefit obligation, the actuary projects the salary levels using an estimate of future salary increases. Using the salary projection, the actuary creates an estimate of the final average pay or the final-year salary. The projections for salary levels are used to project the benefit obligation liability.

Let's look at an example of the calculations for the different pension obligation measures using ten employees.

Let's suppose that the Safari Group hired ten employees in 1995. The company has a defined benefit pension plan with the predefined benefit formula as follows:

2.0% × Final year salary × Years of credited service

Let's now say that all ten employees are scheduled to retire in 2030 after 35 years of service. These employees' retirement period is estimated to be on the average 30 years (we are taking an average here for simplicity; in actuality, the actuary would do the calculation separately for each employee). At the end of 2005, after ten years of service, the base salaries of the ten employees totaled $700,000. The projected salary at retirement for the ten employees totaled $1,465,645. The average salary increase assumption being used here is 3.0% per year. The interest rate assumption for this example is 4%.

So, what is the projected benefit obligation for the ten employees?

1. First, determine retirement benefits earned to date (after ten years of services at the end of year 2005):

   2.0% × 10 years × $1,465,645 = $293,129 (or $ 29,313 per person per year)

2. Next, find the present value of the retirement benefits as of the retirement date:

   n= 30 years; i =4%; $293,129 × 17.29203* = $5,068,795 ($506,880 per person)

   Retirement benefits are scheduled to be paid out for 30 years.

   *Note 1: Using appropriate PV tables discount factor for 30 years; present value of an ordinary annuity of $1.

3. Next, find the present value of retirement benefits as of the current date:

n = 25 years; i = 4%; \$5,068,795 × .37512° = \$1,901,406
(\$190,141 per person PBO at the end of year 2005)

°**Note 2:** Using appropriate PV tables discount factor for 25 years; present value of \$1.

From year to year, the estimate for the projected benefits obligation changes. This is because the actuary has to add an additional year of service and the participating employee is one year closer to retirement. So, the present value increases. The other factors that change the PBO estimate from year to year are the gains or losses on pension assets, prior service cost, and the benefits paid to employees who retired during the current year.

So, the PBO changes because of the following:

- **Service cost:** At the end of a year, an additional year has expired for pension obligation calculation purposes. So, the change in the pension obligation reflects the increase in the PBO estimate resulting from the additional year of service. Another year of service will change the calculations in this manner:

  At the end of the year 2006, the calculations demonstrated for the ten employees will change in this manner:

  1. 2.0% × 11 years × \$1,465,645 = \$322,442 (or \$32,244 per person per year)

  2. n = 30 years, i = 4.0%; \$322,442 × 17.29203° = \$5,575,677 (or \$557,568 per person)

  °**Note 3:** the same discount factor for 30 years shown in the previous calculation.

  3. n = 24 years, i = 4.0%; \$5,575,677 × .39012° = \$2,175,183 (\$217,518 per person PBO at the end of the year 2006)

  °**Note 4:** Using appropriate PV tables discount factor for 24 years; present value of \$1.

The PBO has increased from \$1,901,406 to \$2,175,183; an increase of \$273,777 (\$27,378 per person).

- **Interest cost:** Another reason the PBO estimate increases is because of interest cost. Because the PBO is a liability, interest on the liability changes from year to year. This estimate is calculated by multiplying the discount rate by the PBO balance existing at the beginning of the year. The calculations in Exhibit 10-2 demonstrate that PBO changes are reflecting an additional service year and the interest cost for the ten employees.

Exhibit 10-2 PBO at the end of 2006

PBO at the end of the year 2005 is	\$1,901,406
Additional year of service cost: 2.0% × 1 year × \$1,465,645 × 17.29203 × .39012 =	\$197,745
Interest cost = \$1,901,406 × 4% =	\$76,056
PBO at the end of year 2006 =	\$2,175,207°

°(Rounding difference)

- **Prior service cost:** Sometimes the sponsoring organization might amend the plan during a given year by changing the plan formula. When the new defined benefit formula is applied during the current year, the PBO estimate changes. The estimate going forward might either increase or decrease. Plan designers might designate these benefit plan changes to be on a proactive (going forward) or retroactive (going back) basis. The PBO estimates made during the current period can change based on the retroactive or the proactive designation. This change element is called the prior service cost change. To demonstrate how the plan changes affect the pension benefit obligation when changes are made on a retroactive basis, consider the calculation for the ten employee example shown here.

Let's say in our example plan design changes the benefit formula (changed January 2, 2006) as follows:

2.5% × Years of credited service × Final year pay (instead of 2%)

Now we see how the formula change affects the PBO:

1. 2.5% × $1,465,645 × 10 years = $366,411
2. $366,411 × 17.29203° = $6,335,990
3. $6,335,990 × .37512° = $2,376,766

Prior service cost then is = $2,376,766 − $1,901,406 = $475,360 ($47,536 per person)

°Note 4: From PV tables discount factors (see previous explanations).

So, now we see the PBO at the end of the year 2006 as shown in Exhibit 10-3.

Exhibit 10-3 PBO at the end of year 2006 with formula change

PBO beginning of the year 2006	$1,901,406
Prior Service Cost	$475,360
PBO including prior service cost at the beginning of 2006	$2,376,766
Now service cost for the year 2006: 2.5% × 1 year × $1,465,645 × 17.29203 × .39012	$247,149
and interest cost = $2,376,766 × 4%	$95,071
PBO at the end of the year 2006	$2,718,986

$2,718,986 is changed from $2,175,207 because of formula change.

Let's assume that in our example it is now year 2007. The end of year 2007 calculation is (for the ten person case) as shown in Exhibit 10-4.

Exhibit 10-4 PBO at the end of 2007

PBO at the beginning of the year 2007	$2,718,986
Service cost for the year 2007 is: 2.5% × 1 year × $1,465,645 × 17.2903˚ × .40573˚	$257,045
Interest cost $2,718,986 × 4%	$108,759
PBO at the end of the year 2007	$3,102,790

˚**Note 5:** From PV tables discount factors for 30 years and 23 years, respectively.

- **Gain or loss on the PBO:** If the actuary revises his or her calculation assumptions during the current year, this might result in a gain or a loss. The actuary might change the following assumptions:
  - A change of life expectancy
  - The assumption as to when retirement will actually occur
  - A change made in the assumed discount rate

If any of these assumption changes are executed, the PBO obligation can show a gain or a loss. Let's see an example of this factor in the ten-employee example we are using.

Now let's assume that a change is made for the final-year salary from $1,465,645 to $1,550,000 in the year 2007.

The PBO with the revision will be as follows

2.5% × 12 years × $1,550,000 = $465,000

$465,000 × 17.29203˚ = $8,039,990

$8,039,990 × .40573˚ = $3,262,065

˚**Note 6:** From PV tables discount factors for 30 years and 23 years, respectively.

The PBO increase because of the revised assumption to final-year salary by = $3,262,065 − $3,102,790 = $159,275 ($15,928 per person).

Exhibit 10-5 shows a summary of the change.

Exhibit 10-5 PBO end of year 2007 with Salary assumption increase

PBO at the beginning of the year 2007	$2,718,207
Service Cost	$257,045
Interest Cost	$108,759
Salary Assumption Increase (or loss on PBO)	$159,275
PBO at the end of 2007	$3,243,286

- **Payment of retirement benefits:** This is the change in the PBO that takes place when employees retire during the current period and retirement benefits are paid out to these employees resulting in reducing the pension benefit obligation.

So, in summary, the PBO changes because of the factors listed in Exhibit 10-6.

Exhibit 10-6 Factors affecting PBO

Service cost =	(+)
Interest cost =	(+)
Prior service cost =	(+)
Increase or decrease due to revisions =	(+/−)
Retiree benefits paid =	(−)

Aggregate Calculation

Our example here has focused the calculations for ten employees only for ease of understanding. Normally, the actuary makes the estimates and projections for the entire employee population covered under the defined benefit pension plan.

Let's assume that the aggregate (total of all employees) calculations for the Safari Group are as shown in Exhibit 10-7. The changes in the PBO for the Safari Group during the year 2007 are shown; all amounts are assumed.

Exhibit 10-7 Aggregate PBO Calculations

	$ in millions
PBO at the beginning of the year	166
Service cost, 2007	10
Interest cost, 2007 $166 mil. × 4%	6.6
Less (gain) on PBO	6
Less: Retiree benefits paid	(5)
PBO at the end of the year 2007	$183.6

Pension Plan Assets

Calculation of the pension obligation is one thing, regardless of whether the obligation is the vested benefit obligation, or the accumulated benefit obligation, or the projected benefit obligation. The other thing is having enough funds to pay the obligations when necessary.

So, the defined benefit plan has to accumulate enough assets to be able pay the benefit obligations. The balances in the pension plan assets have to be reported in the footnotes of the company's financial statements.

A trustee holds the assets of the pension plan. The pension plan trustee accepts the employer's contribution to the plan and invests the funds accumulated and pays out pension benefits to retired employees. The trustee is normally a bank or a company that provides services as a pension plan trustee. The trustee, on the advice of a pension plan advisor, invests pension plan assets in stocks, bonds, and other types of income-producing assets. The investment advisor or manager influences pension plan investments by directing the trustee to invest the funds as advised.

The investment advisor or manager acts in accordance and within the structure developed by a retirement committee. The retirement committee sets up an appropriate retirement funds investment policy. This committee also establishes the ongoing funding policy for the pension plan. For example, they might lay out a policy that states that the company will fund each year's incremental service cost and also a portion of the prior year's service cost if the plan formula is or has been changed. They will also advise whether retroactivity will be applied. The goal is to ensure that the pension asset balances are sufficient to be able to pay the benefits as and when they become due. The pension plan assets fluctuate based on dividends earned, interest, and market-price appreciation.

Each year, the actuary calculates whether the company needs to contribute more funds to be set aside to pay the benefits. To do this, they need to estimate an expected rate of return that the accumulated funds will produce. This is because the higher the expected return, the more funds will be available to pay out in benefits and the less current contributions will be needed from the company. If the estimate of the expected rate of return does not materialize, the company might need to make additional contributions from general funds to ensure that there are enough pension plan assets to meet the obligations. In the recent past, rate-of-return estimates have been around 3% to 9%, with 6.0% being the median percentage. These are the estimates actuaries have used.

So, during any given calculating period, if the actuary calculates that the plan assets will not suffice to meet the projected benefit obligation, the pension plan is underfunded. Over the past few years, the reality has been that defined benefit plans have remained underfunded. The reasons for underfunding have been many, including the main ones listed here:

- Because of limited cash availability, companies have been unable to continue funding pension plans. Therefore, the underfunding condition has been difficult to remove. The inability to replenish the plan with additional contribution funds got aggravated over the years, and many companies therefore have had to convert defined benefit plans to defined contribution plans or completely disband defined benefit pension plans.

- From year to year, actuaries have found that their assumptions for plan calculations have needed to be revised (and mainly downward). This downward adjustment has been made specifically for the rate-of-return assumption, mainly because investments have suffered from increased market volatility.

- Union pressure to change benefit formulas upward. This has increased the projected pension benefit obligation and increased the underfunding situations.

With the passage of ERISA, minimum funding standards have been introduced to protect plan participants. But the bust and boom scenarios of the stock market have created projected benefit obligation overfunding and underfunding. In addition, companies have diverted pension funds when there has been overfunding situations. The diversion of funds has reduced the long-term viability of the plans over an extended period of time. This has resulted in many firms being in an underfunded situation. Sponsoring companies have had financial troubles, and therefore the pension plans were disbanded. PBGC insurance got triggered. Excessive demands on the PBGC have also negatively impacted the whole system. The PBGC benefit amount in case of a sponsor disbanding their plan is $3,500 a month. Often, this payment is much less than the promised benefit. And because calls to PBGC to pay more and more retirement benefits for bankrupt plans have increased, PBGC has had to increase per-participant premiums. Thus, in a circular manner, the defined benefit plan environment has become problematic, leaving companies no other option than to discontinue defined benefit pension plans and to introduce defined contribution plans instead.

But, there is still no requirement to report pension plan obligations or the accumulated pension plan assets directly in the financial statements in any reporting period. Organizations need to report only the net difference between the two amounts, either as net pension liability or a net pension asset depending on the funding status of the plan.

Let's now demonstrate aggregate calculations with the Safari Group example.

The Safari Group decides that it will fund a portion of each year's service cost. Let's say that the retirement committee has decided to fund the plan with $5 million for the year.

Let's assume that the plan assets at the beginning of the year 2007 were $170 million. The expected return was 7%, but the actual return in 2007 was 8%. And let's assume that the company paid out $2 million in retirement during the year 2007.

Exhibit 10-8 shows the plan's assets at the end of 2007.

Exhibit 10-8 The Plan Assets at Year's End 2007

	$ in millions
Plan assets at the beginning of the year 2007	$170
Return on plan assets 8%	13.6
Cash contributions in 2007	5
Less: Retiree benefits paid	(2)
Plan assets at the end of year 2007	$176.6

And let's assume that the PBO at the end of the year for the entire employee population was $183.6, as indicated in Exhibit 10-7. The plan is now underfunded. Companies are required to recognize on their balance sheets the underfunded or overfunded status of their defined benefit plans. This status is recorded on the balance sheet as the netted amount of the fair values of plan assets and the projected benefit obligation.

The Pension Expense

The pension expense relates directly to the changes in the projected benefit obligation and the change in plan assets discussed in the previous sections. Once calculated, the pension expense is directly reported as a period expense on the current period's income statement. The pension expense reported on the income statement is a combination of changes that took place in the pension obligation, the pension plan assets, and the current-year increase in the employer's obligation attributed to the employee service during the current reporting year. The pension expense then is considered as a current period compensation expense along with other total compensation expenses such as wages, salaries, sales commissions, incentives, bonuses, and the various other forms of compensation discussed in this book. So, in essence, the accounting process is matching all the forms of total compensation with the services provided by employees during that specific time period.

Exhibit 10-9 explains the derivation of the pension expense.

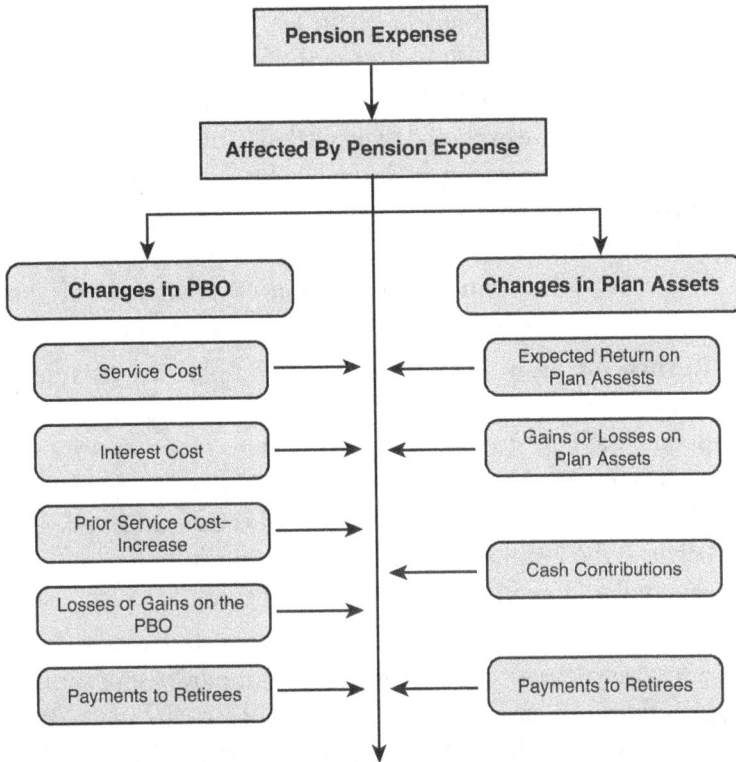

Exhibit 10-9 Factors affecting the Pension Expense

We will now discuss each component of the pension expense:

- **Service cost:** This is the change in the PBO attributable to the employee service that was provided during the current reporting year for which the financial statements are being prepared. More precisely, the service cost is said to be the actuarial present value of retirement benefits based on a predetermined benefit formula applied to the employee service rendered during the past year. FASB has adopted a benefits/year-of-service actuarial method. The important point to note here is that the service cost or the present obligation has to be calculated using the future compensation levels

- **Interest cost:** This is the cost that is calculated by multiplying the actuary's discount rate (interest rate) by the beginning-year projected benefit obligation. This is the interest for the period on the PBO outstanding during the period. FASB states that the assumed discount rate should reflect the rates at which pension benefits are expected to be settled. Companies usually look for rates of return on high-quality fixed-income investments currently available in the market. Note that the interest cost is combined with the other components of the pension expense and reported as part of the pension expense and not shown separately in the income statement as an interest expense.

- **Return on plan assets:** The return on plan assets is derived from investing the plan assets in various investment instruments, such as, stocks, bonds, and various other securities. But each year there has to be a reconciliation of the expected rate of return used versus the actual rate of return achieved. This is because the employer contributions and actual returns on the accumulated pension assets increase the pension plan assets.

We know that if the plan assets are invested wisely and the assets accrue positive returns that the employer sponsoring the plan does not have to contribute as much to the plan. Positive returns reduce the cost of the pension plan, and so the amount to be reported as pension expense will be reduced by positive investment returns. The actual returns earned on the plan's assets increase the fund balance and as a result reduce the employer's cost of providing employee pension benefits.

In the Safari Group example, the expected return is used in deriving the pension expense. In the example, the expected rate of return was 7% on the beginning of the year plan assets of $170 million. $170 million × .07 = $11.9 million.

Then there is the question of how and when to reconcile differences between the actual rate of return and expected rate of return that was used in the estimates. FASB has required that the expected rate of return be used in the calculation of the pension expense. This seems counter logical because the pension expense is reduced by the actual rate of return on plan assets and the charge to pension should reflect the actual return. But

FASB guidance says otherwise. The difference between the actual rate of return and the expected rate of return is considered a gain or a loss on plan assets.

- **Amortization of prior service cost:** If a plan sponsor for whatever reason changes the pension benefit formula during a given reporting year, the actuary has to change the pension benefit obligation to reflect that change. Sometimes a plan sponsor changes the benefit formula during a given year but because of the terms of a union contract or for just good employee relations the plan sponsor agrees to retroactively give credit for prior service years. Of course, such action might not work with the employee if the employer revises the formula downward. In this case, the expedient path would be that the reduced formula would take effect only going forward. In any case, normally the formula is revised upward, with the pension benefit obligation increasing.

But how does the accounting convention treat the increased pension obligation? The increased obligation can be reported entirely as a current period expense in the year of the plan amendment. But under FASB, the increased costs associated with plan amendments cannot all be carried to expense in the year of the amendment but must be amortized. The time period to amortize these costs is over the time the employees who benefit from the changes will work for the company.

Also note that under FASB the unamortized balance of prior service cost is not an asset, although it is being amortized, but it is carried as a shareholder equity account under *accumulated other comprehensive income* (AOCI).

Suppose, for example, that in aggregate the prior service cost (which was explained in the ten-employees example) is $5 million at the beginning of 2007. Also assume that the average service period remaining for all employees at Safari Communications is 15 years. Then, the current-year pension expense for the amortization of prior-year service cost will be as follows:

$5 million / 15 years = $333,333, and this will be the number that will be used as part of this year's pension expense.

- **Amortization of a net loss or net gain:** Gains or losses occur when the assumptions used to calculate both the pension obligations and the pension assets are revised during the current year. Accounting conventions, like the prior service costs, do not allow the entire gain or loss resulting from updating the pension obligation to be reported on the income statement as a pension expense in the year the changes are made. However, it is reported as other comprehensive income on the statement of comprehensive income. Then it is carried as Net Loss – AOCI or a Net Gain – AOCI depending on whether there are greater losses or gains. These amounts are reported as part of AOCI on the balance sheet in the Shareholder's Equity section.

A case can be made that these gains or losses should be shown as part of the current-year earnings because these gains or losses affect the net cost of providing the defined benefit plan. But FASB designates that the income statement recognition for both the gains and losses be delayed.

The current delayed recognition of gains or losses achieves income smoothing, but this stance is not true to the accounting principle, referred to as the matching principle. But the practical justification for the delay principle is the fact that over time, gains and losses cancel each other out. And if that were the case, why subject corporate income statements to nonoperational fluctuations via the changes in the pension benefit account?

So, in any year when the gain or loss is excessive, there needs to be recognition in the pension expense account.

SFAS 87 arbitrarily assigns a 10% threshold to the excess evaluation. When the PBO or the pension asset gain or loss at the beginning of the year is more than the 10% threshold, then there needs to be recognition. This 10% threshold is called a corridor. The corridor states that 10% of either the PBO or the pension asset, whichever is higher at the beginning of the year, will be taken as a pension expense. The excess is charged to income over a period of time and not all at once. The amount of the excess that is charged to income is the excess divided by the average remaining service period of all active employees who would be scheduled to receive retirement benefits. The calculation of the amortized amount for the amortization of a net loss or net gain is shown in Exhibit 10-10.

Let's say that the Safari Group had a cumulative net loss position.

Exhibit 10-10 The Corridor Calculation

Prior Net Loss position (previous losses exceeded previous gains)	$20 mil.
10% of $170 million is greater than 10% of $166 million "the corridor"*	$17 mil.
Excess at the beginning of the year	$ 3 mil.
Average remaining service period	/ 15 years
Amount amortized to 2007 pension expense	$200,000

*°**Note 7:** In the example, the aggregate numbers were $170 million plan assets at the beginning of the year and $166 million PBO at the beginning of the year.

So, for this example, the summary of pension expense in 2007 is as shown in Exhibit 10-11.

Exhibit 10-11 Summary of Pension Expense in 2007

	($ in millions)
Service cost	10
Interest cost	6.6
Expected return on plan assets	(11.9)
Amortization of prior service cost – AOCI	.333
Amortization of net loss – AOCI	.200
Pension expense for 2007	$5,233

Note that numbers for Exhibit 10-11 came from Exhibit 10-7.

So, the Net Loss – AOCI account at the end of 2007 will be as shown in Exhibit 10-12.

Exhibit 10-12 Net Loss – AOCI Account

	($ in millions)
Net Loss – AOCI at the beginning of 2007	20
Less: 2007 amortization	(.333)
Plus: 2007 loss on PBO (assumed for illustration)	3
Less: 2007 gain on plan assets ($13.6m – 11.9m)	(1.7)
Net Loss – AOCI at the end of 2007	$20,967

The Accounting Record-Keeping

Here we include a brief review of the required journal entries for pension accounting. As discussed previously, gains or losses resulting from (1) changing PBO assumption and (2) from the return of assets being either higher or lower than expected are not immediately charged to pension expense in any given year. They are reported as part of *other comprehensive income* (OCI) on the statement of comprehensive income.

If a loss occurs, because of a change in assumption, an increase (credit) in the PBO account is recorded, and an associated decrease (debit) is recorded to the OCI account. If a change in assumption causes a gain in the PBO account, a debit is recorded, and a credit is recorded to the OCI account.

If there is a gain because the actual returns were higher than the expected return, the plan assets increase. The increase in the plan assets is the difference between the expected and the actual return. In this case, the PBO account is debited and a credit entry is made to the OCI account reflecting the gain. If the actual return was the less-than-expected return, a debit entry is made to the OCI account and a credit to plan assets is recorded.

There is also a need to make a change in the prior service account for any new prior service cost when it occurs. For this, a debit entry is made to Prior Service Cost – OCI (increase because of plan revision) and a credit entry is made to the PBO account.

As indicated, prior service cost as well as gains or losses when they occur are reported as OCI on the statement of comprehensive income. The OCI items accumulate as Prior Service Cost – AOCI and net loss (or gain) – AOCI. When this account is amortized, the amortization amounts are also reported in the Statement of Comprehensive Income. Amortization reduces Prior Service Cost – OCI and Net Loss – AOCI. Because these accounts have debit balances, the amortization amounts are credited. Net gain amortization is debited because net gain has a credit balance.

The funded status of the plan is reported in the balance sheet, and that is the difference between the PBO and the plan assets.

When the company contributes additional funds to the plan, the plan assets are debited and cash is credited.

To record a pension expense, the following entries need to be made.

1. Pension expense (debit).

2. Plan assets (expected return on assets) (debit)

3. Amortization of prior service cost – OCI (for a given year) (credit)

4. Amortization of net loss – OCI (for a given year) (credit)

5. PBO (service cost + interest cost) – credit (an increase)

On a typical balance sheet, the Net Pension Liability (which has been explained before) is reported in the Liabilities section of the balance sheet. And in the Shareholder's Equity section, you would find the following accounts reported under Accumulated Other Comprehensive Income:

- Net Loss – AOCI
- Prior Service Cost – AOCI

ERISA, FASB, and *American Institute of Certified Public Accountants* (AICPA) have established requirements for financial statement issuance for defined benefit pension plans. We briefly review these required statements in the next section.

Statement of Accumulated Plan Benefits for Defined Benefit Pension Plans

In addition to other reporting and disclosure requirements, defined benefit pension plans are required to report the actuarial present value of accumulated plan benefits for the beginning and the ending of the plan year. In addition, the change to the *present value of accumulated benefits* (PVAB) from year to year has to be reported. Note that this amount is not the actual plan liability. The PVAB reflects only those benefits that have accumulated as of a specific date. The PVAB can be reported on the same page as the Statement of Net Assets Available for Plan Benefits, or it can be reported in a separate statement. It can also be reported in a footnote. The report needs to show numbers for (1) vested benefits for participants currently receiving benefits, (2) other vested benefits, and (3) nonvested benefits. The method of calculation and significant assumptions used to calculate the PVAB needs to be reported in a footnote.

Statement of Changes in Accumulated Plan Benefits for Defined Benefit Pension Plans

Here information on the changes in the PVAB from the previous to the current reporting period can be presented as a separate financial statement or in the footnote. This can be presented in a narrative or a reconciliation format. Any changes in accumulated plan benefits made during the plan year needs to be reported as of that year, and there is no requirement for retroactive reporting. Any significant factor, whether affecting independently or in conjunction with other factors, needs to be identified. Minimum disclosure requirements for this statement include (1) plan amendments, (2) changes in the nature of the plan (for example, resulting from spinoffs and mergers), and (3) changes in actuarial assumptions. Other changes in accumulated benefits and benefits paid, including actuarial gains or losses, as a result of changes in the discount rates need to be disclosed as well.

Reporting Requirements for Defined Contribution Plans

In defined contribution pension plans, amounts contributed by participants and the investment results of the accumulated funds and forfeitures allocated all affect the plan balances.

The required disclosure requirements are as follows:

- Amount of unallocated assets
- The basis used to allocate assets to participant accounts when there is a difference in the allocation basis from that used to record assets in the financial statements
- Net assets and significant components of the changes in net assets for nonparticipant-directed investment programs
- Amounts allocated to participants who have withdrawn from the plan
- Nonparticipant-directed investments that represent more than 5% of total net assets

Note also that an auditor's report on employee benefit plan financial statements is normally included as part of the annual reports as per ERISA standards. These audit reports need to conform to requirements of SFAS No. 58 – Reports on Audited Financial Statements.

Accounting Standards Affecting Pension Plans

In September 2006, SFAS 158, Employers' Accounting for Defined Benefit Pension and Other Postretirement Plans – An Amendment of FASB Statements No. 87, 88, 106, 132 (R), was issued. This statement significantly changed balance sheet reporting of defined benefit pension plans.

The instability in the defined benefit pension plan environment resulted in FASB reforming pension accounting. With the passage of SFAS 158, this was accomplished. Before SFAS 158, certain events, such as plan amendments or actuarial gains or losses, were granted delayed balance sheet recognition. Therefore, the plan's funded status (plan assets minus obligations) was rarely reported on the balance sheet. SFAS 158 requires companies to report the plan's funded status either as an asset or a liability on the balance sheets.

The framework for pension accounting under *Generally Accepted Accounting Principles* (GAAP) was first established with the standard SFAS 87. The focus of SFAS 87 was obtaining a stable and permanent measure of the pension expense. Pension expense was included in net income – net periodic pension cost. This smoothed out the volatile components of the pension costs (for example, actuarial gains and losses, prior service, and actual return on planned assets). To connect the pension to the balance sheet, SFAS recognized the cumulative net periodic cost (accrued or prepaid pension cost) on the balance sheet instead of the actual funded status of the plan.

SFAS 158 improves financial reporting by more clearly communicating the funded status of the defined benefit pension plans. Under SFAS 158, companies with defined benefit pension plans must recognize the difference between the plan's projected benefit obligation and the fair value of the plan assets, either as an asset or a liability. The unrecognized prior service costs and actuarial gains and losses that were previously reported in the footnotes are now recognized on the balance sheet, with an offsetting amount in accumulated other comprehensive income in shareholder's equity.

The pension expense included in net income remains SFAS 87's net periodic pension cost. This remains a function of service cost, interest cost, expected return on pension plan assets, and amortization of unrecognized items. However, actuarial gains or losses and prior service costs that arise during a period are recognized as part of comprehensive income amortization of actuarial gains or losses; prior service costs require reclassification adjustment to comprehensive income.

Key Concepts in This Chapter

- Income replacement ratio
- Defined contribution pension plans
- Loans from defined contribution pension plans
- Defined benefit pension plans

- FASB standards for the accounting of pension plans
- Pension benefit obligation
- Accumulated benefit obligation
- Projected benefit obligation
- Pension Benefit Guarantee Corporation
- Service cost
- Interest cost
- Prior service cost
- Gain or loss on the PBO
- Pension plan assets
- The pension expense
- Return on plan assets
- Amortization of prior service cost
- Amortization of a net loss or net gain
- Statement of accumulated plan benefits
- Changes to accumulated plan benefits
- Reporting requirements for defined benefit pension plans
- Actuary's role in costing defined benefit pension plans

Part II

The second part of this book covers compensation, benefits, and *human resource* (HR) management topics that are on the periphery of the accounting and finance disciplines. It also covers some concepts that make a connection between HR management and accounting but are not part of current accounting principles or standards. Specifically, you will learn about HR accounting. HR accounting has been a subject of interest for many years. However, because the ideas presented are not accepted within the current *Generally Accepted Accounting Principles* (GAAP) standards, the subject has remained in the domain of academic research and discussion. This part also examines the concept of HR analytics (metrics).

HR executives should use the basic financial concepts underlying return on assets to determine human asset *return on investment* (ROI). HR professionals should calculate human asset ROI as the profit generated by an HR program divided by the investment made for that program.

It can be difficult to figure out what to include in the "investment" amount or how to attribute the profit to the HR programs. However, it is important that there is a metric of the HR program ROI because it allows senior management to evaluate the effectiveness of these "soft" programs. It assists with quantifying the benefits the HR department provides the organization. In periods of tight budgets, such an analysis can assist HR departments to avoid budget cuts.

Let's first start with the concept of HR analytics.

11

Human Resource Analytics

Aims and objectives of the chapter

- Discuss human resource analytics
- Establish the need for HR effectiveness metrics
- Discuss the effectiveness of benchmarking HR Metrics
- Consider HR effectiveness metrics with regard to internal efficiency and effectiveness
- Discuss internal HR operational metrics
- Examine total compensation effectiveness metrics
- Discuss the span of control management effectiveness metric
- Discuss how perceptions about HR effectiveness metrics have changed

More than ever before, the *human resource* (HR) function is being challenged by senior business executives, such as *chief executive officers* (CEOs), *chief operating officers* (COOs), and *chief financial officers* (CFOs), to demonstrate the value of the human capital employed and the value of the HR function using the language of business: accounting. Business success in general is measured, evaluated, and scrutinized using concrete numbers, as in dollars and cents. Why not demand from the HR function the same analytical rigor?

The emphasis on valuing, evaluating, and measuring HR investments stems from the fact that management throughout the world clearly recognize that the effectiveness of their HR assets can be a major competitive advantage. The effectiveness of human resources (the employees) can be the main contributing factor in becoming a successful organization. Therefore, business leaders have said that managing their human resources is their most important responsibility.

The Background for the Use of HR Analytics

An organization's financial effectiveness is evaluated through the use of financial ratios. The discipline of using financial ratios is a key tool in the evaluation of the financial success or failure of any business (both for-profit and nonprofit organizations). Financial ratios are also used to value a business (its assets and liabilities). Various stakeholders, both internal and external, use financial ratios to judge organizational performance. The stakeholders can be investors, stock analysts, business valuation specialists, investment bankers, internal management, government regulators, and many others. In other words, financial ratios are integral to managing and evaluating a business or even a nonprofit organization. The discipline of financial metric analysis and evaluation by using financial ratios has widespread usage.

The use of quantitative metrics is common, except for the HR function. The utilization of metrics and reporting on them for human resources is lagging. In comparison, metrics drive performance in other business functions such as sales, finance, operations, supply chain management, and marketing. As organizational resources become scarce, all staff functions (information technology, research and development, and human resources) are also being scrutinized as to their abilities to add value. The efforts expended by these functions toward the achievement of organizational objectives are being questioned.

A lack of data and appropriate information systems that might otherwise facilitate the collection and reporting of HR analytics and metrics often hamper HR personnel. This lack of effective and relevant data has prevented the HR department from "coming to the table." Whatever data the HR function can collect and report is out of sync with the information and data structures of the entire organization. Therefore, the HR function is often not regarded as a strategic function. Instead, the HR function is regarded as a purely operational and administrative function.

The data the HR function usually develops and disseminates is mainly tactical and operational. Examples include performance appraisals, healthcare costs per employee, turnover rates, absentee rates, cost per hire, workers' compensation costs, to name a few.

The Need for HR Analytics

HR metric systems are needed for two main reasons. The first is the evaluation of the effectiveness of the actual investments made in human capital. The second is the evaluation of the HR function itself. This chapter first covers the issues of measuring the effectiveness of human capital investments. The focus then turns to measuring the effectiveness of the HR function. The chapter closes with a discussion about compensation and benefit program metrics.

There is a need to use quantifiable metrics and financial ratios to determine the value of the two dimensions mentioned in the preceding paragraph. There is a need to use human capital management analytics.

In recent years, this topic has elicited a great deal of conversation. It has been discussed widely, in seminars, conferences, journal articles, books, and on the Internet. The use of HR metrics is not a new phenomenon. Discussion on this topic has continued steadily from the 1960s.

Early approaches centered on auditing the HR function. Then in the 1970s and 1980s, more value-added approaches started being utilized. Competitive HR benchmarking, HR satisfaction surveys, and HR cost monitoring and HR key indicators started being discussed and used.

Although the concepts were being discussed, the actual usage was found in only a few companies in the 1960s and 1970s. But since the mid-1980s, the discussion about HR metrics has become more intense. We also see a wider use and increased sophistication of the concepts. Concepts such as *return on investment* (ROI), evaluation of the HR departments as a profit center, balanced scorecards, and human capital metrics are now in the forefront of HR thinking.

Therefore, more and more HR professionals will be challenged to show the value of the investments in human capital assets quantitatively. The challenge will also be to show the ROI for human capital initiatives.

Measuring the Effectiveness of HR Investments

HR professionals will add value by not only deciding what to measure but also by deciding how to interpret the data and compare the data to benchmarks within industry segments. In addition, HR professionals need to focus on improving the methodology for securing the type of information the organization needs to achieve its overall goals. The concept being advocated here is that HR professionals should look at improving their metric data systems from being just tactical and operational to being integrated with the strategic organizational data system that is used for overall financial performance evaluation. This involves tying HR metrics with key financial success factors that are normally used to measure business or organizational success.

Conceptual connections between HR plans, programs, and activities and business performance need to be understood and developed, as has been demonstrated in Chapter 2. And HR metrics are needed that capture the impact of HR investments on business performance. This chapter describes some of these connected metrics. Let's first look at metrics that lend themselves to effective industry benchmarking, and then consider various HR value indicators.

Benchmarking HR Effectiveness Metrics

Benchmarking is the process of comparing an organization's processes and related performance metrics, first to the standards within the same industry group and then with the standards across all industry groups. Also *market intelligence* and *competitive intelligence*—comparing to direct competitors and the industry—is a common practice in benchmarking. In the financial area, organizations compare financial performance with those of others in the same industry group and then across all industries.

HR professionals should use benchmarking, and if they already are, they should enhance the analytical rigor in their benchmarking efforts. The analytical rigor should be commensurate with that used by accounting, investment, and finance professionals. Metrics that you can use for benchmark comparisons include the following:

- **Revenue per employee:** A company's sales in relation to the number of employees they have. This is an overall measure of an organization's employee productivity.

- **Profit per employee:** A precisely defined metric using *earnings before interest, taxes, depreciation, and amortization* (EBITDA) in the numerator.

- **Number of employees per HR staff:** A very useful HR department effectiveness measure. In the past, the industry average for this ratio was 100 employees to 1 HR staff member. Actual practice varied. In recent times, with the advent of HR department automation, a good target for this ratio is approximately 80 employees to 1 HR staff.

- **Total HR department expenses versus total operating expense:** A measure of the operational efficiency of an organization's HR department.

- **Training investments:** A measure of the total training dollars divided by total headcount.

- **Total compensation:** A measure of total compensation as a percentage of net income before taxes.

- **Internal placement:** A measure of the percent of management positions filled internally.

- **Employee benefits costs:** A measure of employee benefit costs as a percentage of total payroll cost.

Supporting the benchmarking contention, Dr. Jac Fitz-enz, a leading proponent of HR metrics and the founder of Saratoga Institute,[1] has often suggested that HR metrics should look toward integrating the metrics with the entire organizational metric system instead of just focusing on internal HR department metrics.

---

[1] Saratoga Institute was sold to PricewaterhouseCoopers, and this service is now part of PwC's Human Capital Consulting Services.

Exhibit 11-1 is adapted from an article Dr. Fitz-enz wrote for *HR Focus* magazine. It gives a sample of metrics recommended by Dr. Fitz-enz. Dr. Fitz-enz endorses the concept of benchmarking the metrics.

Exhibit 11-1 HR Business Performance Metrics Suitable for Benchmarking[2]

HR Performance Area	Method of Calculation
Human value added	Revenue – Operating expense – Pay and benefits = Adjusted profit ÷ Full-time equivalent employees
Return on human capital invested	Revenue – Operating expense – Pay and benefits = Adjusted profit ÷ Pay and benefits
Time to fill openings	Total calendar days from each requisition opening to accepted offer ÷ Number of openings filled
Turnover cost	Cost to terminate + Cost to hire + Vacancy cost + Productivity loss = Total ÷ Employees lost
Volunteer turnover rate	Total voluntary employee separations ÷ Total number of employees
Return on training	Depends on the type of training done
Cost per employee hired	Advertising expenses + Agency fees + Employee referral bonuses + HR recruiters pay and benefits + 10% misc. costs = Total ÷ Total number of employees hired
Pay and benefits as % of operating expense	Total pay and benefit expenditures ÷ Total operating expense
Healthcare costs per employee	Total healthcare benefits expenses ÷ Total number of employees

[2] Source: Adapted from Jac Fitz-Enz, "Top 10 Calculations for Your HRIS," *HR Focus*, April 1998, p. S-3.

We have thus far discussed metrics appropriate for external benchmarking; after all, much has been written about developing outward-looking metrics appropriate for benchmarking. But there is another reason HR analytics are necessary: to measure HR effectiveness, not just for benchmarking purposes but also for the optimization of human resources and HR management. In other words, although it is necessary to develop metrics for external comparisons, it is also vital to use HR metrics to effectively and efficiently manage human resources internally. So, organizations need to develop a comprehensive HR metric structure for both external comparisons and for internal management use.

What follows is a comprehensive review of all HR effectiveness metrics that are appropriate for both internal and external purposes. Notice that some of these metrics are also listed as benchmarking metrics (for external comparisons). Also within this category of HR effectiveness metrics one can include those that evaluate HR department efficiencies.

Human Capital Effectiveness Metrics

As previously mentioned, HR effectiveness metrics are those measures that are used to evaluate the overall organizational human resource effectiveness. In other words, they are an evaluation of the effectiveness of an organization's human capital investments. These metrics include the following:

- **Revenue per employee (revenue factor):** Also used in benchmarking.
- **Expense factor:** Current literature on HR effectiveness advocates the use of total operating expenses dividing by the total headcount. A better measure for the expense factor might be total HR-related expenses (as discussed in previous chapters) divided by the total headcount. Of course, total HR-related expenses are not aggregated in *Generally Accepted Accounting Principles* (GAAP)-based accounting consolidations. HR departments, by analyzing journal entries and ledger accounts, can calculate the aggregate total HR-related expenses.

- **Profit per employee:** This is an income factor. For this metric, many hold that the total operating income should be used. However, *total operating income* can mean many things. Total operating income can be gross profit, or net cash operating income (net income adjusted for noncash items), or *net operating income after taxes* (NOPAT), or net income before taxes (that is, *earnings before interest and taxes* [EBIT]), or *earnings before interest, taxes, depreciation, and amortization* (EBITDA). Clearly for a financial metric to evaluate HR effectiveness, one needs to select a metric that correlates directly with the efforts of the human resources of the company. Therefore, the most effective profit metric that correlates clearly with the organization's HR efforts is EBITDA, because this measure excludes the extraneous accounting and tax-related issues. Profit per employee is also an appropriate external benchmarking factor.

A case can be made, though, that discounted free cash flow, a true metric of the intrinsic value of a company, should be used. Therefore, another effective metric of HR effectiveness is discounted free cash flow divided by the total headcount. And for that matter, organizations can use any metric of economic value added as an HR effectiveness indicator.

The next metric category (turnover rate) can be used to evaluate human asset retention and depletion. These effectiveness metrics have been around for a while. But with the new emphasis on the value of human resources as a core facilitator of organizational value, they are now looked at in a new light.

- **Turnover rate:** The number of employees terminating per 100 employees employed within a given time period. It can be broken into two components: voluntary turnover rate and involuntary turnover rate. Some organizations add the two types of turnover and calculate a total turnover rate per 100 employees.

Note that the metrics described so far are just descriptive statistics. Unless you convert these statistics to a normative model or a predictive model, they might not be of much value. Normative and predictive models not only analyze the present but also suggest different alternatives for future action using a standard decision criterion.

Organizations can build a model to predict voluntary employee turnover. The first step in this model is to hypothesize, based on exit interviews, the possible causes of voluntary turnover. When the appropriate sets of causes are conceptually agreed to, a correlation matrix can be developed with voluntary turnover rates and data on causes from the exit interviews. The data on causes can be derived from the use of a semantic differential scale (a type of scale that is designed to measure the connotative meaning of concepts, which are meant to capture attitudes). Of course, the semantic differential scale needs to be built into the exit interview questionnaire. This resulting correlation matrix indicates those hypothesized causes for voluntary turnover that have the largest correlation with the voluntary turnover rate.

The next step in the analysis is to develop a predictive voluntary turnover model, as follows:

$$Y = a + b\,x_1 + b\,x_2 + b\,x_3 \text{-----} b\,x_n$$

Where Y = Voluntary turnover rate

$\quad$ a = Intercept

$\quad$ b_{1-n} = Slopes of the independent variables

$\quad$ x_{1-n} = Reasons and causes or Independent variables

Another important point to consider with regard to the dimensions of HR effectiveness is what element should be the denominator of the ratio calculation. Is total headcount appropriate, or would *full-time equivalent* (FTE) be a more appropriate metric? PwC–Saratoga Institute advocates the use of FTE in the denominator. The FTE number could be a better data point because nowadays most organizations use a flexible workforce, with a variety of employee working arrangements (full time, job share, part time, temporaries, telecommuters, flexible-schedule employees, and others). No matter the working arrangement the various employees work under, all of them are contributing to the HR effectiveness of the organization.

Internal HR Operational Metrics

Traditional HR management operational metrics focus on the efficiency, quality, and the speed of delivering HR services. To facilitate this type of analysis, statistical models are built to analyze the costs and benefits associated with specific HR activities.

The typical metrics used are as follows:

- **HR process cycle time:** The cycle time for each HR process, such as selection and staffing, benefit claims administration, and payroll and salary administration. Cycle time refers to the average time required to complete the activity, start to finish.

- **The HR service quality:** Assessed via the use of internal customer satisfaction surveys.

- **HR process costs:** The cost of the various HR processes, such as staffing, benefit claims administration, and payroll and salary administration.

- **Offer-acceptance ratios:** For staffing effectiveness.

- **Training evaluation:** Also called the development rate. It is calculated as the number of employees trained divided by total headcount (that is, access to training).

- **Training costs:** The average dollar amount spent for training an employee. Training efficiency requires that this factor should show a declining rate with the passage of time. The training cost factor is calculated by using the average training dollar and dividing it by the number of employees trained.

Total Compensation Effectiveness Metrics

Total compensation and benefit effectiveness metrics represent the final category of HR effectiveness metrics.

Some researchers contend that the value of human capital is best measured by using compensation data. Compensation data is the proxy value of human capital. Compensation is a monetary metric, and so it can be used as a value metric. Within this context, some of the metrics of compensation and benefit effectiveness that can be applied to the valuation of human capital are as follows:

- Compensation to revenue ratio factor
- Compensation to total expense ratio factor
- Executive compensation to the number of executives ratio factor
- Span of control factor (a managerial effectiveness indicator)

Compensation to revenue factor is a metric of total compensation costs as a ratio of total revenue. Improving organizational efficiencies should reduce this ratio over time. It is undesirable to see compensation expenses growing at a higher rate than the revenue growth rate. Many consider this ratio a valid employee-productivity metric.

Compensation to total expense factor is also an employee-productivity metric. Because of improving organizational efficiencies, this metric should show a downward trend over time. Many consider this to be a valid HR effectiveness metric. It is calculated by dividing total compensation expenses by total expenses. Note that *total expenses* in accounting terminology include both the cost of goods sold and the period expenses. Therefore, all income statement expenses are used as the denominator.

Total compensation expenses include all elements of compensation as described in this book

- Base salary
- Incentives
- Employee benefits
- Executive compensation
- Sales compensation
- Expatriate and international compensation
- Equity compensation
- All pay adders, such as overtime pay

Executive compensation expenses to the number of executives factor has gained importance as a metric because of the recent public outcry about excessive executive compensation paid to a handful of executives. For this metric, total compensation paid to vice presidents and above is divided by the number of executives. This metric can readily be used to compare with the ratios of comparable

organizations. Another ratio used to determine the relationship of
executive compensation to the pay of the total employee population is the ratio of senior executives' total compensation as a ratio of
the lowest-paid employee. The ratio establishes a reasonableness of
executive pay indicator. A modified version of the ratio is the total
compensation of the top ten executives as a ratio of the bottom ten
executives.

The United States often ranks number one (for unreasonableness)
when calculations are made using this ratio. In 2010, for instance,
CEO pay in the United States was 325 times that of the average
worker pay, according to the annual Executive Excess survey published by the Institute for Policy Studies, a Washington, D.C.-based
research group critical of high executive pay. According to a February
2007 Heritage Institute summary of various survey data, the multiple
has increased from about 24 in 1965 to 262 in 2005.

In an August 2008 article,[3] Graef Crystal, a renowned executive compensation consultant, indicated that the larger the company
in sales size, the larger the differential between CEO and average
worker pay. For the denominator, he used the 2007 Bureau of Labor
Statistics average American worker annualized pay of $36,100. For
the numerator, he used the pay of CEOs of very large companies.
For the company with the highest sales rank, the differential was
525; for the company with the lowest sales rank, the ratio was 162.

Executive compensation surveys also provide industry average
data on the various executive compensation elements. For example,
an examination of executive compensation might indicate that perquisites make up only 5% of the average of the total executive compensation package, or that the annual incentive compensation is 50% of
total cash compensation.

Span of control factor is a management effectiveness metric. Common practice suggests that there is an optimum number of employees
that one manager or supervisor can manage. With corporate delayering initiatives, this number has been increasing in recent years. In
the past, an optimum number of employees supervised by a single

[3] Found on the Internet: www.Graefcrystal.com/images/CEO_worker_pay_ratios_
web_7_1_.08.pdf.

manager or supervisor was approximately 6 employees. Nowadays, this ratio has gone up to 10 or 12 employees. The logic of this change is (1) the increasing use of automation and information technology, (2) enlightened management practices, (3) improving worker skills, and (4) the need to manage costs.

Another dimension of the span of control ratio is total managerial compensation dollars divided by the number of managers. This is the average total compensation for the management employee group. This metric can also be compared with other comparable companies.

Other effectiveness metrics used by compensation professionals to evaluate compensation programs include the following:

- **Average performance rating:** Average performance rating is the sum of performance ratings divided by the number of employees.

- **Average merit increase:** Average merit increase is the sum of all merit increases granted divided by the number of employees.

- **Grade creep:** Grade creep or inflation is the number and percentage of employees in each grade from one year to the next.

- **Compa-ratio:** Compa-ratio is the average salary divided by the midpoint within each grade, pay program, job family, and in the company as a whole.

- **Market index:** Market index is the average salary divided by the job or position's market average salary.

- **Actual incentive compensation payout as a percentage of target payout:** Incentive payout percentage is the actual average incentive compensation payout divided by the target incentive payout. This metric can be calculated in total dollars or by using the average actual payout and the average target payout.

- **Change in incentive compensation payout as a percentage of the change in net income:** Incentive payout effectiveness is a metric that evaluates the alignment of incentive compensation paid out versus net income. In recent times, especially in executive compensation, the increases in incentive compensation payouts have been higher than the growth in net income. In public companies, compensation committees of the board of directors are charged with the fiduciary responsibility to monitor and attest to the reasonableness of executive compensation. The compensation committees should ask to regularly see a presentation of these metrics to monitor the reasonableness of executive compensation.

A Changed Paradigm

Most often, a company's compensation staff focuses on objectives from one angle only: competitiveness. Compensation professionals consider their job is primarily to ensure that pay packages are externally competitive. Questions commonly addressed by the compensation staff center involve the following:

- Are salaries commensurate with the averages in the relevant market?
- Are the company's programs similar in features to that of our competitors?
- What is the company's ability to pay? What can we afford to pay?

These are appropriate questions. But human resources employed by an organization are primarily responsible for increasing revenue and the value derived by various stakeholders. The human resources in an organization drive the top line and the bottom line. They are responsible for creating new products, making the products, selling the products, and maintaining customer satisfaction.

Therefore, in analyzing HR effectiveness ratios, focus needs to be placed both on the numerator and the denominator of the ratio.

In other words, compensation professionals should focus on not only the supply side (of human resources) of the equation but also pay attention to the demand side.

The supply side has traditionally received the most attention. On the supply side, compensation and benefit professionals design programs to attract and retain the numbers and types of employees an organization needs.

The demand side considers what employees need from their compensation programs and which types of compensation plans and programs create the highest satisfaction levels for the employees. By focusing on the demand side, organizations can motivate employees to enhance productivity and improve the top line. Various consulting companies have developed and marketed programs that assist clients to design programs that address both the supply side and the demand side. These programs often encourage employee input into the compensation design process. The demand side focuses on employee performance.

Key Concepts in This Chapter

- The need for HR analytics
- Measuring the effectiveness of HR investments
- Benchmarking HR effectiveness metrics
- HR effectiveness metrics
- Revenue per employee
- Profit per employee
- Training investments
- Total compensation costs
- Internal placement effectiveness
- Employee benefit costs
- Expense factor
- Turnover rates
- Internal HR operational metrics
- Training evaluation
- Training cost factor
- Total compensation effectiveness metrics
- Span of control
- Compensation program effectiveness metrics

12

Human Resource Accounting

Aims and objectives of this chapter

- Define human resource accounting
- Explain the conceptual basis for HR accounting
- Explain the debate with respect to HR accounting
- Describe HR accounting methods
- Review cost-based models
- Discuss the economic value models for HR accounting
- Explain the limitations of each of these models

Thus far in this book we have been discussing *human resource* (HR) management topics that have accounting and finance implications. The basis of the discussion has been within the structure of current accounting principles and practices as defined by *Generally Accepted Accounting Principles* (GAAP) and *International Financial Reporting Standards* (IFRS).

The Background

This chapter covers HR accounting, a paradigm-shifting proposition that proposes capitalizing HR expenditures.

Although the previous chapters in this book covered many concepts for the accounting of human resources, the term itself is specifically used by proponents of capitalizing HR expenditures. They use the term *human resource accounting* to identify this paradigm-shifting concept.

The proposition suggesting the capitalization of HR expenses has been around since the 1960s (although mainly in academic circles). As proposed, HR accounting is a system of identifying, gathering, and reporting of data on the economic investments in human assets. This is an effort to analyze and report on the investments in human resources in a manner that is not a part of the current accounting standards and principles. *Human resource accounting* (HRA) uses current accounting and finance principles covering the capitalization of expenses and applies those concepts to first quantifying the cost and then valuing the human resources employed.

Fundamentally, the HRA has a two-pronged conceptual basis:

- **The quantification of the cost of human resources:** Covers all the expenses an organization incurs for acquiring, motivating, retaining, maintaining, developing, and redeploying its HR assets.

- **The valuing of human resources:** An analysis of the *return on investment* (ROI) received from HR investments. HRA suggests that the value can be measured by calculating the present value of an employee's total compensation income earned over the employee's service period.

As indicated, HR accounting has been around for a while, but mostly relegated to academic dialogue. HRA as a concept was first developed as a research effort at the University of Michigan. Rensis Likert, founder of the University of Michigan Institute of Social Research, along with some colleagues at Michigan (R. Lee Brummet, William C. Pyle, and Eric G. Flamholtz), was responsible for the original work on HRA. The term *human resource accounting* was first used in a paper in 1968.[1] That paper is the earliest study dealing with HR measurements.

This chapter reviews HRA and discusses its efficacy, applicability, and its drawbacks.

---

[1] Brummet, R.L., Flamholtz, E.G., and Pyle, W.C., "Human resource measurement: A challenge for accountants," *Accounting Review,* April 1986, pp. 217–224.

The Debate

Some say that current accounting principles as codified in the U.S. GAAP and the IFRS is a legacy of the manufacturing era. Since the early 1970s, the manufacturing era has given way to a service economy. Ever since the advent of the use of technology, automation, robotics, and other process efficiencies, the need for relevant know-how has risen exponentially. Given these structural transformations, it can be said that an organization's real investments, its assets, and ultimately its value lie in its human resources. However, the accounting profession has not placed human assets in the same place on the balance sheet (or in business valuations) as physical assets.

A manufacturing organization's core assets are its physical assets: property, plant, and equipment. For service-based and knowledge-based organizations, the core assets are the HR assets. In service and knowledge organizations, human capital is the most important asset employed in extracting value from the organization. This is especially true in purely knowledge-based economics. Imagine Intel, Google, and Facebook without human capital. Without their human talent, those companies would possess minimal value.

Others say that organizational decision makers currently lack complete information on the effectiveness and efficiency of human capital expenditures. But, currently, in financial statements the value of HR assets is not recorded.

The paradigm-shifting concept of HRA is a methodology to bridge this gap. So, HRA is the process for recording, reporting, and analyzing HR expenditures using the language of finance and accounting.

Nevertheless, in the absence of legitimate recognition by the accounting profession for this structural accounting principles shift, HRA will remain the domain for academic discussion and dialogue. Change in this area is slow to come.

HRA proponents suggest that intellectual capital of an organization consists of its human capital and its organizational capital, which is the sum of customer satisfaction, the efficiency of internal processes, and the ability of the organization for continuous learning and development (a learning organization).

Others have postulated that the human capital of an organization can be looked at from a longitudinal point of view—or a human asset life cycle view (see Appendix in Chapter 2, "Business, Financial, and Human Resource Planning"). In this conceptual structure, human assets are acquired, onboarded, motivated and retained, maintained, developed, and redeployed. Thus, human capital assets have a life cycle just like any other physical capital assets.

There is a twofold uniqueness to human capital. Human capital and thus human assets have longer life cycles and most probably appreciate rather than depreciate. Physical assets can only depreciate.

The accounting profession contends that human capital as contained in skills, knowledge, abilities, and competencies of an individual employee is hard to replicate. The accounting profession will argue that the value of one human capital unit (an employee) compared to another is not comparable. One employee's contribution can be greater than another employee's contribution. This issue in itself makes it difficult to calculate human asset values accurately. Human capital valuation is therefore hard to quantify. The future benefit to be derived from HR investments is hard to determine. As a result, the accounting profession has avoided including human capital in the financial and accounting records and statements. Under current GAAP principles, all monetary outlays for HR-related costs are considered as period expenses and not as assets.

The problem with this way of thinking is that the more an organization invests (or, based on current accounting thinking, spends), the more an organization's current net income decreases. The logic here is hard to rationalize. The human resources of an organization (its human capital investments) with their individual and joint effort, skills, experiences, abilities, knowledge, and competencies are solely responsible for creating and adding value to an organization. Yet the current accounting system considers those expenditures as immediate expenditures. This, in turn, reduces the financial value of the organization because current expenditures decrease current income. How can an expense increase and decrease organizational value at the same time?

Furthermore, in analyzing the financial value or viability of an organization, analysts currently use many ratios. But none of these measures consider HR contributions or the human capital value. All of these ratios are based on hard physical capital values only. ROI is also based on investments only in physical capital.

The most glaring outcome of this logical conundrum is found in reduction-in-force decisions (layoffs). When organizations decide to lay off employees, the short-term immediate cost savings is what motivates the decision. The objective of making this decision is primarily to show a short-term increase in profitability. But is this analysis complete? What about the longer-term implications? In the long term, there will be many incremental costs in reacquiring, retraining, and paying pay premiums for replacement hires. One cannot also ignore the negative impact on the remaining employee's motivation and morale. So, shouldn't this decision be made with a longer-term perspective?

When investors are considering long-term investments, the data from HRA will provide valuable information about the long-term viability of the enterprise. And shouldn't we use a capital budgeting approach in making this decision? This chapter's appendix lays out a model for such an analysis.

HR Accounting Methods

Many computational models have been used for the calculations of the value human resources in an organization. Generally, these models can be grouped into two categories: cost-based models and value-based models. Within each category, you can find various individual models. The following subsections briefly cover each of these models.

The first category of models is cost-based models. Here you can find models that focus on capitalization of historical costs, replacement cost models, and opportunity cost models. The second category of models is value-based models. In this category, you can find the present value of future earnings model (the Lev and Schwartz model), the reward valuation model (the Flamholtz model), and the group-based valuation model.

Cost-Based Models

Acquisition Cost Model

The acquisition cost model was developed starting in 1967, at the University of Michigan, by a research team that included Rensis Likert, R. Lee Brummet, William C. Pyle, and Eric G. Flamholtz. Brummet, Flamholtz, and Pyle published a seminal article in the area of HR measurement in the *Accounting Review*,[2] where they introduced the acquisition cost model. Their research was based on work they had done on employee valuation at the R.G. Barry Corporation of Columbus, Ohio.

The method measures the organization's investment in employees using the five HR functions:

- Recruiting and acquisition
- Formal training and familiarization
- Informal training, informal familiarization
- Experience
- Development

The model suggested that instead of charging the HR process costs to the income statement they should be capitalized in the balance sheet. Like all other asset accounts, the researchers suggested that HR assets should also be amortized over a determined useful life. It was suggested that the amortization process should also be done over a period of time. The period of time was the difference between the date of hire and the retirement date. It the employee terminates any time during this period, an impairment calculation can be done and an impairment expense taken during the termination year (similar to methods used to account for a physical asset).

For example, suppose that a company had hired an employee at age 35 on January 1, 1991, for an annual salary of $100,000, and the employee left the company after 20 years of service, on December

---

[2]   Brummet, R.L., Flamholtz, E.G., and Pyle, W.C., "Human resource measurement: A challenge for accountants," *Accounting Review*, April 1968, pp. 217–224.

31, 2010 (normal retirement age is age 60). The company would have amortized $80,000 as of 2010, so the unamortized amount of the annual salary of $20,000 should have been charged to the income in the year 2011.

In essence, the human asset value is amortized annually each year over the expected length of the service of the individual employee, and the unamortized cost is shown as the investment in the human asset on the balance sheet. If the employee leaves the organization (that is, human assets expire) before the expected service life period, the net value of that specific human asset is charged against current revenue as a current expense.

This model has also been referred to as the *capitalization of historical costs model*. The original classification of the costs by the researchers seemed somewhat esoteric. A better categorization is the sum of all costs related to acquisition (recruitment, selection, and onboarding), total rewards, maintenance (employee benefits and services), training (both in-house and outside) and development, and redeployment.[3] These costs taken together would represent the real value of the human resources of an organization.

Another category of costs to consider within the acquisition cost methodology is learning costs. From a managerial accounting point of view, a clear estimation of learning costs is necessary to derive a good prediction of product costs. So, concepts such as the learning factor and experience curves should be brought in to more effectively estimate the true costs of the organization's learning and development efforts.

The acquisition cost model of HRA is simple and easy to understand and satisfies the basic matching accounting principle for costs and revenues. But, the model has some drawbacks. Historical costs are sunk costs and are irrelevant for decision making. So, the model fails to value human resources accurately from the point of view of using relevant costs. Another conceptual drawback of this model is that because no distinction is made for the differing value of individual human resources (some human resources in an organization are of a higher value than others because of their advanced knowledge,

---

[3] This is a different classification of HR costs than that presented by Brummet, Flamholtz, and Pyle.

skills, and abilities) and because training costs (specifically) for these employees will be lower (they already possess the much needed knowledge and know-how), they will be given a lower value. Intrinsically, employees with advanced knowledge, skills, and abilities have a higher value for the organization.

Another criticism of this model is that this method measures only the costs to the organization but completely ignores any measure of the value of the employee to the organization.[4]

Replacement Cost Model

The replacement cost model takes into consideration the costs that would be incurred to replace one individual with another (or one group of employees with another). However, the replacement is based on the exchange of identical *knowledge, skills, and abilities* (commonly called KSAs). The costs included in replacement costs include the termination costs associated with the terminating employee or the group of employees plus the costs of hiring and training the replacement.

Proponents suggest that the concept of replacement cost has two manifestations: position and personal. So, individual replacement costs cover the costs that have to be incurred to replace an employee by another employee who can provide the same set of services as that of the individual being replaced. Positional replacement costs refer to the cost of replacing the set of services being rendered by an individual occupying a specific position. The positional replacement cost takes into account the position in the organization currently held by the employee. In contrast, personal replacement costs are costs for any specific individual being replaced by another specific employee capable of rendering the specific services. This personal replacement is not connected to any particular position. For practical reasons, this is too fine a distinction and would create data-tracking difficulties.

This is a per-person cost method compared to the average cost method employed by the historical cost method. So in this method,

---

[4] Cascio, W.F., *Costing Human Resources: The Financial Impact of Behavior in Organizations, 3e,* 1991, PWS-Kent Pub. Co., Boston.

you use the average HR costs for a specific position or employee, which could be held by either one person or a number of employees.

Note here the specific difference between a position and a job. A job entails the roles and responsibilities and the skills required for a specific job. The job can be benchmarked against similar jobs in other organizations. A position includes the cumulative job responsibilities, duties, and tasks entrusted to a specific employee. The individual components that make up the position can be benchmarked. The position provides a more dynamic and flexible framework within which to make salary decisions. For example, clerk is a job, whereas a payroll clerk is a position.

The replacement cost model can also be built around competencies within an organization. Competencies refer to the optimum set of knowledge, skills, and abilities and associated behavioral indicators that are necessary to achieve the company's strategic and operational business objectives.

The problem with this model is that the determination of the replacement cost of an employee is highly subjective. This is because the collection of the replacement cost data is not a normal part of regular accounting systems or even a part of regular HR information systems. Procedurally, both these systems do not keep track of which terminating employee is being replaced by which new hire. To match replacements, a system can be developed to do the necessary data tracking. For senior management personnel, this replacement tracking will not be very difficult.

Opportunity Cost Model

The opportunity cost model states that the human resource of an organization has to be valued on the basis of the economist's concept of opportunity cost. This is the value of the benefit foregone by putting it to an alternative use. This is measured by the net cash inflow that is forgone by redirecting a resource from one use to another. So in the HR area, it is the value lost by assigning an employee to one assignment as opposed to another.

The value of an employee is determined by the alternative best use of that employee's knowledge, skills, and abilities in the organization.

The opportunity cost value may be established by competitive bidding within the firm, so that, in effect, managers bid for any scarce employee. This model advocates setting up a market where a competitive bidding arrangement establishes a value for the human resource. Managers bid for a scarce resource and establish a bid price for that resource. The net cash inflow is calculated by the increased profit the hiring entity derives from acquiring that scarce resource. The human asset therefore will have a value only if it is a scarce resource (that is, when its employment in one division denies it to another division).

A selection process is set up to operate this system. A human asset has value only if it is a bid-for scarce resource. The others are not. Only scarce human resources are used in the model. Readily recruited human resources are not scarce and are excluded. Therefore, this approach is concerned with only one section of the human resources in an organization. Of concern are only those internal human assets who have profit-generating special skills. In addition, the special skills can be hired from the external labor market.

Value-Based Models

Present Value of Future Earnings Model

This model of HRA was developed by Lev and Schwartz in 1971 and involves determining the value of human resources by calculating the present value of estimated future earnings discounted by the firm's cost of capital.[5] Exhibit 12-1 shows the expression used to calculate the expected value of a person's human capital.

$$E(V\tau) = \sum_{t=\tau}^{T} P_\tau(t+1) \sum_{t=\tau}^{t} \frac{I_t}{(1+r)^{t-\tau}}$$

Exhibit 12-1 Calculating Human Capital

---

[5] Lev, B., and Schwartz, A., "On the use of the economic concept of human capital in financial statements," *Accounting Review*, January 1971, pp. 103–112.

Where $E(V\tau)$ is the expected value of a person's human capital and $P(t)$ is the probability of a person dying at age t. $V\tau$ is the human capital value of a person τ years old. $I(t)$ is the person's annual earnings up to retirement, r is a discount rate specific to the person, and T is the retirement age.

Lev and Schwartz used employee compensation as a proxy for the HR value. Estimated future earnings of an employee were used as a substitute for economic value. According to the authors, "the value of human capital embodied in a person of age r is the present value of his remaining future earnings from employment."[6]

The present value model ignores the probability that an individual may leave an organization for reasons other than death or retirement. It also ignores the probability that people may make job or position changes during their careers. Service life is overstated, which results in inflating the value of human capital. It is important to calculate a person's expected realizable value and not just the conditional value (the value based on the person's current employment condition).

Reward Valuation Model

The reward valuation model is also known as the stochastic rewards valuation model or the Flamholtz model.

Flamholtz advocated that an employee's value to an organization is determined by the services the employee delivers to the organization. This takes into account the probability that an individual is expected to transit through a set of mutually exclusive organizational roles or employment states during a given time interval. The assumption here is that an employee provides value to the organization as the employee holds various jobs and positions as he or she moves along a career progression. The realizable value and the conditional value can be calculated as follows:[7]

---

[6] Lev and Schwartz, *"On the Use of the Economic Concept of Human Capital,"* p.105.

[7] Flamholtz, E.G., *Human Resource Accounting: Advances in Concepts, Methods and Applications,* 3e, 1999, Kluwer Academic Publishers, Boston, pp. 180–181.

1. Define the mutually exclusive transition states or service states.

2. Determine the value of each state to the organization.

3. Estimate a person's expected tenure in an organization.

4. Find the probability that a person will occupy each possible state at specified future time periods.

5. Discount the expected future cash flows to determine their present value.

The first step identifies time periods or stages when an employee can generate an employment service value to the organization. The second step calculates the value the organization derives by the employee occupying each specific service state. These are service state values. The third step estimates the employee's total tenure within the organization. In the fourth step, a probability determination is made that a specific employee will remain in that service state at specific future times.

What is the probability that an employee holding a marketing manager position now will remain in that marketing manager position at the end of a specific time period? What is the probability that an individual will leave the organization? These are example of some analytical questions that are posed. Finally, the expected future values are discounted to derive the present value of future benefits.

In this model, the value of each service state is an implied value of what a person in that service state will do during a specific period. The four possible value states are

- Remain in the present position
- Be promoted
- Be transferred
- Leave the organization

These state values form the basis of the valuation in this model.

The major drawback to this model is the difficulty of calculating any realistic probabilities for each likely service state. The methodology for the determination of a monetary value equivalent of each service state is not clearly provided in this model. Also, because this model has an individual employee orientation, it ignores team effort and activities.

Valuation on a Group Basis

Proper valuation of human resources is not possible unless the contributions of individuals as a group are taken into consideration. An individual's expected service tenure in the organization is difficult to predict, but on a group basis it is easier to estimate the percentage of people in that group who are likely to leave the organization at any specific time. Group valuation of HRA attempts to calculate the present value of the entire group in a service state. You can calculate the group-based present value as follows:

1. Ascertain the number of employees in each group.
2. Estimate the impact of the group using a probability estimate of the termination of an individual group member.
3. Estimate an economic value of each member in the service state.
4. Estimate the value of the entire service state by multiplying the result of the first three steps.

Although the group method simplifies the valuation process in HRA, it ignores the exceptional qualities of specific skilled employees. The performance of a group may be seriously negatively affected if a skilled member leaves (thus reducing the value of the entire group).

Comments on HRA

The theoretical discussion on HRA has value. Why the accounting profession has been slow to embrace these concepts remains a big question. The theoretical constructs of HRA have yet to meet the requirements of current accounting measurement standards. Specifically, the current standards emphasize that accounting principles need to meet the following principles:

- Relevancy for organizational decision making
- Verifiable by independent sources

- Free of subjective bias
- Quantifiable in meaningful accounting terms

Recently, there has been a movement toward adoption of more complex measurements compared to the historical costing methods. Time value of money and present value calculations have come into more use by the accounting profession. There has also been a lot of consideration given to the use of fair value measurements. This trend has been accentuated by the convergence efforts between GAAP and IFRS. The fair value measurements are made at each balance sheet date. Many items on the balance sheet that are now noncurrent are being measured at the present value of future cash flows. We have talked about these initiatives in various sections of this book.

So, as the accounting profession diversifies their thinking and becomes accustomed with different and even complex measurement systems, a possibility exists that they will embrace similar approaches taken to measure HR asset values.

Also in current accounting practice it is fairly routine to determine values of intangible assets using accepted accounting measurement techniques. These approaches are even sanctioned by the *Financial Accounting Standards Board* (FASB). It can be argued that the human capital asset is the most important intangible asset in any organization. Given these arguments, it is hard to see why any accountant would consider HRA an unrealistic concept.

Key Concepts in This Chapter

- Human resource accounting
- Capitalization of HR expenses
- Why the accounting profession is yet to buy in to HRA
- HRA methods
- Acquisition cost model
- Replacement cost model
- Opportunity cost model
- Present value of future earnings model

- Reward valuation model
- Valuation on a group basis
- Limitation of HRA
- Valuation of HR assets

Appendix: No Long-Term Savings from Workforce Reductions

Nowadays, more than ever, we see a widespread use of a very short-term business practice: workforce reductions. It seems this practice is quite popular. Business pundits have even coined extraordinary words to describe the practice. Words such as *rightsizing, restructuring, downsizing,* and *delayering* are now commonly used to describe workforce reductions. The words being used have legitimized a practice that in reality is just short-term cost reduction. The widespread global use of these practices has climbed steadily over the past two decades. This has resulted in an acceptance of these actions as a common management practice. But when is common practice common sense?

The argument here is that such a practice is ineffective from the human side of the enterprise. The widespread use of reductions in force has emotional, psychological, economic, and social consequences that are far reaching. Use of this management practice destroys people and communities.

In addition to the devastating human consequences, a case can be made that this practice does not fulfill its intended purpose (saving money). Sure, it saves expenses in the short term. It makes income statements look good immediately. However, you cannot be sure about the impact of this short-term cost reduction on the balance sheet. And as discussed previously, accountants are yet to look at human capital investments as assets.

The use of this practice can make business leaders look competent in the eyes of shareholders in the short run. However, long-term investors might recognize that this practice does not really save money. Another key question is how this action affects the intrinsic value of a company over the long term. It can be argued that it ends up increasing long-term costs. Yet, this practice has become a reality in business decision making, especially in bigger organizations.

Workforce reductions result in direct long-term consequences and costs. Very few organizations creatively explore alternatives to saving on expenses before executing the workforce-reduction cost-saving program.

The workforce-reduction decision has resulted in business leaders weakening their organizations through repeated downsizing exercises. In the process, these executives have earned enormous compensation and also fame and glory for "turning the company around." When HP brought in a new CEO in the late 1900s, the company underwent major reorganization, which involved massive layoffs and off-shoring of the jobs of long-tenured HP employees. These efforts were fruitless because of many other ineffective management decisions. The legendary high-technology company lost 50% of its stock value, resulting in a high-profile CEO termination.

From an analytical point of view, long-term cost savings accruing from massive layoffs is not a reality. Using the concepts of HRA, a financial model can be developed that can prove that over an extended period of time, reduction in force actions do not save money. In fact, they cost more in the long run. The present value concept has been used to develop the following model shown in Exhibit 12-2.

Exhibit 12-2 An HRA Model

Savings from layoffs (immediate short-term impact):

> Direct labor expenses (–)

> Associated benefits costs (–)

Short-term and long-term costs incurred as a result of layoffs:

> Separation payments (+)

> Replacement hiring costs (+)

> In/out additional compensation costs (+)

> Replacement hires training costs (+)

> Replacement productivity ramp-up costs (+)

> Loss from unused office and other facilities (+)

> Key employee additional retention costs (+)

> Remaining employee demoralization cost (+)

Now do a present value analysis, as shown in Exhibit 12-3.

Exhibit 12-3 PV Calculations of Savings and Costs

	Yr 1	Yr 2	Yr 3	Yr 4	Yr 5
Savings $					
Costs $					
Net Savings $ Or Net Cost $					
PV net savings or costs @ an appropriate discount rate					

So, if you calculate the impact of workforce-reduction policies using this model, you might see a different reality.

After all, the fundamental value measure of a company is its intrinsic value. Intrinsic value enhancement is mainly a result of increasing free cash flows. So, managers can enhance company value by focusing on increasing the size of expected cash flows. Also, the true value of a company is based on future cash flows and not just cash flows in the immediate, short-term time period.

Conclusion

This book has focused on applying finance and accounting principles to HR management systems. From that perspective, it is a technical book.

More often than not, the soft side of human resources is emphasized in practice. But HR management has a harder side, too. This book has attempted to explain the hard side, with an emphasis on the compensation and benefit function.

As discussed at the beginning of this book, the discipline of HR management has multidisciplinary underpinnings. The HR profession is guided by influences from psychology, economics, sociology, philosophy, mathematics, and statistics, as well as from accounting and finance. Many stakeholders suggest that accounting and finance are the languages of business and organizations. In many ways, accounting and finance are core functions in the management of nonprofits as well. HR management is a very important component for both for-profit and nonprofit organizations. Therefore, HR management should also use the core language of organizational management. This book encourages and has attempted to facilitate the use of this language by HR professionals.

We focused on compensation and benefits because this is where accounting and finance has the most impact. The hope with this book is that in ongoing HR management education, especially compensation management, this book can be used to add to the required technical know-how.

The topics and subjects covered in the book are not new. The ideas and concepts can be found in many textbooks and other publications. In this book, we have attempted to compile all relevant topics, ideas, thoughts, concepts, principles, and subjects in one text. We focused on the core dimensions of compensation and benefits management. We covered accounting and finance implications in base, incentive, sales, international, and equity compensation. We also covered accounting and finance implications of employee benefit plans.

Our primary objective was to develop a single-source publication to serve as a knowledge repository and a reference source. Overall, our hope is that this book will be the impetus to help develop the accounting and finance knowledge of HR professionals.

HR professionals come to this discipline from various paths. There is no discernible singular career path to becoming an HR professional. Quite often, therefore, HR professionals lack accounting and finance knowledge and know-how. This clearly hinders HR professionals in many ways. Some of these hindrances can be seen in HR professionals lacking credibility with senior management. HR professionals are mainly considered "soft-side" professionals and considered advisors and counselors but not core decision makers. Therefore, HR professionals are not always brought to the "decision-makers table." One of the main ways to change these perceptions is for the HR professional to talk the language of business in a credible fashion using accounting and finance knowledge and know-how. We hope this book facilitates that end. For the HR professional, this knowledge enhancement is not a want, but a need.

An HR Finance and Accounting Audit

We conclude with various questions HR professionals should ask themselves with respect to applying accounting and finance principles to global HR management systems. If an HR professional does not have adequate answers to these questions, he or she should take the necessary steps to develop the requisite skills and knowledge to implement these principles. The questions are in no particular order:

- Does your organization have an adequate system of accurately projecting total compensation expenses that is tied in to the organization's financial budgeting system?
- If your organization has a defined benefit plan, do you participate in cost determination activities? Do you understand the

funding issues of the plan? Do you understand the calculations involving the ongoing pension expense?

- Are you aware and knowledgeable about the financial triggers used in the determination of sales commissions earned?

- If your organization sends expatriates overseas, who manages the expatriate tax program? Do you understand the specifics of the calculations involved?

- From an accounting point of view, what are the implications of capitalizing HR expenses for your organization?

- Do you know the difference between the VBO, ABO, and PBO in pension accounting?

- Does your organization have a stock option program? Do you know how the stock option expenses are calculated for that program?

- Do you know how the intrinsic value of any business is calculated?

- Do you know how the economic value of any business is calculated?

- Do you understand the various financial ratios commonly used to evaluate the performance of a business?

- Are the linkages between HR programs and the intrinsic value of your organization clearly delineated?

- Can you suggest ways in which HR programs can add economic value to the organization?

- Can you justify HR programs using ROI methodologies and capital budgeting techniques?

- Do you know and understand the details of the stock option pricing models?

- What are specific connections between HR programs and the financial ratios used to measure operating profits?

- In what ways can the HR function improve the company's free cash flow position?

- Do you exclusively rely on outside consultants for technical accounting and financial issues that need to be addressed for HR programs?

- Does your organization regularly monitor and then report performance on HR metrics to senior management?
- Do you engage in industry benchmark comparisons for HR metrics?
- Do you annually engage in employee benefits program costing in coordination with your outside vendors?
- Do you participate with the senior management team in developing linked incentive compensation financial triggers?
- Do you understand the tax implications of your compensation and benefit programs?
- Are you knowledgeable about governmental reporting requirements for (DOL and ERISA) your compensation and benefit programs?
- Are you knowledgeable about accounting requirements under the current accounting standards (GAAP and IFRS)?
- Do you know how your equity compensation programs affect the company's balance sheet, especially the Accumulated Paid-in Capital account?
- Do you know how your equity compensation program affects your company's earnings per share?

If your knowledge is limited in answering these questions, a good place to start is this book.

References

Articles

Aboody, D. "Market Valuation of Employee Stock Options," *Journal of Accounting and Economics,* 22 (1996): 357–91.

"Accounting for Employee Benefit and Stock-Based Compensation Under IFRS, Implications and Consideration for U.S. Companies," Towers Watson (2010).

"Accounting for Employee Stock Options," A CBO Paper, Congressional Budget Office, Congress of the United States (2009).

"Authoritative Accounting and Reporting Standards For Employee Benefit Plans," FASB Accounting Standards Codification™, Employee Benefit Plan Audit Quality Center, AICPA.

Baker, T., D. Collins, and A. Reitenga, "Stock Option Compensation and Earnings Management Incentives," *Journal of Accounting Auditing Finance,* 18, no. 4 (2003): 557–82.

Balachandran, B.V., and R.T.S. Ramakrishnan, "Internal Control and External Auditing for Incentive Compensation Schedules," *Journal of Accounting Research (Studies on Economic Consequences of Financial and Managerial Accounting: Effects on Corporate Intensives and Decisions)* (1980): 140–71.

Balsley, H., "Using EVA to Align Management Incentives with Shareholder Interests," Harvard Business School, Student Paper (Dec. 2005).

Barocas, V., and A.M., Rappaport, "Applying Strategic Management Principles to the Design and Management of Employee Benefits," *Human Resource Planning,* 16(1), The Human Resource Planning Society (1993).

Barth, M.E., "Fair Value Accounting: Evidence from Investment Securities and the Market Valuation of Banks," *Accounting Review,* 69 (1994): 1–25.

Barth, M.E., W.H. Beaver, and W. Landsman, "The Market Valuation Implication of Net Periodic Pension Cost Components," *Journal of Accounting and Economics,* 15 (1992): 27–62.

Becker, B.E., M.A. Huselid, P.S. Pickus, and M.F. Spratt, "HR as a Source of Shareholder Value: Research and Recommendations," *Human Resource Management,* 36(1), Spring 1997: 39–47.

Bhayani, R., A. Fluke, and W.P. Murphy, "Diving into the Hypothetical APIC Pool: A Guide to the Tax Consequences of FAS 123 (R)," *WorldatWork Journal,* 16, no. 3, 3rd Quarter (2007).

Blankley, A.I., and E.P. Swanson, "A Longitudinal Study of SFAS 87 Pension Rate Assumptions," *Accounting Horizons* (Dec. 1995): 1–21.

"Bonus Programs and Practice," a research report by WorldatWork, Scottsdale, AZ, Apr. 2011.

Boudreau, J.W., "'So What?': HR Management as a Change Catalyst," Working Paper # 95-34, Presented in the Symposium, "Measuring the Impact of HR Practices in Future Organizations," Academy of Management National Meeting, Vancouver, British Columbia (Aug. 1995).

Boyee, J.E., "What Spendable Income Overseas Really Means," *Compensation Review* (1972): 20–26.

Brummet, R.L., Flamholtz, E.G., and Pyle, W.C., "Human Resource Measurement: A Challenge for aAccountants," *Accounting Review,* April 1986, pp. 217–24.

Bullen, M.L., and K. Eyler, "Human Resource Accounting and International Development: Implications for Measurement of Human Capital," *Journal of International Business and Culture Studies.*

Bulow, J., "What Are Corporate Pension Liabilities?" *Quarterly Journal of Economics* (Aug. 1982): 435–42.

Caligiuri, P.M., and S. Colakolu, "A Strategic Contingency Approach to Expatriate Assignment Management," *Human Resource Management Journal,* 17, no. 4 (2007): 393–410.

"Changing Patterns of Retirement," *The Actuary,* Society of Actuaries, 35, no. 6 (Sep. 2001).

Chanin, J., R. Parke, and D. Mirkin, "Insight—Expert Thinking from Milliman," *Want to Manage Employer Healthcare Costs? It Starts with Managing Utilization,* March 18, 2010, http://insight.milliman.com/article.php?cntid=7217.

Cliche, S., L. Gignac, and D. Bult, "Changes to Accounting for Employee Benefit Plans Under IFRS," Mercer Communique, Calgary, Edmonton, Ottawa, Toronto, Halifax, Quebec City, Vancouver.

Coller, M., and J.L. Higgs, "Firm Valuation and Accounting for Employee Stock Options," *Financial Analyst Journal*, 53 (1997): 26–34.

Comprix, J., and K.A. Muller, "Pension Plan Accounting Estimates and the Freezing of Defined Benefit Pension Plans," *Journal of Accounting and Economics*, 51, nos. 1–2 (2011): 115–33.

Conglan, A.T., and S.K. Sen, "Salesforce Compensation: Theory and Managerial Implications," *Marketing Science*, 8, no. 4 (Fall 1989).

Conlin, B., "Best Practices for Designing New Sales Compensation Plans," *Compensation and Benefit Review* (Feb. 22, 2008).

Cruz, C., and J. Karayan, "Having Your Cake and Eating It Too: Avoiding the S Corporation Single Class Stock Rules While Grunting Stock-Like Incentive Compensation," *The Cal Poly Pomona Journal of Interdisciplinary Studies*, 10, Fall 1997.

Dalrymple, D.J., P.R. Stephenson, and W. Corn, "Gross Margin Sales Compensation Plans," *Industrial Marketing Management*, 10, no. 3 (Jul. 1981): 219–24.

DeGraff, J.E., "Single-System Expatriate Compensation," *Cornell HR Review*, Cornell University, TLR School (2010).

Derek, J., "Expat: Worth His Money, or an Expensive Luxury?" *Accountancy, U.K.* (Jul. 1984): 75–78.

Dhaliwal, D.S., "Measurement of Financial Leverage in the Presence of Unfunded Liabilities," *The Accounting Review*, (Oct. 1986): 651–61.

Ding, S., and P. Beaulieu, "The Role of Financial Incentives in Balance-Based Performance Evaluations: Correcting Mood Congruence Biases," *Journal of Accounting Research*, no. 5 (2011): 1223–47.

Durkee, D.A., J.E. Groff, and J.R. Boatsman, "The Effect of Costly vs. Costless Pension Disclosure on Common Share Price: The Case of SASF 36," *Journal of Accounting Literature*, 7 (1988): 180–96.

EBRI Databook on Employee Benefits, Chapter 28, Employee Benefit Research Institute, Update (Mar. 2008).

"Employer Health Benefits," 2011 Annual Survey, Kaiser Family Foundation and Health Research and Educational Trust.

Erickson, M., M. Havlon, and E. Maydew, "Is There a Link Between Executive Compensation and Accounting Fraud?" *Journal of Accounting Research*, 44, no. 1 (2006): 113–43.

"ERISA and Health Plans," Employee Benefit Research Institute, Special Report, Issue Brief Number 167 (1995).

"Expatriate Compensation: How Should We Compensate An Employee on a Foreign Assignment?" SHRM Knowledge Center, SHRM (Jun. 2005).

"Exploding the Myth that Employees Always Prefer DC Plans," A Mercer Perspective on Retirement, Mercer Human Resource Consulting (May 2004).

Farley, J.U., "An Optimal Plan for Salesman Compensation," *Journal of Marketing Research* (1964).

FASB Statement No. 123 (R), *Share-Based Payment: A Road Map to Applying the Fair Value Guidance to Share-Based Payment Awards, Second Edition,* Deloitte & Touche LLP, 2006.

Federal Register, Vol. 72, No. 230, November 30, 2007, Notices 67765.000.

Fitz-Enz, J., "Top 10 Calculations for Your HRIS," *HR Focus,* April 1998, S-3.

Flamholtz, E., and E.D. Main, "Current Issues, Recent Advancements, and Future Directions in Human Resource Accounting," *Journal of Human Resource Costing and Accounting,* 4, no. 1 (Spring 1999).

Gaver, J.J., K.M. Gaver, and J.R. Austin, "Additional Evidence on the Association between Income Management and Earnings-Based Bonus Plans," *Journal of Accounting and Economics* (Feb. 1995): 3–28.

Gerhart, B., and G.T. Milkovich, "Organizational Differences in Managerial Compensation and Financial Performance," *Academy of Management Journal,* 33, no. 4 (1990): 603–91.

Gopalakrishnan, V., "The Effect of Cognition vs. Disclosure on Investor Valuation: The Case of Pension Accounting," *Review of Quantitative Finance and Accounting,* 4 (1994): 383–96.

Gopalakrishnan, V., and T.F. Sugrue, "An Empirical Investigation of Stock Market Valuation of Corporate Projected Pension Liabilities," *Journal of Business Finance and Accounting,* 20 (Sep. 1993): 711–24.

Gould, E., "A Decade of Declines in Employer-Sponsored Health Insurance Coverage," Economy Policy Institute, EPI Briefing Paper #337 (Feb. 2012).

Haile, S., "Challenges in International Benefits and Compensation Systems of Multinational Corporation," *The African Economic and Business Review,* 3, no. 1 (Spring 2002).

Hamlni, A.R., and G.E. Calvasina, "Currency Fluctuations and the Management of Expatriate Assignment Cost," *Proceeding of the Academy for Studies in International Business,* 5, no. 2 (2005).

Hestwood, T.M., and B.D. Biswas, "Human Resource Planning and Compensation: A Developing Relationship," American Compensation National Conference Presentation, 1979.

Hestwood, T.M., and B.D. Biswas, "Projecting Base Payroll Costs," *Compensation & Benefits Review,* 7, no. 3 (1975): 47–63.

Hicks, S.W., "Accounting and Reporting by Health and Welfare Plans," *Journal of Accountancy,* 174, no. 6 (1992).

Holthausen, R.W., D.F. Lacker, and R.G. Sloan, "Annual Bonus Schemes and the Manipulation of Earnings," *Journal of Accounting and Economics,* 19 (1995): 29–74.

"Insurer Reports Wider Annual Deficit," *Washington Post,* November 16, 2010.

Ittner, C.D., D.F. Larcker, and M.W. Meyer, "Performance, Compensation, and the Balanced Scorecard," Unpublished, Wharton School, University of Pennsylvania, 1997.

"The Job of an Actuary in the New Millennium," *Probe,* 46, no. 11 (Jul. 20, 1999): 1–2.

John, G., and B. Weitz, "Sales Force Compensation: An Empirical Investigation of Factors Related to Use of Salary Versus Incentives Compensation," *Journal of Marketing Research,* 26, no. 1 (Feb. 1989): 1–14.

Joseph, K., and M.U. Kalwani, "The Role of Bonus Pay in Salesforce Compensation Plans," *Industrial Marketing Management,* 27, no. 2 (Mar. 1998): 147–59.

Khincha, H.P., "Taxation of Employee Stock Option Plans: International Principles," *Revenue Law Journal,* 12, no. 1 (2002).

Kochanski, J., and D. Insler, "The Compensation Scorecard: What Gets Measured Gets Done," Sibson Consulting, A Division of Segal, 2010, SHRM Online Compensation Discipline.

Kodwaui, A.D., and R. Tiwari, "Human Resource Accounting–A New Dimension, Institute of Management Technology (IMT)," Paper presented at Canadian Accounting Association (CAAA) 2006 Annual Conference (Jan. 2007).

Koss, S. "Which Is Best? Anniversary vs. Focal (Common Date)" (2009).

Kouhy, R., R. Vedd, T. Yoshikowa, and J. Innes, "Human Resource Policies: Managerial Accounting and Organizational Performance," *Journal of Human Resource Costing and Accounting,* 13, no. 3: 245–63.

Landua, S.E., and B.A. Benedict, "Going Global with U.S. Employee Stock Plans," Pillsbury Winthrop Shaw Pittman LLP Advisory, Executive Compensation and Benefits (May 2011).

"Leading by Example, Leading Practices for Employee Health Management," U.S. Chamber of Commerce and Partnership for Prevention (2007).

Ledford, G.E., "Managing Unit Incentives the Corporate Level, *WorldatWork Journal,* 21, no. 2, 2nd Quarter (2012).

"Liability Recognition for Certain Employee Termination Benefits and Other Costs to Exit an Activity (Including Certain Costs Incurred in a Restructuring)." EITF 94–3. Norwalk, CT: Financial Accounting Standard Board (1994).

Lindenberger, W., and K. Lindenberger, "Finance Is From Mars, Human Is From Venus," *Workspan: The Magazine of WorldatWork* (2009).

Lowe, K.B., J. Milliman, H. CieriDe, and P.J. Dowling, "International Compensation Practices: A Ten-Country Comparative Analysis," *Human Resource Management*, 41, no. 1 (Spring 2002): 45–66.

Maciosek M.V., A.B. Coffield, N.M. Edwards, M.J. Goodman, T.J. Flottemesch, and L.I. Solberg; "Priorities among Effective Clinical Preventive Services: Results of a Systematic Review and Analysis. *American Journal Preventive Medicine*, 31, no. 1 (2006): 52–56.

Madhani, P.M., "Rebalancing Fixed and Variable Pay in a Sales Organization: A Business Cycle Perspective," *Compensation and Benefits Review*, 42 (Feb. 2010): 179–89.

Makridis, T., "Accounting for Share-Based Compensation Awards, Survey of Relevant Accounting Guidance," Presentation made at the San Francisco NASPP Chapter Meeting (Feb. 2009).

Martin, L.G., and G.V. Henderson, "On Bond Ratings and Pension Obligations: A Note," *Journal of Financial and Quantitative Analysis* (Dec. 1983): 463–70.

"Maximum Monthly Guarantee Tables." Pension Benefit Guaranty Corporation.

McBride, J.R., *International Employment Conditions, Resource Guide*, Wellesley, MA: Employment Management Association (1985).

Milkovich, G.T., and M. Bloom, "Rethinking International Compensation," *Compensation & Benefits Review*, 30 (Jan. 1998): 15–23.

Miller, S., "Employers Accelerate Effects to Control Health Plan Costs, Consumer-Directed Plans, Wellness Intensives Added in Record Numbers in 2011," Society for Human Resource Management, SHRM Online Benefits Discipline (Nov. 2011).

Mittelstaedt, H.F., "An Empirical Analysis of the Factors Underlying the Decisions to Remove Excess Assets from Overfunded Pension Plans," *Journal of Economics and Accounting*, 11, no. 4 (Nov. 1989): 399–418.

"New Insights Into What Is Known About Retirement Planning," Defined Contribution Insights, Profit Sharing Council of America (May/Jun. 2005).

"Option-Pricing Models: Using Option-Pricing Models to Value Employee Share Options," Ernst & Young, International Financial Reporting Standard Group (2009).

Oxley, L., L. Trinh, and J. Gibson, "Measuring Human Capital: Alternative Methods and International Evidence," *Korean Economic Review,* 24, no. 2 (Winter 2008): 238–343.

Parameswaran R., and K. Jothi, "Human Resource Accounting, The Chartered Accountant," The Institute of Chartered Accountant of India, New Delhi (Jan. 2005).

Park, C., "Prevalence of Employer Self-Insured Health Benefits: National and State Variation," *Medical Care Research and Review,* 57, no. 3 (Sep. 2000): 340–60.

Pearson, A., "A Global Payroll Challenge," *Pay and Benefits Magazine* (Apr. 2011).

"Pension actuaries should take bigger role," *The Actuary,* Society of Actuaries, 34, no. 2 (Feb. 2000): 5.

Plan Accounting–Defined Contribution Pension Plans (Topic 962), Financial Accounting Series, Accounting Standards update, No. 2010-25, Sep. 2010, Reporting Loans to Participants by Defined Contribution Pensions Plans, A Consensus of the FASB Emerging Issues Task Force, An Amendment of the FASB Accounting Standard Codification.

Polovina, S., and H. Thomas, "Global Mobility: Through the Looking Glass," *International HR Journal,* 21, no. 2, (Spring 2012): 13–17.

Pownall, G., C. Wasley, and G. Waymire. "The Stock Price Effects of Alternative Types of Management Earnings Forecasts," *Accounting Review,* 68 (1993): 896–912.

"Private Company Incentive Pay Practices," WorldatWork Research Report (Oct. 2007).

Randall, V.R., "Managed Care, Utilization Review, and Financial Risk Shifting: Compensating Patients for Health Care Cost Containment Injuries," *University of Puget Sound Law Review* (1994).

Rappaport, A.M., and D. Fuerst, "Defined Benefit Plans–Still a Good Idea," *Global Report on Aging, Special Issue,* AARP (2004).

Rappaport, A.M., and P.W. Plumley, "The Education of the Actuary in the Future," Transactions of the Society of Actuaries (Jan. 1975).

Rappaport, A.M., and B. Vorwaller, "Key Issues in Plan Design for the 1990s and Beyond," in *Driving Down Health Care Costs Strategies and Solutions.* New York: Panel Publishers, 1993: 359–72.

Reichelstein, S., "Providing Managerial Incentives: Cash Flows Versus Accrual Accounting," *Journal of Accounting Research,* 38, no. 2.

Reynolds, C., "Compensating North American Expatriates," *How To Series for the HR Professional,* WorldatWork (2006).

Ryals, L.J., and B. Rogers, "Sales Compensation Plans: One Size Does Not Fit All," *Journal of Targeting, Measurement and Analysis for Marketing,* 13, no. 4 (Jul. 2005): 354–62.

Rynes, S.L., A.E. Colbert, and K.G. Brown, "HR Professional Beliefs about Effective Human Resource Practices: Correspondence Between Research and Practice," *Human Resource Management,* 41, no. 2 (2002): 149–74.

"Salaries as a Percentage of Operating Expense," SHRM Metric of the Month, Society for Human Resource Management (Nov. 2008).

Scammon. D.L., "Self-funded Health Benefit Plans: Marketing Implications for PPOs and Employers," *Journal of Health Care Marketing* 9, no. 1 (1989): 5–14.

Schieber, S.J., "The Sleeping Giant Awakens: U.S. Retirement Policy in the 21st Century," *Compensation & Benefits Review,* 28 (Jan. 1996): 20–31.

Schraeder, M., and J.B. Becton, "An Overview of Recent Trends in Incentives Pay Programs," *Coastal Business Journal,* 2, no. 1 (Fall 2003).

Schuster, J.R., and P.K. Zingheim, "Sales Compensation Strategies at the Most Successful Companies," *Personal Journal* (Jun. 1986): 112–16.

"Share-Based Compensation Plans and International Financial Reporting Standards: Tax Implications for Financial Reporting, System, and Plan Design," Deloitte Development LLC, Tax Services (2008).

Slottje, D., "Human Capital Measurement: Theory and Practice," *Journal of Economics Surveys,* 24, no. 2 (Apr. 2010): 201–205.

Smis, R.H., and M. Schraeder, "Expatriate Compensation: An Exploratory Review of Salient Contextual Factors and Common Practices," *Career Development International,* 10, no. 2 (2005).

Smith, D.M., and F. Gehlen, "Attempting to Control Health Care Costs: Again, Consumer Driven Health Care Plans and Health Savings Accounts," *Graziadio Business Review,* 7, no. 3, Pepperdine University (2004).

Smith, M., and B. Stradley, "New Research Tracks the Evaluation of Annual Incentive Plans," *Executive Compensation Bulletin,* Towers Watson, 2010.

Snapka, P., and A. Copikova, "Balanced Scorecard and Compensation," 2011 International Conference on Business and Economics Research, IPEDR, 16 (2011).

Stanton, M.W., "Reducing Costs in the Healthcare System: Learning from What Has Been Done," Research in Action, Agency for Healthcare Research and Quality, 9 (Sep. 2002).

"Tailoring Health Care Benefits to Your Employees: Managing Employee Health and Health Benefit Costs Through Vendors Partnerships and Simple, Data Driven Strategies," National Business Coalition on Health, Washington, D. C. (Jan. 2010).

"The Tax Implications of Expensing Stock Option–Global Equity Compensation Programs," *A & M Tax Advisor Weekly*, Alvarez & Marshal Tax Advisory Services LLC., 24, (Jun. 2006).

Theeke, H., and J.B. Mitchell, "Financial Implication for Accounting for Human Resources Using a Liability Model," *Journal of Human Resource Costing and Accounting*, 12, no. 2 (2008): 124–37.

Treasury Inspector General for Tax Administration, Statistical Trends in Retirement Plans, August 9, 2010, Reference Number: 2010-10-097.

Wallace, J.S., "Adopting Residual Income-Based Compensation Plans: Do You Get What You Pay For?" *Journal of Accounting and Economics*, 24 (1997): 275–300.

Werner, S., and S.G. Wand, "Recent Compensation Research: An Eclectic Review," *Human Resource Review*, 14, no. 2 (Jun. 2004): 201–27.

Winer, L., "A Sales Compensation Plan for Maximum Motivation," *Industrial Marketing Management*, 5, no. 1 (Mar. 1976): 29–36.

Wright, P.M., and G.C. McMahan, "Exploring Human Capital: Putting Human Back into Strategic Human Management," *Human Resource Management Journal*, 21, no. 22 (2011): 93–104.

Wyman, T., "Ten Ways Employers Can Control Healthcare Costs," PeoriaMagazines.com, Central Illinois Business Publishers, Inc. (2012).

Yeung, A.K., and B. Berman, "Adding Value through Human Resources: Reorienting Human Resource Management to Drive Business Performance," *Human Resource Management*, 36, no. 3 (Fall 1997): 321–35.

Zajac, E.J., and J.D. Westphal, "The Cost and Benefit of Managerial Incentives and Monitoring in Large US Corporations: When Is More Not Better? *Strategic Management Journal*, 15 (1991): 121–42.

Books

Armstrong, R., B. Hams, C. Ivancic, L. Rodgers, and C. Rosen, *The Handbook of Incentive Compensation*, The National Center for Employee Ownership, 2009.

Arnold, J., and S. Turley, *Accounting for Management Decisions*, Upper Saddle River, NJ: Prentice Hall, 1996.

Atkinson, A.A., R.S. Kaplan, and S.M. Young, *Management Accounting, 4th Edition*, Upper Saddle River, NJ: Prentice Hall, 2004.

Atkinson, A.A., R.S. Kaplan, E.M. Matsumura, and S.M Young; *Management Accounting: Information for Decision-Making and Strategy Execution, 6e*, Upper Saddle River, NJ: Pearson, 2012.

Beam, B.T., and J.J. McFadden, *Employee Benefits, 6th Edition,* Real Estate Education Company, a division of Dearborn Financial Publishing, Inc., 2001.

Berger, L.A., and D.R. Berger, editors, *The Compensation Handbook, A State-of-the-Art Guide to Compensation and Design, 4th Edition,* New York: McGraw-Hill, 2000.

Besley, S., and E. Brigham, *The Essentials of Managerial Finance, 13th Edition,* Mason, OH: Thomson Southwestern, 2005.

Biswas, B., "Compensating the Multinational Executive," Doctoral Dissertation, San Francisco: Golden Gate University, Sep.1986.

Bodie, Z., A. Kane, and A.J. Marcus, *Essentials of Investments, 8th Edition,* New York: McGraw-Hill Irwin, 2010.

Cascio, W.F., *Costing Human Resources: The Financial Impact of Behavior in Organizations, 3e,* Boston: PWS-Kent Pub. Co., 1991.

Cichelli, D.J., *Compensating the Sales Force: A Practical Guide to Designing Winning Sales Compensation Plans,* New York: McGraw-Hill, 2004.

Commission Accounting–System Administration Manual, Richmond, VA: Appx Software Inc., 1995.

Copeland, T., T. Kollen, and J. Murrin, *Valuation: Measuring and Managing the Value of Companies, 3rd Edition,* New York: John Wiley & Sons, 2000.

Cummings T.G., and C.G. Worley, *Organization Development and Change, 5th Edition,* St. Paul, MN: West Publishing Company, 1989.

Dowling, P.J., M. Festing, and A.D. Engle, *International Human Resource Management, 5th Edition,* Mason, OH: Thomson Learning, 2008.

Ehrhardt, M.C., and E. F. Brigham, *Financial Management: Theory and Practice, 13th Edition,* Mason, OH: South-Western Cengage Learning, 2011.

Ellig, B.R., *Executive Compensation, Fully Revised and Expended Edition of the Classic Best Seller,* New York: McGraw Hill, 2007.

FASB Proposals of Stock Option Expensing, Hearing Before the Subcommittee on Commerce, Trade, and Consumer Protection of the Committee on Energy and Commerce, House of Representatives, One Hundred Eighth Congress, Second Session, Serial No. 108–99, July, 2004.

Fitz-enz, J., *The ROI of Human Capital: Measuring the Economic Value of Employee Performance,* AMACOM, 2009.

Fitz-enz, J., and B. Davison, *How to Measure Human Resources Management, 3rd Edition,* New York: McGraw-Hill, 2002.

Flamholz, E.G., *Human Resource Accounting: Advances in Concepts, Methods and Applications, 3rd Edition,* Boston: Kluwer Academic Publishers, 1999.

Garrison, R.H., E.W. Noreen, and P.C. Brewer, *Managerial Accounting, 14th Edition,* New York: McGraw-Hill Irwin, 2012.

Gerhart, B., and S. Rynes, *Compensation: Theory, Evidence, and Strategic Implications (Foundations for Organizational Science),* Thousand Oaks, CA: Sage, 2003.

Gomez-Mejia, L., and S. Werner, editors, *Global Compensation: Foundations and Perspectives,* Part of Rutledge's Global Human Resource Management Series, 2008.

Harrison, W.T., and C.T. Horngren, *Financial Accounting, 7th Edition,* Upper Saddle River, NJ: Prentice Hall, 2008.

Herod, R., *Expatriate Compensation: The Balance Sheet Approach,* Global HR Management Series, Society for Human Resource Management, 2008.

Herod, R., *Expatriate Compensation Strategies, Applying Alternative Approaches,* Society for Human Resource Management, 2009.

Herod, R., *Managing the International Assignment Process, From Selection Through Repatriation,* Global HR Management Series, Society for Human Resource Management, 2009.

Hicks, S.W., "Accounting and Reporting by Health & Welfare Plans," AICPA Federal Government Division, edited by Linda A. Volkert, CPA, AICPA Technical Information Division.

Kieso, D.E., J.J. Weygandt, and T.D. Warfield, *Intermediate Accounting, 14th Edition,* Hoboken, NJ: John Wiley & Sons, 2012.

Kimmel, P.D., J.J. Weygandt, and D.E. Kieso, *Financial Accounting: Tools for Business Decision Making, 6th Edition,* Hoboken, NJ: John Wiley & Sons, 2011.

Lewis, B., editor, *The Management of Expatriates,* London: Institute of Personnel Management, 1982.

Martocchio, J.J. *Strategic Compensation: A Human Resource Management Approach, 5th Edition,* Upper Saddle River, NJ: Prentice Hall, 2009.

Mathis, R.L., and J.H. Jackson, *Human Resource Management, 13th Edition,* Mason, OH: Cengage Learning, 2010.

McCoy, T.J., *Compensation and Motivation: Maximizing Employee Performance with Behavior-Based Incentive Plans,* New York: Amacom Books, 1993.

Milkovich G.T., and J.M. Newman, *Compensation, 9th Edition,* New York: McGraw-Hill Irwin, 2008.

Richer, H., *Aligning Pay and Results: Compensation Strategies That Work from the Boardroom to the Shop Floor*, AMACOM, published in cooperation with the American Compensation Association, 1999.

Rosenbloom, S., editor, *The Handbook of Employee Benefits, Design, Funding, and Administration, 5th Edition*, New York: McGraw-Hill, 2001.

Rynes, S.L., and B. Garhart, *Compensation in Organizations Current Research and Practice*, San Francisco: Jossey-Bass, 2000.

Slater, J., *College Accounting: A Practical Approach, 11th Edition*, Upper Saddle River, NJ: Prentice Hall, 2010.

Spiceland, D., J. Sepe, M. Nelson, and L. Tomassini, *Intermediate Accounting, 5th Edition*, New York: McGraw-Hill Irwin, 2009.

Subramanyam. K.R., and J.J. Wild, *Financial Statement Analysis, 10th Edition*, New York: McGraw-Hill Irwin, 2009.

Taylor, G.W., and F.C. Pierson, *New Concepts in Wage Determination*, New York: McGraw-Hill, 1957.

Teagne, B.W., *Compensating Key Personnel Overseas*, New York: Conference Board, 1972.

Torlsion, I., *Living Abroad: Personnel Policy in the Overseas Setting*, New York: John Wiley & Sons, 1982.

Waring, B.M., *Pension Finance: Putting Risks and Costs of Defined Benefit Plans Back Under Your Control*, Research Foundation of CFA Institute, Hoboken, NJ: John Wiley & Sons, Inc., 2012.

The WorldatWork Handbook of Compensation, Benefits & Total Rewards, WorldatWork, Hoboken, NJ: John Wiley & Sons, 2007.

Zingheim, P.K., *Pay People Right, Breakthrough Reward Strategies to Create Great Companies*, San Francisco: Jossey-Bass, 2000.

Websites

Bontis, N., "Human Capital Study: Written Report," McMaster University, www.bontis.com, sponsored by Accenture, Institute for Intellectual Capital Research, Saratoga Institute, 2001.

California Teachers' Association Retirement Employee Web site: http://ctainvest.org/home/CalSTRS-CalPERS/about-calstrs/calstrs-retirement-benefit.aspx.

Coleman, S.,"Recruiting Rants and HR Commentary," The Recruiters Lounge Blog, http://Xpatulator.com.

Crystal, G., "CEO Pay Ratios: It All Depends," Crystal Reports, 2008, http://graefcrystal.com/image/ceo_worker_pay_ratios_web_7_1_08pdf.

Flaherty, J., "How Employers Are Controlling Healthcare Costs Today by Communicating with Their Employees," Guest Article, Winter, Wyman News & Views, www.winterwyman.com/index.cfm/AboutUs/How_Employers_Are_Controlling_Healthcare_Costs_Today_By_Communicating_With_Their_Employees.

Harding, L., "Can International Payroll Accelerate the Success of Your Global Expansion," Northeast Human Resource Association, Web Article, 2011.

"HR Measurement and Metrics, Gaining HR a Seat at the Strategy Table," Biskman International, www.bisknan.com, 2008.

"HR Metrics: Moving Beyond Absenteeism + Turnover Statistics," Koenig + Associates, Inc., www.koenig.ca/files/HR_Metrics.pdf.

"Internationally Mobile Employee and Pensions, 2010–10–08," Swiss Life Network, www.employeebenefits.co.uk.

Investments and Pension Europe, Magazine, December 1999, www.ipe.com/magazine.

Johnson, N., "Tax Considerations of the Personal Use of Company Vehicles," posted at www.normaujohnsoncpa.com/fft.htm.

Liccione, W.J., "A Framework for Compensation Plans with Incentive Value, Performance Improvement," *International Society for Performance Improvement*, 46(2), February 2007. Published online in Wiley Inter Science (www.interscience.wiley.com).

Marcinko, D.E., "What Is An IBNR Claim?" on the Medical Executive Post... Insider News and Education for Doctors and their Advisors Blog, October, 2008.

Summaries on International Financial Reporting Standards, AS19-Employee Benefits.

"Taxation of U.S. Expatriates," Global Tax Network U.S. LLC (GTN) at www.GTN.com.

U.S. Healthcare Costs, Kaiser EDU.org, *Health policy explained*, www.kaiseredu.org/issue-modules/us-health-care-costs/background-brief.aspx.

Walken, M., "Tying Compensation to the Balanced Scorecard," Yahoo! Contributor Network, September, 2008.

"What Is Human Resource Accounting," *Chartered Club Blog*, www.charteredclub.com/what_is_human_resource_accounting/2012.

"Will Tax Equalization Reduce Your U.S. Tax Costs?" Expatriate Tax Services LLC, www.expatriatetaxservices.com/articles/show.aspx?id=17.

Index